On Four Modern Humanists

On Four Modern Humanists

HOFMANNSTHAL

GUNDOLF

CURTIUS

KANTOROWICZ

EDITED BY ARTHUR R. EVANS, JR.

PRINCETON, NEW JERSEY

PRINCETON UNIVERSITY PRESS

MCMLXX

Library of Congress Card: 76-90945
International Standard Book Number: 0-691-06174-2

Publication of this book has been aided
by the Whitney Darrow Publication Reserve Fund
of Princeton University Press

Printed in the United States of America
by Princeton University Press, Princeton, New Jersey

This book has been composed in Linotype Baskerville

Table of Contents

I

Hugo Von Hofmannsthal as a Critic

By Egon Schwarz

I I

Friedrich Gundolf

By Lothar Helbing and C. V. Bock

I I I

Ernst Robert Curtius

By Arthur R. Evans, Jr.

I V

Ernst H. Kantorowicz

By Yakov Malkiel

Index

Preface

THIS BOOK is intended as a contribution to the cultural history of our epoch and, more particularly, to our present-day reflection upon the crisis of European humanism brought about by two World Wars and the advent of the totalitarian state. It is made up of four intellectual biographies, by different hands, of distinguished German-speaking men of ideas who, with the exception of Hofmannsthal—here treated as a critical essayist, a neglected aspect of his many-sided accomplishments—are known only by name to the great majority of serious English and American readers.

In their various intellectual ways, be it cultural criticism, the historical monograph, or the literary essay, the works of these German humanists, who were all "good Europeans," find a general coherence and a certain family likeness in being at one and the same time conservative in temper and forward-looking in the urgency and intensity of their inquiries. That is, the achievements of each can be seen not only as a persevering effort to perpetuate the tested values of the past, but also as an important contribution to the fostering and assessment of twentieth century modernism in its search for experimental forms of expression and contemporary styles of thought.

A more specific, particularized unity is given to their lives and work by the fact that each one of these men, in varying degrees, came under the personal and powerful influence of Germany's poet and sage, Stefan George; and so, in an ancillary way, this group of studies may assist in the historical evaluation, now under way, of the cultural effects of George and his circle.

PREFACE

I am pleased to acknowledge the considerable aid given to my editorial efforts by Professor Theodore Ziolkowski, who first conceived the general plan of this book and has steadily encouraged its progress; by Miss R. Miriam Brokaw, Princeton University Press' able Associate Director and Editor; and by its brilliant and energetic Staff Editor, Sarah George.

My warmest thanks, too, to my wife, Catherine, for all kinds of help.

THE EDITOR

On Four Modern Humanists

Hugo Von Hofmannsthal
as a Critic

By Egon Schwarz

RANGE

Every . . . perfect thing we find lying in our path is a fragment that has strayed from a strange harmonious world, like meteorites which have somehow fallen down upon the paths of our earth. The task is now to call forth from the lost fragment, through a great exertion of the imagination, a momentary vision of that strange world. Whoever can accomplish this and is capable of such an exertion and concentration of the reproductive imagination will be a great critic. He will also be very just and very conciliatory because he will measure every work of art by an ideal, but a subjective ideal gained from the artist's personality, and he will sense the beauty of all that has been conceived and born in truth.[1]

THESE WORDS, written by the young Hugo von Hofmannsthal and published in a Viennese journal in 1894 under the pseudonym "Loris,"[2] aim at describing the

---

[1] From an essay entitled "Walter Pater," first published in *Die Zeit* (1894); now in *Prosa I*, ed. Herbert Steiner (Frankfurt: S. Fischer, 1950), p. 203. All translations are mine.

[2] In his youth Hofmannsthal used the pseudonym "Loris Melikow" or simply "Loris" (borrowed from a Russian general, Count

critical stance of Walter Pater. But they reveal several features just as characteristic of Hofmannsthal himself.

One of these is Platonism, a characteristic to remain with him to the end of his days in spite of many troubling challenges:[3] art partakes of perfection and perfection in turn exists in a higher realm of the spirit, "a strange harmonious world." Tokens from this sacred sphere descend upon our commonplace earth only infrequently and mysteriously. The observer does not examine the laws governing their trajectory. He is content with noticing that they arrive "somehow." His task is to create for his readers, through an extraordinary exertion of his imaginative powers, a momentary vision of the spiritual world whence these fragments came. He who is capable of such feats of restoration, Loris decrees, is a great critic.[4] He might as well have said "poet"

Loris-Melikow) because Gymnasium students were not allowed to publish under their own name in Imperial Austria. The last of his publications signed "Loris" appeared in 1897.

[3] Neo-Platonism would be the more accurate term. The great self-analytical summary of his life's work written in 1916 still bears the following neo-Platonic motto, taken from Gregory of Nyssa's *Vita Mosis*: "Quocirca supremae pulchritudinis amator quod jam viderat tamquam imaginem eius quod non viderat credens, ipso frui primitivo desiderabat." ("Since he was such a lover of the highest beauty that he took what he had already seen to be an image of what he had not seen yet, he desired to enjoy the original.") *Aufzeichnungen* (Frankfurt: S. Fischer, 1959), p. 213.

[4] It is no wonder that Hofmannsthal chose to write about Pater: the critical principles the Austrian writer proclaims here can also be attributed to the Englishman. "Pater believed that criticism should be 'itself a kind of construction or creation, as it penetrates, through the given literary or artistic product, into the mental and inner constitution of the producer, shaping his work.' Pater's aim in his critical essays was accordingly creative—to catch a writer's spirit by retracing his steps of creation; structure was the key to soul, to the perfect word as it existed in the mind of the artist." J. Gordon Eaker, *Walter Pater: A Study in Methods and Effects* (Iowa City: University of Iowa Humanistic Studies, 1933),

for even though he is speaking of "reproductive imagination" the poet's mission on earth is likewise that of a mediator. The meteorite, to remain within the same metaphor, is of his own making but it is incomplete, a mere atom from that yonder world, allowing creator and receiver alike no more than a glimpse.

Similarly expressive of Hofmannsthal, and of impressionistic criticism in general, is the demand that the yardstick by which art is measured should be gained by an immersion in the work itself and not brought to it from without. The standards of judgment, no matter how benevolent and lenient with the imperfect condition of everything that takes on discernible shape, must be derived from an ideal. But the ideal ought not to be an alien abstraction; it should be a living form distilled from what the artist intended and not so much from what he accomplished.[5]

Even the seemingly innocuous postulate at the end of this amazing passage, half hidden by the syntax, rather than openly proclaimed, is profoundly Hofmannsthalian. An insistence on the ethical origins of beauty is certainly not startling nor is it necessarily alien to Pater, Impressionism, or earlier intellectual currents; but we

---

p. 33. For further parallels between Hofmannsthal and Pater, cf. the section entitled "Critical Attitude" in this study, p. 52.

[5] There is a large supply of treatises on Impressionism in art and literature. Richard Hamann's and Jost Hermand's *Impressionismus* (Berlin: Akademie Verlag, 1966) offers an exhaustive typology of its manifestations in German art and culture. I should also like to quote from an article by Robert Soucy, "Proust's Aesthetic of Reading," in *The French Review* 41 (1967): 54, where "immersion in a text" is also connected with the impressionist aesthetic as I am claiming here: "There is another side to reading which Proust regards as equally important—and here Proust was very much in tune with Impressionism—which consists of temporarily annihilating one's subjectivity before the artistic vision of the author, of getting 'outside oneself' and into the mental world of another."

shall have occasion to observe that it is central to Hofmannsthal's personal development.

Hofmannsthal as a critic? This sounds like Leonardo as a designer of military fortifications or Casanova as the author of a Venetian history: both undeniable dimensions of the men but not the accomplishments that are conjured up immediately by the mere mention of their names. Of the millions of opera-goers who are fond of, say, the *Rosenkavalier (The Cavalier of the Rose)*, not all remember the name of the librettist. But the educated among them know that without his unique collaboration with the composer there would be neither this opera nor such favorites of the repertoire as *Ariadne, Die Frau ohne Schatten (The Woman Without a Shadow), Arabella,* or *Die ägyptische Helena.*

There also is a growing awareness that, together with Max Reinhardt, Hofmannsthal is the founder of the Salzburg *Festspiele,* the oldest and most prestigious of Europe[6] and that he wrote three distinguished morality plays for the occasion, thus rejuvenating the age-old theatrical form, *Jedermann;* its sequel, *Das Salzburger Grosse Welttheater (The Salzburg Great Theatre of the World);*[7] and the apocalyptic tragedy *Der Turm (The*

[6] Hofmannsthal himself described the idea behind the Salzburg festivals in several essays written from 1922 to 1928: "Die Salzburger Festspiele," "Das Salzburger Grosse Welttheater," "Das Salzburger Programm," "Das Publikum der Salzburger Festspiele." References to the festivals can also be found in Hofmannsthal's five letters to the American magazine *The Dial* (1922-24), especially "Brief III" (which forms part of "Die Salzburger Festspiele" above), as well as in his articles on "Max Reinhardt" and "Reinhardt bei der Arbeit," which were also originally written for American newspapers. All are now in *Aufzeichnungen.*

[7] Trans. T. Gwynn Jones (Llangollen: Welsh National Theatre, 1936), and included in *Hugo von Hofmannsthal: Selected Plays and Libretti,* ed. Michael Hamburger (New York: Pantheon Books, 1963). This volume also contains "The Tower," a transla-

Tower). The latter two were fashioned after decades of creative effort from the Calderonian plays *El gran teatro del mundo* and *La vida es sueño.*[8] But it is the former, *Jedermann,* embedded in the European *Everyman* tradition, that has become the center of the Salzburg *Festspiele* and has grown so well-known that it is regarded by countless spectators as an anonymous gift of nature for their edification. Thus the name of Hofmannsthal is paradoxically overshadowed even by his most popular contribution.[9]

Above all, Hofmannsthal is for the literate public the author of a series of delightful comedies, the precious possession of a national literature not exactly abounding in comic masterpieces. It does not take great literary sophistication to recognize that in a play like *Der Schwierige (The Difficult Man)* the highest demands of what the French call "le comique sérieux" have been met: wit is wed to philosophical profundity, social satire coupled with character portrayal, symbolism with a touch of lightness and gaiety altogether rare in German letters. Similarly, *Der Unbestechliche* of 1922-23, largely true to such French models as Molière and Marivaux, can be regarded as a variation of the farcical *servo padrone* theme and is nevertheless, to the initiated observer, a political allegory with strong theological overtones. Knowing that Hofmannsthal wrote

---

tion of the first version of "Der Turm." The 1927 version was translated by Alfred Schwarz in *Hugo von Hofmannsthal: Three Plays* (Detroit: Wayne State University Press, 1966).

[8] For a study of Hofmannsthal's relation to Calderon, see Ernst Robert Curtius, "George, Hofmannsthal und Calderon" in *Kritische Essays zur europäischen Literatur* (Bern: Francke, 1950); as well as Egon Schwarz, *Hofmannsthal und Calderon* (The Hague: Mouton, 1962).

[9] Since the première of August 22, 1920 on the Domplatz, the play has experienced numerous performances in Salzburg and elsewhere.

these plays immediately after World War I, at a low point of his country's history and cognizant of Novalis' prescription that one must write comedies after a lost war, helps us understand this strange but eminently successful double perspective.

However, those who are old enough to remember directly or who are otherwise familiar with the *fin de siècle* know that the original Hofmannsthal cult goes back to the 1880's and had as its object a pupil of the Viennese Academic Gymnasium. At the ripe age of seventeen, when he still wore short trousers[10] and had a nurse to watch over his comings and goings, he wrote the most intoxicatingly mellifluous German poems since Goethe, or at least Brentano, and such enchanting lyrical one-act plays that he immediately became the darling of the fastidious avant-garde of the day. Such precociousness was paralleled in literary history only by *Wunderkinder* like Keats and Rimbaud, and Hofmannsthal's contemporaries did not hesitate to assign him the same rank as that of these famous predecessors. His early fame was obscured when he ceased writing poetry and turned to nonlyrical pursuits which his erstwhile admirers did not understand. One of them, the Austrian writer and critic Hermann Bahr, went so far as to proclaim regretfully that Hofmannsthal should have died at twenty-five to retain his place of glory in the history of literature.

It was not until after World War II—when people in Germany and Austria were searching for models to venerate, writers who had lived in the European tradition and had at least endeavored to come to grips with

[10] Stefan Zweig paints a vivid picture of Hofmannsthal's literary début in Vienna in his autobiography, *Die Welt von gestern. Erinnerungen eines Europäers* (Hamburg: G. B. Fischer, 1953), pp. 52-57.

the disintegrating forces of the century—that Hofmannsthal was rediscovered and a new vogue instituted. The fifteen-volume edition of his works, published by S. Fischer, uniting for the first time what had been scattered in a great many diffuse publications, helped make a large-scale post-war occupation with Hofmannsthal feasible. Not disconnected with this movement, largely academic and scholarly in character, was the publication of several volumes of Hofmannsthal's correspondence with a series of more or less famous contemporaries such as Rudolf Borchardt, Arthur Schnitzler, Eberhard von Bodenhausen, Carl Burckhardt, Helene von Nostitz, Edgar Karg von Bebenburg, Leopold von Andrian, Stefan George, Richard Strauss,[11] and several others. (Incomplete collections of Hofmannsthal's epistolary exchanges with the latter two had appeared in the late thirties but these publications were overshadowed by National Socialism and the outbreak of World War II.)[12] Thus many people have become acquainted

[11] *Hugo von Hofmannsthal – Rudolf Borchardt. Briefwechsel*, ed. Marie Luise Borchardt and Herbert Steiner (Frankfurt, 1954). *Hugo von Hofmannsthal – Arthur Schnitzler. Briefwechsel*, ed. Therese Nickl and Heinrich Schnitzler (Frankfurt, 1964). *Hugo von Hofmannsthal – Eberhard von Bodenhausen. Briefe der Freundschaft*, ed. Dora Bodenhausen (Düsseldorf, 1953). *Hugo von Hofmannsthal – Carl J. Burckhardt. Briefwechsel*, ed. Carl J. Burckhardt (Frankfurt, 1956). *Hugo von Hofmannsthal – Helene von Nostitz. Briefwechsel*, ed. Oswalt von Nostitz (Frankfurt, 1965). *Hugo von Hofmannsthal – Edgar Karg von Bebenburg. Briefwechsel*, ed. Mary E. Gilbert (Frankfurt, 1966). *Hugo von Hofmannsthal – Leopold von Andrian. Briefwechsel*, ed. Walter H. Perl (Frankfurt, 1968). *Briefwechsel zwischen George und Hofmannsthal*, ed. Robert Boehringer (1st edn. Berlin, 1938; 2nd augmented edn. Munich and Düsseldorf, 1953). *Hugo von Hofmannsthal – Richard Strauss. Briefwechsel*, ed. Franz Strauss (Berlin, Vienna, Leipzig, 1926); Complete Edition, ed. Willy Schuh, under the supervision of Franz and Alice Strauss (1st edn. 1952; 2nd edn. 1955; 3rd augmented edn., Zurich, 1964).

[12] There are two volumes of letters from Hofmannsthal's youth:

with yet another aspect of his *oeuvre*, with Hugo von Hofmannsthal as a master of the epistolary style, which allowed him to turn forth different facets of his personality in each encounter with another individual. At the same time every one of these correspondences is a cultural monument illustrating the epoch from a great variety of points of view.

Confronted with a profusion of more familiar forms, Hofmannsthal's admirers rather neglected a very significant portion of his productivity, his critical essays. While the studies of his poetry, his Greek dramas, his morality plays, his comedies crowded shelf after shelf in the world's important libraries, relatively little attention was paid to his essayistic *oeuvre* in spite of the fact that it fills five of the fifteen volumes of the Steiner edition. There are a few dissertations dealing with Hofmannsthal's criticism, a few articles scattered in the learned journals,[13] but the effort has been reluctant and must be continued before its results can be said to be adequate. The reason for this may be sought in the fact that the essay, a form occupying an indeterminate zone between journalism and creative writing, between factual report-

---

Briefe 1890-1901 (Berlin, 1935) and *Briefe 1900-1909* (Vienna, 1937). For a complete list of Hofmannsthal correspondences, up to the date of its publication, see Werner Volke, *Hugo von Hofmannsthal in Selbstzeugnissen und Bilddokumenten* (Reinbek by Hamburg: Rowohlt, 1967), p. 181-82.

[13] I am especially indebted to Hilde D. Cohn's article "Loris. Die frühen Essays des jungen Hofmannsthal" in *Publications of the Modern Language Association* 53, no. 4 (1948): 1294-1313; Richard Exner's articles "Probleme der Methodik und der Komposition in den Essays von Thomas Mann und Hugo von Hofmannsthal" in *German Quarterly* 30, no. 3 (1957): 145-57; and "Zur Essayistik Hugo von Hofmannsthals" in *Schweizer Monatshefte* 42, no. 2 (1962): 182-98; as well as Mary E. Gilbert, "Hofmannsthal's Essays, 1900-1908: A poet in Transition" in *Hugo von Hofmannsthal: Studies in Commemoration* (London, 1963), p. 29-52.

ing and imaginative elucidation of the world by an idiosyncratic personality, has never found much acclaim in the German-speaking world where more clear-cut categories seem to be preferred. Another impediment to a wide acceptance of Hofmannsthal's critical writings may have been, paradoxically, their brilliance. "Most people are prone to despise gracefulness," Richard Alewyn, one of the best connoisseurs of Hofmannsthal, quotes from Stendhal. He continues in his own words: "A deep distrust is rooted in the Protestant and especially the German genius against gracefulness. It much rather condones what is too obscure and difficult than the too bright and the too light. It is reluctant to recognize seriousness and depth without the predominance of loud pathos and heavy-handedness. It is hard for it to admit that something that glitters could be gold."[14]

Hofmannsthal's critical essays glitter and are gold at the same time. It is in them that he can give free rein to an important impulse of his versatile mind which, without such liberation, might have become detrimental to his poetry, his dramatic works, and even his epistolary communications with friends and acquaintances: an unusually keen intelligence. It is once more Alewyn who puts this trait into proper perspective. "Hofmannsthal," he declares, "is one of the foremost in a generation of modern creative writers[15] who are exceptionally intelligent and therefore great essayists. In the German language Thomas Mann and Robert Musil belong to this category; in French, Valéry and Sartre; in English, T. S. Eliot and W. H. Auden. This intelligence does not necessarily speak for their rank as poets

[14] Richard Alewyn, "Der Tod des Aestheten" in *Über Hugo von Hofmannsthal,* 2nd rev. edn. (Göttingen: Vandenhoeck & Ruprecht, 1960), p. 64. My translation.
[15] The German word is "Dichter."

and creative writers, but it certainly does not speak against it either."[16]

This passage is part of an attempt to characterize Hofmannsthal as a writer of letters, and it cannot be denied that the great Austrian exhibits remarkable critical acumen in his epistolary *oeuvre*. However, in a survey of Hofmannsthal's achievement as a critic, his essayistic work will be the primary concern. Criticism, for the purpose of this exploration, must be defined as any conscious confrontation on the part of the author with a literary, artistic, cultural, or even political phenomenon. It is clear then that from this point of view it would be legitimate to look for Hofmannsthal's critical utterances in his diaries, aphorisms, and even his poetic and dramatic works. For practical reasons, however, the majority of examples will be taken from his essays. They are of sufficient breadth and versatility to reveal his thought in many nuances.

We do not intend to confuse, if we can avoid it, Hofmannsthal's essays with his criticism. There are essays which cannot be regarded as critical in any sense. It ought, however, to be pointed out that his essays were the chief vehicles of Hofmannsthal's critical thought and that therefore the synonymous use of expressions like "critical essays," "essays," and "criticism" must be condoned as a pardonable practice in dealing with this author.

From 1891, when he was seventeen, till 1929, the year of his death, Hofmannsthal wrote critical essays dealing with French, English, German, Italian, Slavic, and even ancient letters. They range from poetry to biography, from the epic to the theatre, from literature to linguistics, as well as from books to such non-verbal arts

[16] "Unendliches Gespräch," *Über Hugo von Hofmannsthal*, p. 19.

as music and pantomime, dance and painting. His gallery of portraits includes not only Goethe and Balzac, Ibsen and Swinburne, Stefan George and d'Annunzio, Shakespeare and Calderón, Oscar Wilde and St.-John Perse, but also Beethoven, Gustav Mahler, Eleonora Duse, Ruth St. Denis, and so many others that they cannot be enumerated. Yet he is also willing, and in his mature years increasingly so, to abandon the world of art and books altogether and to describe places he visited or to address himself to problems of civilization touching upon the political questions of his day. His characterizations of Greece or Sicily, his distinction between Prussians and Austrians, his observations about language, his visions of Europe, and his warnings of the future belong to the most illuminating and often moving utterances of that period of history. And all of this is done with style and charm, humility and wisdom, an endless supply of information, and an inexhaustible wealth of humanity. Hugo von Hofmannsthal is a great European critic and a thorough acquaintance with his essayistic work is a complete education in itself.

INTELLECTUAL DEVELOPMENT

Beginnings

Two things seem to be modern today: the analysis of life and the flight from life. Slight is the pleasure in action, in the play of the external and internal forces of life. . . . One engages in the anatomy of one's own psychic life, or else one dreams. Reflection or imagination, mirror image or dream image. Modern are old furniture and young neuroses. It is modern to hear the psychological grass grow and the splashing in a purely phantastic world of miracles. Paul Bourget and Buddha are modern; splitting atoms and playing ball with the universe; modern is the dissection of a whim, a sigh, a scruple; and modern is the instinctive, almost somnambulistic devotion to every manifestation of beauty, to a color scheme, a sparkling metaphor, a marvelous allegory.[17]

Anyone endowed with some historical sense will immediately recognize the coquettish aestheticizing quality of these sentences and be able to assign their origin to the last decade of the nineteenth century. Hofmannsthal began his career as a writer in the wake of *fin-de-siècle* Impressionism and *l'art pour l'art.*[18] A whole generation found itself mirrored in his early work, complete with the glory and the misery of its aestheticism. Like a second Midas, that élite of artists transformed into beauty whatever it touched, and it starved to death from a want of life. They loved Hofmannsthal for his ability to capture their precious predicament in delicate words and exquisite images, and they lavished fame and admiration upon him. But a great deal of this was a misunderstanding. Every artist first stirs his wings in the atmosphere of his times before he learns how to soar above it. Every writer first toys with the ideas of his contemporaries. Goethe's Leipzig writings are Rococo and Hölderlin's early poems are undistinguishable from those of Schiller. Werther was misunderstood by the sentimentalists of the 1770's just as was Hofmannsthal's "fool" by the aesthetes of the 1890's. The inadequacies of life in eighteenth-century Germany and the gifted individual's contempt for them were so movingly portrayed in Goethe's novel that his contemporaries donned Werther's blue tail-coat, yellow vest, and trousers as marks of protest. When the Werther fashion extended

[17] "Gabriele d'Annunzio I," *Prosa I*, p. 149.
[18] Cf. Richard Alewyn, "Der Tod des Ästheten," *Über Hugo von Hofmannsthal*, p. 65.

further, resulting in an epidemic of suicide, Goethe felt compelled to add as a motto to the second edition a cautionary poem which ended in Werther's exhortation to the reader: "Be a man and do not follow after me."[19] Goethe regarded Wertherism, carried to its logical conclusion, as a disease, and he was able to diagnose it so well because he had had it himself. By the very act of describing it, he proved his convalescence. Similar was the lot of Hugo von Hofmannsthal. His admirers were able to recognize in *Der Tor und der Tod (Death and the Fool)* only the unfulfilled yearnings and frustrations of "the beautiful life," not its guilt. They thought the poet commiserated with them when he was actually taking them to task. He was Claudio's judge as well as his creator.[20]

Almost eight decades have elapsed since the publication of Hofmannsthal's first one-act play, *Gestern*,[21] and the case for his early insistence on the immorality of an ivory-tower art has long since been vigorously made. Had his contemporaries paid more heed to his essays and their unequivocal language, instead of misinterpreting the more ambiguous imagery of his poems and short lyrical plays, the question could have been settled right at the beginning. Years of controversy could have been avoided. No matter what subject he chose to dissect critically, be it d'Annunzio's last novel or Oscar Wilde's humiliating fate, in his essays Hofmanns-

[19] This is the last line of a verse motto introducing the second book of the novel. The poem reads:
Du beweinst, du liebst ihn, liebe Seele,
Rettest sein Gedächtnis von der Schmach;
Sieh, dir winkt sein Geist aus seiner Höhle:
Sei ein Mann und folge mir nicht nach.

[20] Alewyn, *Über Hugo von Hofmannsthal*, p. 66.

[21] First published in *Moderne Rundschau* (Vienna, 1891), under the pseudonym Theophil Morren. Now in *Gedichte und lyrische Dramen* (Frankfurt: S. Fischer, 1952), pp. 139-80.

thal never tired of preaching the supremacy of life over art and the artist's obligation towards this life in all its manifestations, the humbler the better. We saw how generously the young poet praised the achievements of Walter Pater. But in one respect, the fundamental one, he found the English writer wanting. "The third book, *Marius der Epikuräer*," he objects, "shows the total inadequacy of the aesthetic creed to build the whole conduct of life upon."[22] Aestheticism is fine in accessory matters, a failure in what counts most. It is characteristic of Hofmannsthal in his twenties to connect everything he sees or reads with his own existential problems and those of his epoch. Thus epicureanism in Pater's work is equated with the aestheticism to which Hofmannsthal was born an heir, from which he dissented, and which he strove all his life to replace with a philosophy committed to what he called "reality" or "existence." "At a certain half-mature age full of yearning and sophistication," he concedes, "the imagination of all of us has sponged voluptuously on Rome in its period of decadence." And then he proceeds to describe the Roman decline with expressions not only full of charm and seduction but clearly calculated to be confused with that other decadence closer to home from which he was struggling so desperately to extricate himself. "As they kept on living," he says of the ancient Romans, strengthening the analogy wherever he can, "not quite real and yet very witty and very beautiful as they were, with a morbid Narcissus beauty, they seemed to be most similar to ourselves." On the one hand the sentences that follow list the beauties of Roman life under Marcus Aurelius, but on the other, replete as they are with lilting sensuous sounds, they are also clearly meant to give an idea of the spell the beau-

[22] "Walter Pater," *Prosa I*, p. 205.

tiful life can cast over the unwary, especially through the incantational repetition of the word "beauty." "Vibrating from the deep traces of beauty, any beauty, the beauty of gently swelling vases and the beauty of rocky cliffs, the beauty of Antinous, the beauty of dying, of being dead, of flowers, of the goddess Isis, the beauty of the great courtesans, the beauty of the setting sun, of the Christian martyrs, the beauty of Psyche, of the crying, wandering naively perverse little Psyche of the *Golden Ass,* any beauty"—but now comes the anticlimax, the thunderclap that topples the flimsy card-house of beauty—"any beauty except the one great, ineffable one of existence; for it is hidden from weak generations."[23]

Many of Hofmannsthal's essays are astutely penetrating, critical scrutinies of writers, dancers, and painters from all countries, but they are also self-revelatory. Much of this criticism is self-criticism.[24] Once the principle has been recognized, it is easy to uncover the pattern even in unexpected places. Take the progression one can observe in the essays on Gabriele d'Annunzio,[25] the darling of the *fin de siècle.* In the first one, written in 1893 at the age of nineteen, Hofmannsthal once more laments the emptiness of the elite of aesthetes to which he pretends to belong: "We have nothing but a sentimental memory, a paralyzed will and the uncanny gift of self-duplication. We watch our own life; we empty the goblet prematurely and yet remain interminably thirsty.... We have no roots in life, as it were, and move

23 *Ibid.,* pp. 205-06.
24 Cf. Hilde Cohn, "Loris."
25 "Gabriele d'Annunzio I," "Gabriele d'Annunzio II," "Der neue Roman von d'Annunzio," and "Die Rede Gabriele d'Annunzios," all in *Prosa I,* pp. 147, 207, 233, and 288 respectively. It is possible to reach important conclusions about Hofmannsthal's development on the basis of these essays alone.

about the children of life like clairvoyant and yet blinded shadows."[26] The rest of the essay is devoted to showing how representative the Italian writer was of this generation. If there is any disharmony, it is not between Hofmannsthal and d'Annunzio but between their generation of artists and life.

The second essay, published only a little later,[27] shows the first signs of critical detachment. D'Annunzio is still praised for having lived by the aesthetic prescription of the age. He is acknowledged as a poet whom "the words with which we designate the joys and pains of life have made tremble, earlier, more strongly and more deeply than life itself." But this artificial anticipation of experience is a deception which cannot be carried on indefinitely. "But life is there nevertheless. Through its mere oppressive, inescapable existence it is infinitely more remarkable than anything artificial and infinitely more forceful and compelling. It has a frightfully stunning abundance and a frightfully demoralizing desolateness. With these two clubs it alternately beats upon the heads of those who don't serve it. But those whose first approach to life is artificial, don't serve it. Life hangs over them menacingly like a storm cloud, and they run back and forth like frightened sheep."[28] The conclusion is inevitable: "There is indeed something rigid and something artificial in Signor d'Annunzio's philosophy of life, and his books are still lacking the ultimate: revelation." The only saving grace is: "But he is still young."[29]

---

[26] *Prosa I*, p. 148. Hofmannsthal is very much aware of the fact that he is speaking of a small, albeit influential minority: "Wir! Wir!" he says. "Ich weiss ganz gut, dass ich nicht von der ganzen grossen Generation rede. Ich rede von ein paar Tausend Menschen, in den grossen europäischen Städten verstreut" (*loc.cit.*).

[27] A year later, in 1894.   [28] *Prosa I*, p. 209.

[29] *Ibid.*, p. 211.

Hofmannsthal returns to d'Annunzio again and again, as if driven by a compulsion. In his third essay, "Der neue Roman von d'Annunzio, *Le vergini delle rocce*"[30] of 1896, the reason for his revisitation becomes clear. Evidently he has not yet said everything that was on his mind, or rather his development has now reached a point where he can demonstrate with deadly outspokenness the sources of his earlier vague malaise: "At that time I found only uncertain and not very precise words for an enormous phenomenon which it will not be easy to ignore when the attempt is made to write the moral and aesthetic history of the present age. . . . The strange, or if you will, the horrible and dreadful thing about d'Annunzio's books was that they were written by one who did not *stand in life*. They were throughout the experiences of a man whose only connection with life had been through watching it. For every creative writer fashions incessantly but one basic experience of his life; and in the case of d'Annunzio this basic relationship to things had been *that he was watching them*."[31] These are portentous sentences. Hofmannsthal has found his own basic experience: that his era was divorced from life. His attempts to remedy this absurdity and to enter life will dominate his intellectual and artistic endeavors henceforth. The pampered *Wunderkind*, the aesthetic darling of the *fin de siècle* in Vienna, professes an ethical rigorism incompatible

[30] *Ibid.*, pp. 233-41.
[31] *Ibid.*, pp. 233 and 234. The italics are Hofmannsthal's own. This is not, however, the end of his admiration for d'Annunzio. The inevitable break came later, in 1912, in the wake of an anti-Austrian outburst on the part of the Italian writer, in Hofmannsthal's "Antwort auf die 'Neunte Canzone' Gabriele d'Annunzios," *Prosa II*, ed. Herbert Steiner (Frankfurt: S. Fischer, 1951), p. 81.

with the atmosphere in the "Capua of the spirits."[32]
A crisis seems inevitable.

Crisis

My case is briefly this: I have completely lost the abil-
ity to think or talk coherently about anything.

At first I became increasingly incapable of discussing
any higher general subject. I experienced an inexplica-
ble discomfort in even uttering such words as "spirit,"
"soul" or "body." . . . the abstract words the tongue must
use after all in order to pass any judgment whatsoever,
disintegrated in my mouth like rotten mushrooms.[33]

The impotence crystallized in these sentences is
known as Hofmannsthal's linguistic skepticism or denial
of speech.[34] The disease had been smoldering all
along, but it was not until 1902 that it broke out with
savage virulence and found inimitable expression in a
brilliant and moving piece, half fiction, half essay, entitled "Ein Brief," which has since attained fame in the
intellectual world.[35] This outbreak of despair had grave

[32] This is Franz Grillparzer's expression to signify the effem-
inating influence of Vienna's intellectual atmosphere with its surfeit of stimuli. Cf. Werner Volke, *Hofmannsthal in Selbstzeung-*
nissen, p. 7.

[33] *Prosa II*, pp. 11-12, from an essay entitled "Ein Brief" but
better known as "The Letter of Lord Chandos" or simply the
"Chandos Letter" which first appeared in 1902.

[34] This phenomenon is well known and much discussed by
Hofmannsthal scholars who usually refer to it as "Sprachskepsis"
or "Sprachverleugnung," for example in the following studies:
Karl Pestalozzi, *Sprachskepsis und Sprachmagie in Werke des*
jungen Hofmannsthal (Zurich: Atlantis, 1958); and Paul Requadt,
"Sprachverleugnung und Mantelsymbolik im Werke Hofmanns-
thals" in *Deutsche Vierteljahrsschrift für Literaturwissenschaft*
und Geistesgeschichte 29 (1955): 255-83; reprinted in *Hugo von*
Hofmannsthal, ed. Sibylle Bauer (Darmstadt: Wissenschaftliche
Buchgesellschaft, 1968).

[35] Proof of the universal significance of this piece of writing
is contained in Donald Davie's book *Articulate Energy: An*

consequences for Hofmannsthal himself. Not only did
he cease to write poetry, the poetry to which he owed
his privileged position among the men of letters in his
time, he turned to other genres, notably drama, as his
principal modes of expression. More significantly, Hofmannsthal also changed his artistic style and basic
outlook upon life, with the result that most of his
earlier devotees no longer understood him and regretfully parted company with their erstwhile idol.

Hofmannsthal's crisis was not merely a private affair.
It was part of a much wider intellectual crisis in Europe
which left its imprint on the writings of Joyce and
Maeterlinck, Kafka and Musil, Rilke, Valéry, and T. S.
Eliot.[36] The fourteen pages of "Ein Brief" are merely
the most striking statement and the most penetrating
analysis of a widespread upheaval in the intellectual
sensibility of Europe at the turn of the century. This is
Hofmannsthal's historical merit, and as a "confrontation with a phenomenon in his culture"[37] one of his
most notable critical achievements.

The essay—best known as "The Letter of Lord
Chandos" because it poses (with subtle hints at Hofmannsthal's own relationship with Stefan George) as a
fictitious communication directed by an Elizabethan

Inquiry into the Syntax of English Poetry (London: Routledge
& Kegan Paul, 1955) where the author discusses the Chandos Letter at the beginning of his introductory chapter on T. E. Hulme
(pp. 1-5). Walter Jens uses the Chandos Letter to characterize
what he calls "the revolution of German prose." "Der Mensch
und die Dinge: Die Revolution der deutschen Prosa" in *Akzente*
4 (1957): 319-21.

[36] Cf. the illuminating treatment of the entire phenomenon by
Theodore Ziolkowski, "James Joyces Epiphanie und die Über-
windung der empirischen Welt in der modernen deutschen Prosa,"
in *Deutsche Vierteljahrsschrift für Literaturwissenschaft und
Geistesgeschichte* 35 (1961): 594-616.

[37] See p. 12 of this essay.

gentleman to Francis Bacon—is more than the lament
of a gifted writer who feels the sources of poetry, his
very medium, language, drying up in his mind. It is a
full account of the writer's development in which we
readily recognize Hofmannsthal's intellectual career,
and it aroused such resonance only because it was
paradigmatic for the development of the European
mind as a whole. The crux of the matter is that in speaking of his earlier works, Lord Philipp Chandos recalls
and is still able to describe the frame of mind or rather
the ecstasies of the soul which accompanied their creation: "The whole of existence appeared to me at that
time in a kind of permanent intoxication as a great
unity: the spiritual and material world seemed not to
be in conflict. . . . I was in the midst of things everywhere
and never became cognizant of anything deceptive. Or
else I sensed that everything might be a parable and
every creature a key to the next. . . ."[38]

It is not difficult to sense that he is speaking here of a
mythical golden age of harmony between the individual
and the universe, which, from the vantage point of the
writer, appears as a lost paradise. It is also an exact
statement of the solipsism of *fin-de-siècle* aesthetics
which disdained the concrete outside world and used its
objects solely as playthings for the uninhibited self-
expression of the "beautiful life." We have touched
upon the most intimate part of Hofmannsthal's private
myth, which is to a large extent expressive of his contemporaries as well. Later in his life, in philosophical
retrospection, he called this trance-like state from which
his early intoxicating poetry flowed "pre-existence" and
labeled it "a glorious, but dangerous condition."[39] The

[38] *Prosa II*, p. 10.
[39] "Praeexistenz. Glorreicher, aber gefährlicher Zustand," in
"Ad me ipsum," *Aufzeichnungen*, p. 213.

glory is easy to understand. The capacity to relate all bodily and spiritual phenomena to one another, not to be bound by the laws of time and gravity, to turn the objects of the world into as many glittering gems by a mere touch of the poetic wand—all of this must swell the ego of the poet, who perpetrates such wonders with a feeling of having magic powers and mastery of the universe. No wonder young Hofmannsthal liked to project himself into the figures of sorcerers and emperors.[40]

We are now beginning to see the danger inherent in such a posture. It consists of a loss of reality, a dearth of respect for the life of things and people, a lack of humility. All of these can be summed up in one familiar term which has been used for centuries to describe just such delusions of grandeur: hybris. We can go even farther and say that the state of pre-existence is not only dangerous, but also sinful, and we are not at all surprised when Lord Chandos describes his inevitable fall from grace in words introducing, unobtrusively but nevertheless unmistakably, religious terminology: "To him who is amenable to such convictions it may appear as the well-laid plan of a divine providence that my spirit had to collapse from such a *blown up presumption* into this extreme faint-heartedness and impotence, which is now the permanent condition of my mind."[41] Fall from grace is the right expression. Chandos hastens to add: "this kind of religious conception has no power over me." But his skepticism is a necessary part of the myth. The prescribed mythological sequence is: Garden of Eden, Fall of Man, and then the endless search for

---

[40] For example in the poems "Ein Traum von grosser Magie" of 1895 and "Der Kaiser von China spricht" of 1897 or 1898, or in the verse play "Der Kaiser und die Hexe" of 1897, all contained in *Gedichte und lyrische Dramen* (Frankfurt: S. Fischer, 1952), pp. 20, 32, and 256-96, respectively.

[41] *Prosa II*, p. 11. Italics mine.

salvation. Hofmannsthal was born a Catholic with, among others, a line of Jewish ancestors. His great-grandfather was raised to the aristocracy by Emperor Ferdinand I, and his grandfather converted to the Christian faith. But this is not the point. It is much more important that he was raised and educated as a member of an enlightened, rationalistic, unbelieving *haute bourgeoisie* in the Austro-Hungarian Empire, and that religion for him was not a natural possession.

After the "Chandos crisis" Hofmannsthal repeatedly returned to religious topics and left behind a precious heritage of modern morality plays. In them there can be no doubt that Christianity plays the metaphorical role of Western tradition in conflict with the pagan non-values of the industrial age, just as there can be little doubt that the author searched for more than the allegorical meaning in Catholicism. Whether he as an individual reached such firmness of faith must and ought to remain an open question. Rather than joining a fruitless controversy, one should listen to the words he puts into the mouth of his double, the younger son of the Earl of Bath, Philipp Lord Chandos: "For me the mysteries of faith are condensed into a lofty allegory which hovers over the fields of my life like a luminous rainbow, invariably distant, always ready to recede if it occurred to me to approach it and to wrap myself in the hem of its cloak."[42] This points to a quest much larger than that of overcoming mere poetic sterility. "The Letter of Lord Chandos" marks the end of the first stage in Hofmannsthal's *oeuvre*. The crisis was not new nor is it over now. It never will be. But from this point on his work is characterized by an unceasing en-

[42] *Loc.cit.* For the pervasive role played by the cloak image in Hofmannsthal's work, consult Paul Requadt's treatise identified in footnote 34.

deavor to subordinate its aesthetic values to an ethical
philosophy, by entering the very premises of life, and to
place art in the service of life.

Maturity

*Connexion with Life. To penetrate from preexistence
to existence.*

*Introversion as the road into existence (The mystical
road.) . . . Letter of Lord Chandos. The situation of the
mystic without mysticism.*

*The road to life and to human beings through sacrifice.
. . . The road to society as the road to the higher self:
non-mystical a) through acting b) through work c)
through the child.*[43]

Art as an *ersatz* religion reached the highest peak
toward the end of the nineteenth century. Its arrogant
practitioners and their acolytes inhabited their ivory
temples in splendid isolation, occupied with their holy
rites and disdainful of everything that was ugly, commonplace, or practical. Their alienation from society
was merely a special instance of a broader phenomenon
in the Western world, the result of rapid economic
changes. From preponderantly agricultural societies,
at harmony with nature in spite of their material want,
they had turned into competitive industrial nations.
From the resulting turmoil and uprooting mankind has
not yet recovered. The disastrous consequences for the
individual and collective psyche are all too evident even
today. At the height of their self-removal from life, the
artists showed the ill effects of such isolation. The
rarefied atmosphere into which they had withdrawn
became unbreathable. They began to perish from spir-

[43] "Ad me ipsum," *Aufzeichnungen*, pp. 214, 215, 217.

itual asthma. Hofmannsthal, one of the youngest and
most adulated, began his arduous descent into the low-
lands, calling for a connexion with life, for a return to
people and society, for a breakthrough from pre-existence to existence. Finding a path, experimenting with
different approaches became his main occupation.

He could not of course undo the spiritual damage
done to his era by social forces beyond the control of an
individual, no matter how gifted. But his greatness lies
in having lent his not inconsiderable strength of creative energy to the task of understanding and healing.
He pictures his transformation in the nature of a sacrifice. He renounces the poetic eloquence belonging to
the period of pre-existence and subjects his language to
the frugality and asceticism proper for the exacting discipline of existence. But language is only symptomatic
in this struggle. This is how Richard Alewyn asses-
ses what the descent into life meant existentially for the
poet: "Thus Hofmannsthal broke out of the dead-end
street of aestheticism. He became aware of its psychic
danger, the danger of impoverishment in the midst of
life. . . . He realized its moral fault which consisted in
avoiding responsibility. . . . Finally, he recognized its
metaphysical error, namely that of ignoring arrogantly
and anxiously the dark side of life and to leave it un-
reconciled and untranscended. . . . Now Hofmannsthal
begins to explore the roads which lead to life: love,
marriage, fatherhood, society, action. . . ."[44] The record
of this development toward maturity is of course present
in the critical essays. Hofmannsthal can speak of "The
Letter of Lord Chandos" as depicting the mystical
way, the way of introversion, into existence, and of
Chandos himself as a mystic without mysticism because
in the second half the protagonist describes a strange

[44] *Über Hugo Von Hofmannsthal*, pp. 159 and 160.

phenomenon, the only experience that helps him transcend the bitterness and humiliation resulting from the emptiness of his inner life. "It is not easy for me to suggest to you what these good moments consist of," he complains. But then he does proffer a few examples. "A watering-can, a harrow abandoned in the field, a dog sunning himself, a pitiable church steeple, a cripple, a small farm house, all of these can become the vehicles of my revelation. . . . It can also be the definite conception of an absent object that is inconceivably chosen to be filled to the rim with that gently and suddenly rising tide of divine feeling."[45]

Simple, everyday things, augmented by some equally unassuming events, like the flight of quails or the physical torment of poisoned rats, things too commonplace or too hideous to have attracted the attention of the aesthete, now become the vehicle of a new mystical experience. Having given up the self-seeking *belparlare* of the earlier magical poetry, Chandos is now rewarded with those rare moments in which things give up to him their essence and he experiences what they are "in themselves." These "epiphanies" have been recognized as similar to states of mind described by other writers.[46] Such mystical moments[47] are not restricted to the Chandos letter: they occur in other of his critical writings,[48] and even in his most light-hearted comedies. Hofmannsthal stuck to a Platonist world view throughout his life, and he does not deny himself the

[45] *Prosa II*, p. 14.

[46] Cf. Theodore Ziolkowski's article identified in footnote 36.

[47] The expression is used and the phenomenon described by Egon Schwarz, "Hofmannsthal and the Problem of Reality," in *Wisconsin Studies in Contemporary Literature* 8 (1967): 485.

[48] For example in "Die Briefe des Zurückgekehrten," *Prosa II*, pp. 279-310; and "Augenblicke in Griechenland," *Prosa III*, ed. Herbert Steiner (Frankfurt: S. Fischer, 1952), pp. 7-42.

privilege of lifting occasionally the flimsy veil that con-
ceals ultimate reality. But the point is that he no longer pretends to have unobstructed access to that realm
of the spirit. In his later works Hofmannsthal is for the
most part content to remain within what ordinary mor-
tals call empirical reality and to show God's workings,
if need be, in our commonplace environment. His conversion could not be called complete if he were not to
explore other ways into life, social approaches to a meaningful existence accessible to someone not endowed
with poetic genius.

In as early an essay as the one on d'Annunzio's novel,[49]
Hofmannsthal's search for the life-giving mysteries
of everyday existence (if such a slightly paradoxical formulation is permissible) becomes apparent. It is touching to see that he is willing to forgive the frightening
rigidity and divorce from life in the earlier d'Annunzio because he thinks he can detect in him a similar turn
toward life. This is how Hofmannsthal recapitulates
a portion of d'Annunzio's novel: "The young noble-
man who is an artist would like a son, resembling himself. This is the eternal manner in which life tends to
perpetuate itself within us. However, when it grows into
such a stubborn passion this desire represents in the life
of a man the intense need for a connection with existence. Finding a mother for one's son means looking for
an action in which to spend one's strength and to come
alive."[50] It is amazing to encounter here, in a critical
essay written in 1896, purportedly about the work of
another, the vocabulary of *Die Frau ohne Schatten*
(The Woman without a Shadow), Hofmannsthal's own
allegorical libretto and fairy tale written in 1913. It is
not necessary to go into an analysis of the precise

[49] From which we have already quoted. Cf. footnote 30.
[50] *Prosa I*, p. 238.

function of the plot of d'Annunzio's novel to understand that Hofmannsthal is projecting his own concerns into whatever may be the immediate object of his occupation at a given moment. These concerns, at first still half-hidden, become much more explicit and elaborate in subsequent essays. But just as significant as the discovery of the ethical mission of the writer and the obligation of literature to serve life, is the exploration of the social dimension of man which Hofmannsthal takes up with increasing earnestness in the years of his maturity. The results are his delightful comedies, all of which are built, however, on a terribly serious historical subsoil. In the essays the expansion of his focus from the individual to society, from the "I" to the "Thou" is evident in his shift of emphasis from literary to cultural criticism. The early essays dealt largely with individuals. Théodore de Banville, Maurice Barrès, Franz Stuck, Eleonora Duse, Walter Pater, and Algernon Charles Swinburne are not only the subjects but also the titles of his critical work.[51] While the interest in individual writers and artists does not entirely subside, it is palpably supplemented by a considerable number of pieces the titles of which alone testify to the newly found responsibility of the artist to the world at large; titles such as "Der Dichter und diese Zeit," "Blick auf den geistigen Zustand Europas," and "Das Schrifttum als geistiger Raum der Nation."[52] Characteristic of this interaction between the individual and the world, on which Hofmannsthal now insists, is the famous "Briefe des Zurückgekehrten" of 1907 where, in the tradition of Montesquieu's *Lettres Persanes*, he has an outsider cast critical glances

[51] All in *Prosa I*.
[52] *Prosa II*, pp. 229-58; *Prosa IV*, ed. Herbert Steiner (Frankfurt: S. Fischer, 1955), pp. 75-80; *ibid.*, pp. 39-413.

at the state of culture, in this case German culture, and find it sadly wanting. "He [Hofmannsthal] rejected the presumption of excluding himself from life. He came to believe that even a poet is not exempted from being a man. Thus he himself went the way which led from the radiance of his youthful *oeuvre* into the unpretentious modesty of his late work. . . . It led from fame to obscurity, from the mythical realm to the human, indeed—*from the temple to the street*."[53] These are still valid words with which to characterize Hofmannsthal's transformation. All we have to add to them is an elucidation. "Street" in this context not only stands for the unsheltered and the commonplace but is also the meeting ground of individuals of all professions and ages, of differing backgrounds and degrees of intelligence, a symbol of society as a whole.

In a series of imaginary conversations which sometimes take the form of communications directed from one friend to another, like the Chandos letter, Hofmannsthal uses his essays as substitutes for more traditional modes of creativity. The inventive freedom, both in character and in situation, which this form allows tips the balance of intellectual-conceptual and intuitive-creative forces making up the essay[54] in favor of the latter. What the essays of this period have in common is a tentative two-fold solution to the impasse Hofmannsthal has reached: a stress upon the religious-mystical process of creation culminating in mystical moments. These in turn may not be entirely compatible with a quest for a starker realism which demands

[53] Alewyn, *Über Hugo von Hofmannsthal*, pp. 160-61. Alewyn's italics because the phrase is taken from Hofmannsthal's sketch "Der Priesterzögling," now in *Dramen III*, ed. Herbert Steiner (Frankfurt: S. Fischer, 1957), p. 493.

[54] Cf. Theodor W. Adorno, "Der Essay als Form" in *Noten zur Literatur I* (Frankfurt: Suhrkamp, 1965), pp. 9-49.

the subservience of individual subjectivity to the inexorable self-sufficiency of the outside world.[55] This quest is metaphorically subsumed under the image of the road to life. Once Hofmannsthal establishes some routine in his two approaches to productivity, which resemble the ancient prescription for a *vita activa* and a *vita contemplativa*, his self-reliance will be restored and result in the sovereign cultural criticism of his maturity.

STATE AND SOCIETY

He who says Austria really says: a thousand years of struggle for Europe, a thousand-year mission through Europe, a thousand years of faith in Europe.

For us, Germans and Slavs and Latins dwelling on the soil of two Roman Empires, chosen to bear a common destiny and inheritance—for us Europe is truly the basic color of the planet, for us Europe will be the color of the stars when from an unclouded sky the stars will again shine above us.[56]

We are better prepared for what will have to come now than anyone in Europe. Stronger than partisanship and ideologies—which are erroneously regarded as the only manifestations of politics—is the fateful mission which demands of us that we absorb Europe into our German character and that we balance this no longer exclusively German nationality with the Slavic element. The ideas of conciliation, of synthesis, of overarching the cleavages have their own effective force, their spon-

---

[55] See Mary E. Gilbert's article (cited in footnote 13) where, among other things, she addresses herself to the question of why Hofmannsthal used the imaginary dialogue in preference to other modes of expression during the years in question (1900-1908).

[56] "Die Idee Europa. Notizen zu einer Rede" (1916), now in *Prosa III*, p. 383.

taneity. This Europe which is about to reconstitute itself needs Austria: a complex of unaffected elasticity, but a complex, a true organism pulsating with its own inner religion without the likes of which no combination of living powers is possible.[57]

There can be no doubt about Hofmannsthal's growing involvement with social issues. The question one has to raise is about the particular form this involvement takes in those writings which can be legitimately called his "criticism." A glance at his essays (some of which were conceived and delivered as public lectures) instructs the reader that the author's politico-cultural concerns appear in them strangely transmuted. Even though highly allegorical in character, some of Hofmannsthal's later dramatic works reflect in amazing concreteness the political concerns of the era. The rise of the lower classes with both its ironic and its turbulent effects is portrayed in the comedy, *Der Unbestechliche.*[58] While groping for a Christian solution, *Jedermann* and *Das Salzburger Grosse Welttheater (The Salzburg Great Theatre of the World)*,[59] present with undisguised censure, admirable in someone identifying himself with the possessing classes, the human and social hybris not merely of the rich, but of the modern rich, skillfully stylized in the direction of imperialist capitalists. In the second of the two plays the Calderonian beggar appears on the scene transformed into a twentieth-century proletarian revolutionary propounding his case against a hypocritical social order in powerful and moving language. His best phrases are clearly borrowed from the *Communist Manifesto*. This figure must be regarded as among the finest and most

[57] "Die österreichische Idee" (1917), *Prosa III*, pp. 405-406.
[58] Now in *Lustspiele IV* (Frankfurt: S. Fischer, 1956).
[59] Both in *Dramen III*.

sympathetic allegorizations of the working classes. It would be difficult to find in all of modern literature, including its avowedly Marxist practitioners, a more forceful portrayal of their plight as well as their dignity preserved under conspicuously unpropitious circumstances.

In the historical tragedy, *Der Turm (The Tower)*,[60] Hofmannsthal finally analyzes with uncommon political astuteness the various socio-political forces vying for supremacy in the Europe of the era. The figure of Olivier is a frighteningly accurate and, in view of the time when the final version was written,[61] a prophetic representation of the totalitarian mentality in its most contemporary manifestation. Beyond that, this work, in spite of its mythological atmosphere, pays attention to such economico-political phenomena as monetary inflation, the corruption of the upper strata of society, and the abdication of the clergy from political responsibility.

None of this topical detail is present in Hofmannsthal's critical writings where the more frankly political the occasion, the more abstract and veiled his mode of expression appears to become. An illuminating example of this approach can be found in his famous essay "Das Schrifttum als geistiger Raum der Nation,"[62] originally a speech delivered in the Auditorium Maximum of the University of Munich on January 10, 1927. It was on the basis of this address that Hofmannsthal was classified as a proponent of the "Conservative Revolution."[63] Today this phrase is used as a label for an in-

---

[60] *Dramen IV*, ed. Herbert Steiner (Frankfurt: S. Fischer, 1958).
[61] 1927.
[62] *Prosa IV*, pp. 390-414.
[63] Cf. Detlev W. Schumann, "Gedanken zu Hofmannsthals Begriff der 'Konservativen Revolution,'" in *Publications of the Modern Language Association* 54 (1939): 853-99.

tellectual movement of the twenties, without a well-defined program but, in spite of its fragmentation and inner contradictions, with certain recognizable historical attitudes. Golo Mann, in his book on German history,[64] attributes some of these to the intellectual leadership of Ernst Jünger but even more decisively to that of Oswald Spengler. "By praising old Prussia but criticizing the monarchy, by ridiculing the ideal of progress, by glorifying war but claiming to be a socialist, by completely overthrowing conventional ways of thinking in politics Spengler became the co-founder of an intellectual movement which the present writer cannot ignore, however confused it was and however little came of it in the end. It was called the 'Conservative Revolution.' A strange combination of words, indicating that its supporters rejected not certain aspects of the Republic but the whole of it, and the whole present; they regarded 'Right' as outmoded as 'Left' and wanted to ask completely new questions and offer completely new ideals. This they all had in common, however much their views differed otherwise. . . . They disliked the face of European democracy; the League of Nations with its impotent hypocrisy; the Reichstag with its intrigues and jobbery. . . . They wanted a new Reich without party squabbles, a Reich of the young and of masculine virtues, a great, proud gathering around a camp-fire instead of the capital Berlin."[65]

In "Das Schrifttum als geistiger Raum der Nation" Hofmannsthal uses the slogan "Konservative Revolu-

---

[64] *The History of Germany Since 1789*, trans. M. Jackson (New York and Washington: Frederick A. Praeger, 1968). See also Bernd Peschken's interesting discussion in his "Zur Entwicklungsgeschichte von Hofmannsthals *Turm*, mit ideologiekritischer Absicht," in *Germanisch-Romanische Montasschrift*, N. F. Bd., 19, no. 2 (1969): 152-78, esp. 177-78.

[65] Golo Mann, *The History of Germany Since 1789*, p. 377.

tion" in such a manner that his identification with at least part of the movement must have been clear to his audience of well-informed students, many of whom probably shared its impulses. His address which contrasts the cultural life of the French nation with that of the Germans culminates in the following apparently laudatory apostrophe: "I am speaking of a process in the midst of which we live, a synthesis as slow and grandiose, if one were able to observe it from without, as it is somber and taxing when one is standing within it. We may call this process slow and grandiose when we consider that even the long period of development from the convulsions of the Enlightenment to our days is merely a section of it, that it really began as an inner countermovement against the intellectual revolution of the sixteenth century which we are accustomed to call by its two aspects Renaissance and Reformation. The process I am speaking about is nothing other than a conservative revolution of a dimension the likes of which European history has not seen. Its goal is form, a new German reality in which the entire nation might participate."[66]

And yet, a reader in the second half of the twentieth century must be allowed his doubts as to the appropriateness of classifying Hofmannsthal as a truly representative proponent of this "conservative revolution." He almost surely agreed with some of its tenets, especially the many ideals that the "conservative revolutionaries" derived from romanticism and its glorification of the past and the social hopes that they nourished with words and concepts from the Middle Ages: ". . . estates versus classes, guilds versus mere associations of interest and so on. Even the idea of the empire came from the Middle Ages and there was mention of the old

[66] *Prosa IV*, pp. 412-13.

Hohenstaufen glory."[67] After all, early attempts on the part of literary historians classified Hofmannsthal as an exponent of Neo-Romanticism which was revived around the turn of the century. And yet there are good reasons for denying Hofmannsthal's full identification with the "conservative revolution." That the mention of this catch-phrase is an isolated instance in Hofmannsthal's *oeuvre*, would prove little. But we have to look beyond slogans. Closer scrutiny reveals that the essay cannot by any stretch of the imagination be read as a declaration of allegiance, not even excluding the final passage already quoted, where the positive attributes are carefully balanced with cautionary adjectives.

Whatever the atmosphere may have been at the moment of the original address, the tone of voice of the entire piece strikes the modern reader as that of the objective analyst, the detached historian. How else is one to explain the qualifying "somber" with which Hofmannsthal characterizes the movement? Seen in this light, even the word "grandiose"[68] loses some of its emotional tone and acquires a quantifying property, indicating the historical significance of the phenomenon described at least as much as its luster and appeal for the current generation. The contrast between French and German culture which gives the essay its internal structure is carried out without the slightest polemical overtone. Like Nietzsche, to whom Hofmannsthal explicitly refers and to whose *Unzeitgemässe Betrachtungen* he owes a great deal of his understanding of modernity, Hofmannsthal respects, even reveres French culture. Its clarity, sense of order, and tradition, which he sees reflected in the spirit of the language and of its writers, are dealt with as wholly ad-

---

[67] Golo Mann, *The History of Germany Since 1789*, p. 378.
[68] *Prosa IV*, p. 412.

mirable characteristics. Echoing the time-honored po-
larities of "being" (*sein*) and "becoming" (*werden*)
"having" (*haben*) and "seeking" (*suchen*), he describes
the Germans in contradistinction to the French as
ardent seekers and soul-searchers. Adroitly, almost im-
perceptibly applying this concept to the intellectual
turmoil of the present, Hofmannsthal then proceeds
to paint a portrait of the types of seekers exemplify-
ing what he will later term the Conservative Revolution. One of these seekers evidently horrifies Hofmannsthal himself. Only secret terror can explain and
justify the use of the summarizing term "somber," mentioned above. In characterizing a leader of youth he
employs ambivalent terminology throughout. He speaks
of him as "the roving intellectual emerging from chaos,
pretending to be a teacher and a leader—with even
bolder demands—with the mark of genius upon his tall
forehead, with the stigma of the usurper in his fearless
eye or his daringly formed ear."[69] "Perhaps he is more
of a prophet than a poet, perhaps he is an erotic dream-
er," Hofmannsthal says in trying to come to grips with
his own vision of the man destined to shape the German future.[70] At any rate, he concludes, such a seeker
is "a dangerous hybrid nature, a lover and a hater and
a teacher and a seducer at the same time."[71]

At the risk of coming into conflict with the traditional view of the famous address, today one can ad-
duce a great deal of evidence for reading it as a warning against the Conservative Revolution rather than
as an exhortation towards it. To enhance the plausibil-
ity of this reading it is sufficient to visualize the psycho-

[69] *Ibid.*, p. 401.
[70] It seems that the character of Julian in *Der Turm* is made up
of some of these characteristics.
[71] Mann, *The History of Germany Since 1789*, p. 402.

logical situation of the speech's origin. Facing a German academic audience with tendencies toward irrationalism and a questionable cult of mystical leadership, of which Hugo von Hofmannsthal was well aware, he tells his youthful listeners about the risks involved in their quest. It is true that he speaks of a reaction against the Renaissance and the Enlightenment, but is it therefore also necessarily true that he shared in the reaction? After all, the words "dangerous" and "seducer" are of Hofmannsthal's own choice.

There exists another argument for the notion that Hofmannsthal spoke to the Munich students as an outsider. That they constituted a *German* audience was said advisedly. Hofmannsthal spoke to them as an Austrian. Large amounts of his spiritual energy went into conceiving, refining, and formulating his notions of what was Austrian as well as understanding the complex relationships between Austrians and Germans. Hofmannsthal's attitude towards the Germans was ambivalent. It ranged from overt hostility[72] to conciliation and an appeal for more attention to Austria on the part of the Germans. "Less and less time and attentiveness remained for Austria," he complains in an essay totally devoted to an analysis of this relationship, "Wir Österreicher und Deutschland." "Austria is the special task given the German mind in Europe,"[73] he concludes. The most famous of his juxtapositions of the two nations, which became an obsession with Hofmannsthal, is contained in "Preusse und Österreicher: Ein Schema" where the bold attempt is made to distill their national characteristics into two opposing columns. While the weaknesses of both are unsparingly

---

[72] For example, in the figure of Baron Neuhoff in the comedy *Der Schwierige.*

[73] (1915), *Prosa III*, p. 230.

exposed, one cannot help but feel that the balance tips in favor of Austria to whom "more humanity" is attributed as against "more efficiency" on the side of Prussia.[74] The source of Hofmannsthal's ambivalence lies of course in history itself which has made Austria a part of greater Germany and at the same time something quite distinct and unique. It is characteristic that the writer of "Die Briefe des Zurückgekehrten" is an Austrian and that a severe critique of the contemporary German scene is entrusted to one who is a part of the nation and yet an outsider. He recalls having asked his father about Austria and receiving this answer: "It is true, down here is Austria . . . and we are Austrians, but we are also Germans, and since the land always belongs to the people who live in it this is also Germany."[75] Hofmannsthal always remained conscious of this ambiguity and of the dangers to conceptual clarity emanating from it. "I am confounding the simplicity of your feelings by postulating a dualism, whereas you wish to see the unity of the language guarantee every other unity with the great German nation," he concedes. But at the same time he insists on separation, demanding that it be accepted as a fact and turned into a benefit: "in the terrible and critical cultural and political situation in which we find ourselves we must know how to preserve this dualism of feeling: our belonging to Austria and our cultural belonging to the German totality."[76]

[74] "Mehr Menschlichkeit," "Mehr Tüchtigkeit." *Prosa III*, p. 407.

[75] *Prosa II*, p. 294. Another time Hofmannsthal expresses this dualism in a kind of mathematical formula: "Deutschheit aber ohne Sehnsucht, ohne Schweifendes, Grösse ohne Titanisches," in "Österreich im Spiegel seiner Dichtung" (1916), *Prosa III*, p. 333.

[76] *Prosa III*, pp. 344-45.

There is much to recommend the idea that Hofmannsthal spoke to the Munich students in his dual role
as Austrian and German.

What was Austria to Hugo von Hofmannsthal? Before
trying to answer this question, one ought to say what
Hofmannsthal was to Austria: by fate and inclination
he became the glorifier of the Austrian mission shortly
before its extinction. As Karl Anton Prince Rohan said
at the poet's death: "L'esprit autrichien perd en Hofmannsthal sa figure spirituelle représentative par excellence."[77] The discussion of the phenomenon Austria
was a favorite intellectual pastime during the early part
of the twentieth century. But with his positive, indeed
optimistic, attitude toward it, Hofmannsthal was a
member of a tiny minority. Austria was perceived by
most intellectuals to be a paradigm of the larger general
decadence. "It is the *Austrian paradox* that in its very
backwardness the monarchy anticipated symptoms of
the general decay; that in Austria, where everything
was retarded, the putrefaction of the capitalist world,
the problems of the last stage came early."[78] One does
not have to be a Marxist like Ernst Fischer, who wrote
these words from the secure knowledge of hindsight, to
view Austria in this fashion. From Grillparzer to Karl
Kraus, from Nestroy to Joseph Roth, proponents and
detractors alike were impressed with the same decline,
the same paralysis of the will.

Robert Musil, hardly a socialist realist, offered the
following devastating diagnosis as early as 1909, thus
antedating many of Hofmannsthal's own essays on
Austria: "This somnolent state which watched over its

[77] "Hofmannsthal et l'Autriche," in *Revue d'Allemagne et des
pays de langue allemande*, 3 (1929): 939. Cf. also page 16 of
Egon Schwarz' article identified in footnote 8.

[78] Ernst Fischer, *Von Grillparzer zu Kafka. Sechs Essays*
(Vienna: Globus Verlag, 1962), p. 294.

peoples with two blind eyes also had real fits of severity and despotism; . . . one may call the spirit of the state absolutistic against its will; it would have preferred to proceed democratically if it had only known how. But who made up this state? It was not supported by a unified nation or a free union of nations which might have used it for their skeleton, it was not nurtured by a spirit born of a private society which, once it has attained a certain strength in an issue, penetrates the state; in spite of many talents in its officialdom and some individual good work it really did not have a brain at all for it lacked a center for the formation of a will and of ideas. It was an anonymous administrative organism; actually a ghost, a form without matter, imbued with illegitimate influences for lack of legitimate ones."[79] And summarizing, he notes: "This grotesque Austria is but a particularly obvious case of the modern world."[80]

The only thing Hofmannsthal had in common with these prophets of doom, whose visions of course turned out to be right in the end, was his conviction that Austria was somehow representative of the European whole, a summary of Europe. For him Austria was not decrepit; old and venerable yes, but certainly not decadent. "The mentality arising among us," he proclaimed, "is the mentality of a young organism much rather than that of a decaying one."[81] Above all, Austria was for Hugo von Hofmannsthal a spiritual synthesis. There was the glittering, culturally saturated capital and the vast untapped strength of the provinces; the German speaking leadership and the multitongued masses of the hinterlands; the historical

[79] Quoted by Ernst Fischer, *Von Grillparzer zu Kafka*, p. 239.
[80] *Ibid.*, p. 238.
[81] "Die Bejahung Osterreichs" (1914), *Prosa III*, p. 193.

traditions on the one hand and on the other a youth-
fulness so virile that Hofmannsthal does not shrink from
calling Austria "a European America"[82] where others
merely saw an ossified Alexandria or mandarinate; a
breathing organism receiving nourishment from the
north and the west while imparting its substance to the
south and the east.

Hofmannsthal was not impervious to severe tensions
between such multiple factors. He saw the Baroque
palaces of the city center and the almost Asiatic bleak-
ness of the suburbs,[83] the luxury of the well-to-do and
the growing misery of the proletarians. He felt the contrast between the ceremonial pomp of the court and
the explosive fermentation of the Slavs, between a
city of music, dance, and theater and the cultural depri-
vation of the masses. He sensed that the security[84] of
the upper classes was threatened by economic catastrophes, the tolerance and psychic sensitivity of Lib-
eralism by a rising anti-semitism and irrationalism in
politics. But he was also convinced that it was Austria's
mission to set an example for Europe by harmonizing
and synthesizing these differences, and he supported the

[82] "Wir Österreicher und Deutschland," *ibid.*, p. 231.

[83] It may not be superfluous to remind the reader that, before
the heavy inroads of industrialization into the European cities,
the suburbs were the abode of the lower classes while the well-to-
do had their houses in the inner city.

[84] Stefan Zweig in his autobiography (identified in footnote 10)
devotes a paean to the feeling of security in his native Vienna in
the period before World War I. As a result of the war experience,
Hofmannsthal condemned a social order based on such a sense
of security. In "Die Idee Europa" (1916) he accuses his civilization of having set up a series of false idols: "Ohne Scheu betete
diese Welt die drei Götzen Gesundheit, Sicherheit und langes
Leben an, Kultus der Sicherheit, des Behagens, Komfort ohne
Schönheit" (*Prosa III*, p. 377). In these "Notizen zu einer Rede"
there are many echoes of a critique of European culture from the
political right, to be adopted by the proponents of a Conservative Revolution after the war.

Austrian war effort because he believed that Austria was fighting to preserve a way of life which alone could save Europe from barbaric chauvinism, crass materialism, and a soulless technocracy.[85] Most of Hofmannsthal's utterances on Austria were prompted by World War I. They must be read and understood as manifestoes of a basically apolitical man, an artist who saw his heritage threatened, came to its defense, and tried to make the best of a difficult situation. It is useless not to admit that viewed from the second half of the century they appear as the least pleasant part of Hofmannsthal's essayistic *oeuvre*. But at the same time it is necessary to stress that in spite of all their partisanship in favor of Austria the essays of those years are conspicuously lacking in belligerency against the other side. In the middle of war hysteria against foreign influences, he expressed himself against a boycott of imported merchandise and, more importantly, he came to the defense of foreign elements in the language;[86] moreover, in 1916 he publicly praised the wonderful cohesion of the French nation, its bold synthesis, offering it as a "great example."[87] Hofmannsthal did not view the war as the collapse of an old order, he merely recognized in it a European catastrophe to test the entire civilization, a crisis in which the false values would be shaken off, and thus the purified true ones prepared for a better synthesis. "It is inevitable that a new epoch of the soul will follow the war,"[88] he was able to declare.

Of those who supported the Allied war aims, Hof-

---

[85] Just as Thomas Mann supported the German war effort in his *Betrachtungen eines Unpolitischen* (written during the war and published in 1919).

[86] "Boykott fremder Sprachen?" (1914), *Prosa III*, pp. 182-88; and "Unsere Fremdwörter" (1914), *ibid.*, pp. 195-203.

[87] "Österreich im Spiegel seiner Dichtung," *ibid.*, p. 343.

[88] "Die Idee Europa," *ibid.*, p. 383.

mannsthal was predestined to take up the dialogue with intellectuals on the other side because of his lack of hostility toward Austria's opponents in the conflagration. He did so in reply to what must have been a challenge by a number of French writers. The little essay is entitled "An Henri Barbusse, Alexandre Mercereau und ihre Freunde" (1919) and concludes on a brotherly note: "The enormity of our situation is without parallel. And this is only the beginning, nothing but the departure. Our road is dangerous: but we shall go it together."[89] Earlier he had confessed: "We are an ambivalent nation, and we have trouble understanding ourselves. Dark guests among the peoples of the earth, we have to endure it when the world distrusts us, even if we have acted and moved sincerely, if unexpectedly."[90] With their slight note of contrition, these words are acceptable from one to whom self-criticism was never alien and who had generous words for the adversary even at the peak of everybody else's belligerency.

Hofmannsthal lived in a time of great historical upheavals. He knew that many conflicting currents of the epoch sought expression through the poetic word.[91] One of the conflicts in the midst of which he stood and which was partially reflected in his own psyche was inherent in Viennese *fin-de-siècle* society. The upper strata of the bourgeois classes in Austria to which Hofmannsthal belonged developed a liberal culture which, in its moral and scientific orientation, was scarcely distinguishable from the Victorianism in other European countries. "Morally it was secure, righteous, and repressive; politically it was concerned for the rule of law. . . . It was intellectually committed by the rule of the mind

[89] *Ibid.*, p. 440.
[90] *Ibid.*, p. 439.
[91] "Der Dichter und diese Zeit" (1907), *Prosa II*, p. 248.

over the body and to a latter-day Voltairism: to social progress through science, education, and hard work."[92] However, by the end of the century this class had withdrawn, because of its political setbacks, from public leadership. In its now prevailing mood of impotent frustration it evolved an introspective, apolitical, aesthetic culture, a belief in art for art's sake which "elsewhere in Europe . . . implied the withdrawal of its devotees from a social class; in Vienna alone it claimed the allegiance of virtually a whole class, of which the artists were a part. The life of art became a substitute for the life of action. Indeed, art became almost a religion, the source of meaning and the food of the soul, as civic action proved increasingly futile."[93]

Consciously or unconsciously, Hofmannsthal tried to mediate between these two tendencies of his own social class. The concept of a multiracial, multinational Austria, reflecting in its variegated cultural background the condition and the potential of Europe, served him to reconcile, to synthesize, the claims of a basically individualist sensitivity to art and poetry and those of a politically active, ethically just social order. The need for this unifying concept made Hofmannsthal blind to the decadence, indeed the disintegration, of his society at a time when other Austrian writers were preoccupied with practically nothing else. When he was finally forced to admit the reality of disintegration because it had actually taken place before his very eyes in the cataclysmic end of World War I, Hofmannsthal's world had fallen apart together with the Habsburg

[92] "Even those who won a patent of nobility were not admitted to the life of the imperial court." Carl E. Schorske, "Politics and the psyche in *fin-de-siècle* Vienna: Schnitzler and Hofmannsthal," *American Historical Review* 46, no. 4 (1961): 933.

[93] *Ibid.*, 934-35.

Empire. The "Austrian ideal"[94] no longer existed and, because of the failure of its model, that other goal of Hofmannsthal's, a culturally unified Europe, had not many hopes of being realized either. Courageous as he was, Hofmannsthal kept reiterating his convictions and confronting them with the modern developments to which he could not close his eyes.[95] But more and more, apocalyptic visions darkened his optimistic thinking. That synthetic creature, Austrian and European, artistic and political man, visionary and social reformer, must give way to the rise of sinister forces. His prototype, Prince Sigismund of Poland in *Der Turm (The Tower)*, dies tragically in resignation at the hands of Olivier, the totalitarian worshipper of brute force to whom the future belongs. The only ray of hope this gloomy tragedy, Hofmannsthal's last message to us, emits is contained in the dying words Sigismund whispers into the ears of his two remaining loyal followers, a doctor and a servant, allegorical representations of the traditionalist-universalist intellectual and the good Austrian people: "Bear witness, I was here even though nobody knew me."[96]

It is possible to say that Hofmannsthal died a tragic premature death.[97] The defeat of the best of his hopes cast a gloom over his last years of life. He had opposed the materialism of his age, and materialism was triumphant. He had feared the increasing technification

[94] "Die österreichische Idee" (1917), *Prosa III*, pp. 402-406.

[95] In his essay "Blick auf den geistigen Zustand Europas" (1921), Hofmannsthal recognizes "dass wir uns in einer der schwersten geistigen Krisen befinden, welche Europa vielleicht seit dem sechzehnten Jahrhundert, wo nicht seit dem dreizehnten, erschüttert haben, und die den Gedanken nahelegt, ob 'Europa,' das Wort als geistiger Begriff genommen, zu existieren aufgehört habe." *Prosa IV*, p. 75.

[96] *Dramen IV*, p. 463.

[97] Egon Schwarz, *Hofmannsthal und Calderón*, p. 21.

of the world, and practically the only principle emerging intact from World War I was an unchecked trend toward technology. He had been against capitalism, socialism, and relativism, and these forces were strengthened rather than weakened by the war. He had wanted to restore commitment, religion, the absolute as guiding principles for mankind. In these endeavors he may have resembled those constituting the Conservative Revolution.

But Hofmannsthal was more complex than that. He cherished the Enlightenment and loved its foremost German representative, Gotthold Ephraim Lessing.[98] He refused to reject the United States and the naive idea of progress for which it stood in the minds of many Europeans. He was an undaunted opponent of bigotry and chauvinism, and to the last he reaffirmed his hope for a Europe unified in spirit even though he was well aware of the threats to it. By instinct and upbringing Hofmannsthal was a man of the middle,[99] a synthesizer

[98] As late as 1929, the year of his death and the 200th anniversary of Lessing's birth, Hofmannsthal wrote a profoundly laudatory, one might say loving, appraisal of the great German author. "Gotthold Ephraim Lessing," *Prosa IV*, pp. 480-85.

[99] Cf. the conclusion of Michael Hamburger's essay "Hofmannsthal and England," in *Hofmannsthal—Studies in Commemoration*, ed. F. Norman (London, 1963), p. 28: "Hofmannsthal was more than a 'good European'; he attempted nothing less than to attain and uphold a Goethean universality in an age of which Yeats wrote:

> Things fall apart; the centre cannot hold;
> Mere anarchy is loosed upon the world.
> The blood-dimmed tide is loosed, and everywhere
> The ceremony of innocence is drowned;
> The best lack all conviction, while the worst
> Are full of passionate intensity.

To this state of anarchy Hofmannsthal struggled to oppose a 'passionate intensity' quite unlike the fanaticism of 'the worst,'

and conciliator, someone who wanted to preserve the old values by cautiously adjusting them to new conditions. It is from Hofmannsthal's criticism that this position of humanistic equilibrium emerges distinctly and admirably.

CRITICAL ATTITUDE

I am absolutely lacking the means as well as the intention of practicing any sort of philosophy of art. I shall not attempt to augment the treasure of your concepts even by a single new one. Likewise, I shall not try to criticize any of the concepts on which your views of these aesthetic things may rest, if they rest, that is, on concepts at all and not, as I secretly and firmly hope, on a chaotic mixture of confused, complex, and incommensurable inner experiences. . . . It is not my ambition to move walls; my ambition is simply to step forth from them at as many different points as possible, and at as many unexpected ones as possible, and thereby to startle you in a not unpleasant manner.[100]

The transition from Hofmannsthal's conception of state and society to his poetics lies in the idea that the creative writer is a seismograph. Every vibration is registered by him, no matter how delicate or how far away. The poet, according to another metaphor, is a deep-sea diver who is capable of living miraculously under the enormous pressure of all the things that exist in the world, whether past or present. Be it ultraviolet rays, skeletons of prehistoric creatures, cities like Athens, Rome, and Carthage, factories or slave markets, every-

---

a passionate intensity tempered with understanding, committed to the centre and yet as all-embracing as the other is exclusive and destructive. . . ."

[100] *Prosa II*, p. 229.

thing is of concern to him; everything clamors to be integrated into the universal order on which he is working all the time.[101] But there is a special connection between the present epoch and a poet like Hofmannsthal. "We are supposed to take leave of a world before it collapses. Many know this and an indefinable feeling makes poets of them,"[102] he wrote in 1905, more than a decade before the historical event that actually swept his world away. The feeling that an epoch was coming to an end, that a peculiar kind of civilization was to be drowned in a historical cataclysm was probably one of the most powerful impulses for Hofmannsthal's criticism. It explains the range as well as the flavor of his critical essays. Indefatigably he sought out the favorite or the most characteristic or even the fortuitous objects that made up this world and preserved them in his mellow prose. It did not matter whether they were sudden apparitions on the artistic horizon of his times, rapidly tiring of too many sensations, or whether they belonged to the canon of venerable cultural possessions of the past. Indeed, it did not matter whether or not they were artistic at all because the landscapes Hofmannsthal knew would disappear together with those who could see and describe them intelligently, incorporating them into the unique universe of the prewar epoch. This wonderful universe was formed of writers and dancers, poems and paintings, cities and countries, past and present, and together they would be demolished by the catastrophes to come. Therefore it was imperative for the lover and connoisseur of them all to visit and revisit them ceremoniously for the purpose of snatching them from the floods. Hofmannsthal, the rescuer, always rushed to the spot of greatest danger. This is why he

[101] *Ibid.*, p. 248.   [102] *Ibid.*, p. 157.

wrote obsessively about Austria during the war that was going to destroy it (embellishing it as one does with something beloved about to be lost), and this is also why he courageously held fast to certain beloved fragments of it still floating about in the postwar chaos.

The impulse to warn of what was coming, to behold a thing of beauty lovingly for the last time, or to save a worthy figure from oblivion also accounts for the *style* of Hofmannsthal's approach. His instrument was not the sharp dissecting knife of the evaluating critic. Hofmannsthal's approving evaluations were completed long before his critical acts. They were the very reasons for his criticism. No wonder he had little use for "the barrenness of concepts."[103] His purpose was a different one: to approach his subject gingerly, to touch it gently, to praise it wistfully, to recreate it—never in its entirety and its full realistic weight, but a fine representative feature of it, a lovely part of its surface, and above all the special atmosphere surrounding it.

All of this resulted in an evocative criticism, full of empathy and mood, of metaphors and similes, devoid of harsh or even firm judgments, and lacking in strict hierarchies. Comprehension, not evaluation, is Hofmannsthal's purpose; images, not concepts, are his tools. His critical essays are sublime and intimate conversations into which the reader feels drawn as an equal partner. In each piece a different mood is created by means of a subtle, irresistible, but ultimately indescribable magic. Each is full of exquisite images, delicate allusions, and hints as vague as they are numerous, all of which result in a strong but indefinite aura. The structure of his essays is not imposed from without, but is internal, by way of association. Many have no clear be-

[103] "Lafcadio Hearns," *ibid.*, p. 106.

ginning and no accentuated end, thus pointing to something infinite. No wonder one speaks of Hofmannsthal's "open form." Vaguely but suggestively one could also speak of his poetic criticism.[104] "Poetic" in this context would mean more evocative than conceptual, relying more on the magic of sound and rhythm than on intellectual analysis, showing a preference for imagery rather than for sharp definitions and witty punch-lines. The "poetic" component of Hofmannsthal's criticism would also explain his preoccupation with inner form and his experimentation with subgenres such as fictitious letters and dialogues, public addresses with their direct involvement of the listener in the thought processes, the *feuilleton*, the preface, and the treatise.

All of this points to a certain tradition in criticism. Donald Davie, a poet and critic himself, drew a picture of the general posture of literary criticism in his native culture[105] that resembles Hofmannsthal's practice in an amazing number of significant details. With the aid of Davie's portrait it is possible to assert that traditional British criticism shares with Hugo von Hofmannsthal its basic scorn of methodology and theory. Both he and the British critics seem to have adopted the attitude, not so much of professional dissecters of literature, but of humble yet attentive readers who simply exhibit the affectionate curiosity of the amateur, in the original sense of the word, and make no claim to superior knowl-

[104] Cf. Elsbeth Pulver, *Hofmannsthal's Schriften zur Literatur* (Bern: Paul Haupt, 1956). Of the numerous other works on Hofmannsthal's poetics I shall only cite Frank Wood's "Hugo von Hofmannsthal's Aesthetics: A Survey Based on the Prose Works," in *Publications of the Modern Language Association*, 55 (1940): 253-65.

[105] Donald Davie, "British Criticism: The Necessity for Humility," paper delivered at the Third Annual Conference of Comparative Literature at the University of Southern California, Los Angeles, in the Spring of 1969.

edge. Both avoid a specialized technical vocabulary,
preferring to voice their insights with the studied simplicity of table talk or the brilliant nonchalance of a
causerie in the salon of a great lady. In short this tradition, into which Hofmannsthal fits with remarkable
ease, has produced an empiricist, nonphilosophical criticism, infinitely more concerned with critical practice
than with finding its own place in a systematic structure of thought. Seen in this light, Hofmannsthal's
early preoccupation with British life and letters takes
on an added significance, especially his familiarity with
Walter Pater—from whom he often quoted, to whom
he devoted a separate essay, and whom he resembled in
a variety of ways, for example in his predilection for
all cultural phenomena, not only literature. Some de-
scriptions of Pater's style sound very much like characterizations of Hofmannsthal as well.[106]

It was unavoidable that Hofmannsthal should also
have had the faults of so many virtues. His aversion to
abstract conceptualization resulted in a lack of intellectual cogency. His affectionate toying with an author
did not permit serious confrontations with the central
issues of his work. Austria is a case in point. Hofmannsthal's desire to preserve what was good in his
native country and the historical moment he chose for
coming to its public defense, precluded the trenchant
analysis of its political and cultural life that we owe
to other critics. Thus he seemed to have been over-
come, in spite of his own fear of doom, by the catastrophes that actually occurred. While he addressed himself to the real hardships and injustices of his epoch in
some of his poetic works, there is no such topicality in
his essays. On the whole, it is possible to say that there
was something traditional, conservative and unaggres-

[106] See note 4.

sive about his criticism, especially when one compares it with that of some of his contemporaries. It must be acknowledged that in spite of his political philosophizing Hofmannsthal did not come to grips with the central phenomenon of our age, technological civilization. Perhaps it is also necessary to say that for these reasons Hofmannsthal's critical essays are not of the highest rank, whereas his poetic and dramatic works are.

And yet on rereading these essays one's own critical objections fade away into the captivation and enchantment of Hofmannsthal's lovely images, the magic of his rhythms, and the purity of his thought.

Friedrich Gundolf

By Lothar Helbing and C. V. Bock*

THE NAME of Friedrich Gundolf is associated with the German public's first encounter with the poetry of Stefan George. Previously, George had been considered by most of his contemporaries as both strange and uncommunicative. Through the typographical layout of his books, but above all through a life withdrawn from contemporary activity in the field of literature, George had consciously deepened the cleft between himself and the Germany of the Wilhelmine period. He had entered into relationships with a very small number of poets, artists, and intellectuals and even then only after careful examination and always with the possibility of withdrawal. Since 1892 he had been publishing the

* This essay, prepared especially for Princeton University Press, has been condensed from the following book in German: *Friedrich Gundolf. Briefwechsel mit Herbert Steiner und Ernst Robert Curtius*, edited by Lothar Helbing and Claus Victor Bock (Amsterdam: Castrum Peregrini, 1962-63). In addition, the essay draws on material from *Gundolf Briefe. Neue Folge*, ed. L. Helbing and C. V. Bock (Amsterdam, 1965). We have received much valuable help from a number of people, but we wish to acknowledge in particular our debt to the Honorary Director of the Institute of Germanic Studies, University of London, for access to the Gundolf archives; and to the Editor, Castrum Peregrini, Amsterdam, for permission to use copyrighted material.

In addition to specific titles referred to in the footnotes, the

Blätter für die Kunst,[1] in order to create a common platform for the new insistence on form which was emerging in his circle of friends.

In 1899, at the age of 31, George became acquainted with Friedrich Gundolf through Karl Wolfskehl.[2] Gundolf was then an eighteen-year-old student from Darmstadt where his father was a professor of mathematics. George "saw in him . . . for the first time ever an incarnation of his dream, a youth already possessing the innate qualities for which the poet himself had had to struggle." He felt him to be his "first spiritual son."[3] The fact that George recognized in the young Gundolf characteristics which he had envisaged and translated into his work distinguished their relationship from all his previous human ties. A feeling of rapture at this

following works dealing with broader but related aspects should be mentioned:

Friedrich Gundolf. Dem lebendigen Geist. Foreword by Erich Berger. Veröffentlichungen der Deutschen Akademie für Sprache und Dichtung, no. 27 (Heidelberg-Darmstadt, 1962). Reprints of *inter alia* "Hölderlins Archipelagus," "Klopstock," "Lessing," "Opitz," "Tieck."

Elisabeth Gundolf, *Meine Begegnungen mit R. M. Rilke und Stefan George; Stefan George und der Nationalsozialismus.* Two lectures with a Foreword by Lothar Helbing (Amsterdam, 1965).

C. Neutjens, *F. Gundolf. Bibliographischer Apparat.* Bonner Beiträge zur Bibliotheks- und Bücherkunde, no. 20 (Bonn, 1969).

Victor A. Schmitz, *Gundolf. Eine Einführung in sein Werk* (Düsseldorf-Munich, 1965).

G. R. Urban, *Kinesis and Stasis.* Anglica Germanica, no. 2 (The Hague, 1962), Chapter IV: "The Idea of Significant Form in the Work of Friedrich Gundolf."

[1] *Blätter für die Kunst,* 1-12 (Berlin, 1892-1919); facsimile edition in 6 vols. (Düsseldorf-Munich, 1968).

[2] See Karl Wolfskehl's essay on Gundolf, "Künder der Grösse," in Wolfskehl, *Gesammelte Werke,* ed. Margot Ruben and C. V. Bock, 2 vols. (Hamburg, 1960), 2: 292-98.

[3] Ernst Morwitz, *Kommentar zu dem Werk Stefan Georges* (Munich-Düsseldorf, 1960), pp. 251-61; both quotations on p. 252.

first recognition coupled with a grave sense of responsibility characterize the twelve poems dedicated to Gundolf at the opening of the *Gezeiten*-cycle in *Der Siebente Ring* (1907).[4] George's anxiety, intensifying from poem to poem, is apparent: would this youth, under the inspiration of an awakening, transforming affection prove himself strong enough to turn what he already possessed innately into the reality of form? The very beginning of their friendship showed this underlying tension, and it remained a determining factor from that time onward. The quatrain, *An Gundolf*,[5] which resulted from their second meeting, warns the young man eager for knowledge and bent on scholarly pursuits about the limitations of an exclusive concern for the past. Against this, George posits creative self-realization in the sphere of the present.

George's nature and Gundolf's were at home in different realms. Roughly one might perhaps say that George's character was terrestrial, always rotating round a concealed core of passion; Gundolf's mind, on the other hand, moved weightlessly like a bird in airy regions. In a telling way, Wolfskehl once referred to Gundolf as winged Ariel, a devoted servant to his master Prospero.

In one of his most revealing prose writings, *Gefolgschaft und Jüngertum*,[6] Gundolf gave expression to his deep knowledge of discipleship as an archetypal mode of existence. The Western world is acquainted with the figure of the Master from the realms of craft and

---

[4] See Stefan George, *Gesamt-Ausgabe der Werke. Endgültige Fassung*, 18 vols. (Berlin, 1927-34), 6-7: 66-83. *The Works of Stefan George*, trans. Olga Marx and Ernst Morwitz (University of North Carolina Press, 1949; new edn., New York, 1966), pp. 183-89.

[5] George, *Gesamt-Ausgabe*, 6-7: 187; *Works*, p. 229.

[6] In *Blätter für die Kunst* 7 (1908-9): 106-12.

sculpture. In Pythagoras, Socrates, Christ, and medieval
mystics such as "Meister" Eckhart, there appears moreover the figure of the charismatic teacher and wise man
who has and is guided by an instinctive knowledge
of the laws of life and the secrets of spiritual generation.
Nowadays one is conscious of such a mentor mainly in
an historical perspective and thinks of a "follower" as
that kind of human being who is enslaved by absolute
dependence and a blind personality cult. Not until very
recently has some idea of the intrinsic value and dignity
of the Master-Disciple relationship begun to reappear
through the promulgation of Confucian, Zen-Buddhist,
and Chassidic writings. In the last year of his life, Gundolf emphasized with pride and sorrow that "there was
a time when I was the Master's only disciple." As outlined in *Gefolgschaft und Jüngertum*, even in the years
of his separation from George, he professed himself to
be loyal to his discipleship to the last: "Whoever finds
his longing for what is eternal fulfilled in this mortal
man and in the message that he brings, whoever sees in
him boundless substance changing into bounded form,
he, for whom this Master is irreplaceable, may call himself a Disciple." He will not "unconditionally accept
what conditions the Master, . . . he will not make virtues of another man's necessities. . . . Whoever serves
without vanity and compulsion may also serve without
blindness; he follows because he has perceived, and be-
lieves because he knows, and knows because he loves."
In this study Gundolf protests against the distortions
of discipleship, orthodox fanatics, and the advocates of
an ideal of individuality mistakenly modeled on Goethe.
He outlines the meaning of discipleship as he had been
able to perceive it: "Sustained chastity, tranquillity, fi-
delity, manliness and all the strength which comes from
renunciation and serving—these qualities alone can

now, still, prepare the soil for new seed. . . . Of Christ's disciples, not one was a genius and, apart from Judas, not one was a personality in the modern sense, but because they—poor fishermen—were loyal and full of service, faith and love, they became in themselves more fulfilled and fruitful in this world than all the so much more gifted Sophists of the Jews and the heathens."[7]

This is not the place to discuss whether George shattered the image of the poet through his position as master and teacher or whether he renewed it in an archaic sense. The Romantic conception of the poet as the lonely *poète maudit* was the antitype of a Europe turned bourgeois and was conditioned by the age. An age which ultimately saw the sense of a life of economic and technical progress accepted that poets would withdraw and set themselves apart. George was profoundly threatened by such isolation, and until the very end he continued to be a rebel against the empty conventions and the cheap conformism of his day. From his seclusion he raised Cassandra-like cries at moments of apostasy and then imperturbably returned to acclaim both Heaven and Man.

Paul Valéry mentions at one point the almost religious veneration of the young men who gathered around their *maître* on those famous Tuesday evenings in the rue de Rome. For Stefan George the guidance of these younger poets, as exercised in the circle around Mallarmé, was an important experience. On his return to Germany, he was sufficiently mature to assume a similar role and to assemble around him a group of companions to whom he demonstrated that a noble life was still possible. George was profoundly convinced that poetry had the power to move body and mind, to

[7] *Ibid.*, pp. 109, 110 and 112.

revive, and to create "new space in the old."[8] He understood poetry as conjuration, as magic runes, as a transmuting force and a communication between one human being and another. All this was not an abstraction, not a dogmatic or gnostic teaching, but a quiet, constant service to the living.

Gundolf was the first to commit himself fully to the guidance of the poet. He discovered that the Master of the word was also a powerful master in life. As for George, it was a great conquest, but he also discovered the limits of all teaching.

Gundolf, skilled in interpreting works of literature, illuminating them as if with cascades of light, was, at the same time, childlike in his defenselessness against the pressures of vulgar reality. His thirst for freedom set him against all priest-ridden toadying and ecclesiastical pedagogy; the constancy of his sensuous response whenever graceful and gentle women crossed his path, the playful brilliance of his quips and wit—all these and other dazzling talents and likable qualities were in fact just so many sources of danger for him. They were, however, counterbalanced by Stefan George's sober realism and discipline which always insisted on solidity, precision, and uncluttered concentration. Without this integrating force, Gundolf might easily have lost himself in Romantic abandon or over-sophistication. He is said to have expressed in conversation the view that without his encounter with George an element in his make-up related to late German Romanticism, a spirit akin to Heine's, would probably have gained the upper hand.

This Romantic inheritance in Gundolf was a lifelong threat and anxiety to him, but at the same time it was to this inheritance that he owed his extraordinary

[8] George, *Gesamt-Ausgabe*, 9: 61; *Works*, p. 305.

ability to feel his way into things, to uncover and echo, to evoke and bring alive the fervor and the greatness of dead poets and their works.

It would be distorting Gundolf's image to forget that the Ariel-like qualities in his character, the soaring power of his mind, had been purchased at a price. He never entered totally into earthly reality. He himself was aware of this, and again and again he was seized by the desire to let himself sink down from the realms of the sidereal into those of the physical and material. It was precisely here that the fate of the Romantics threatened him; instead of coming to terms with the world, they would glide unawares out of the refined air of their spirituality to the bottom of the abyss.

Gundolf has been reproached for failing to complete the transition from youth to manhood. The author of the early poems and essays is, however, not the same person as the author of *Caesar*[9] or the late volumes on Shakespeare.[10] A growing maturity of judgment and expression is visible in every sentence. Ernst Morwitz notes this in a letter to Gundolf dated March 15, 1928, in which he writes: "Although it is not fitting for me to express any criticism, I should nevertheless like to tell you how much I like the change of tenor in your recent *Brentano* essay,[11] a change which derives from an understanding of life and radiates into the style itself. I think that you have developed through the weight of your suffering. Your terminology and comparative method used to proceed from the style alone. It was easily imitated and adapted, and did not always pro-

[9] Friedrich Gundolf, *Caesar. Geschichte seines Ruhms* (Berlin, 1924).

[10] Gundolf, *Shakespeare. Sein Wesen und Werk*, 2 vols. (Berlin, 1928).

[11] Gundolf, *Romantiker*, 2 vols. (Berlin, 1930-31), 1: 277-336. First published in *Zeitschrift für Deutschkunde* 42 (1928).

duce profound results. Now it seems to have given way
to fresh insight. A more mature observation of what is
horrible in life, and your activity despite this horror,
lend your work, which by no means lacks your earlier
precision in abstract matters, a greater maturity and
depth. The feeling of responsibility towards others well
beyond your own personal ken, which is—forgive
me please!—only now becoming apparent in you, justi-
fies the level of criticism which I find beautifully appropriate in the *Brentano* essay as opposed to your
Kleist study.[12] The violence of diction which marked
your *Paracelsus*[13] has now given way to a quieter and
wiser mode, and the effect of this comes across without
any artistic forcedness or cramping terminology. There
is, in short, something new in your *Brentano* study
which was not present before. I believe I can sense
here what in conventional terms might be called
'development.' "[14]

What was felt to be youthful even in the later Gundolf was a feature of the man as a whole. He once wrote
to Ernst Robert Curtius that he envied him for living
secure and free in a solidly established sphere whilst he
himself was a prey to "wide-ranging imagination and
momentum," lacking any "real home in himself" and
having need of "a centre outside himself." By this
centre Gundolf meant a force of gravity which would
hold him firmly to palpable reality.

George could already see all this in the first phase of
their friendship. "Sang und Gegensang," the fifth poem
of the *Gezeiten*-cycle,[15] expresses it to overwhelming
effect. In lines of melancholic renunciation, the "Re-

[12] Gundolf, *Heinrich von Kleist* (Berlin, 1922).
[13] Gundolf, *Paracelsus* (Berlin, 1927).
[14] Gundolf Archives, University of London; with the kind
permission of Ernst Morwitz, New York.
[15] George, *Gesamt-Ausgabe*, 6-7: 72; *Works*, p. 185.

sponse" tells of a soul submerged in the waters. The poet listens at the edge of the gurgling water, struck by the sad song of the soul surging up as if from a deep dungeon. This "Response" is a reply to the question raised with trembling fear in the "Song":

> War das vielleicht *mein* blick—der deiner
> toten augen?
> War das *mein* hauch als du gebrochen sangst?

> Was this, perhaps, *my* glance, caught in your
> lifeless gaze?
> Was it *my* breath that shook your voice with tears?

Among Gundolf's last, unprinted poems written shortly before his death is one that—no doubt unconsciously—takes up the imagery of the "Response" even to its diction. Gundolf sees himself entangled by creepers in marshy water, sliding away from the muddy bank, seized by the gurgling pond, sinking down in the weed. In other poems from the same period it returns again and again, this fear of the uncanny, of the "non," of the flowing away of the Earth which, looking ever more milky pale, thin and sad, is always threatening to disappear from sight; the fear of his own reality becoming buried by an avalanche; the fear of falling into a bottomless well. In a letter he writes: "I have the feeling of hovering on another star. Perhaps on Sirius." And as early as 1910, Curtius quotes with concern Gundolf's confession: "I climbed down listlessly and rested among the phantoms, happy to be one of them."[16] This was long before Gundolf's illness, long before his separation from George, a separation he believed to have been consciously willed by George himself. The light in which he later viewed this development is shown by his

---

[16] *F. Gundolf Briefwechsel mit H. Steiner und E. R. Curtius* (Amsterdam, 1962-63), p. 160.

remarking: "If it is true to say that I fell away from him, it was as a ripe apple falls from the tree when its time has come."

George's concern with Gundolf shows how he could be fascinated by what was foreign to his own rugged and fiery nature. One may recall in this connection his meeting with the young Hofmannsthal, whose graceful charm and sensitive insight derived from the same Jewish heritage as Gundolf's. The combination of youth and intuition had even then filled George with joy at the prospect of a friendship with a fellow-poet. At the time when he made his imperious and yet uncertain approach to Hofmannsthal,[17] George was still unknown and only twenty-one years old. The circumstances of his meeting with Gundolf were much more favorable: Gundolf came from Hessen, as did George, and encountered a poet whose published works were growing in number, a man who was sure of the path he was traveling.

At first, George hoped that he had discovered in Gundolf an original poet. Both George and Wolfskehl addressed him as "Poet" in their letters and dedications.[18] "Poeta Poetae" wrote Wolfskehl in 1899 in the copy of *Ulais* which was intended for Gundolf.[19] In the same year, Gundolf's first eight poems appeared in the fourth volume of the *Blätter für die Kunst*, followed the next year by twelve more. From the fifth to the twelfth and final volume of the *Blätter für die Kunst*, there is none which does not contain some poetic writing by Gundolf—either lyric drama, single scenes,

---

[17] See *Briefwechsel zwischen George und Hofmannsthal*, 2nd enlarged edn. (Munich-Düsseldorf, 1953).

[18] See *Stefan George–Friedrich Gundolf Briefwechsel* (Munich-Düsseldorf, 1962), pp. 29, 31.

[19] K. Wolfskehl, *Ulais* (Berlin, 1897); inscribed copy in Gundolf Archives.

dialogues, songs, or other verses. In 1930 a slim selection of his verse was published in book form.[20] Today it is known that this is only a small fraction of more than a thousand poems written over the course of his life. But despite the facility which Gundolf displayed in writing verse, a facility which never decreased, it became more and more evident that his real talents lay in interpretation.

Gundolf's receptivity, his ungrudging admiration for and ability to surrender himself to the original works of others qualified him to a special degree as a literary historian. His own talent as a poet suffered in consequence. But what was true of him as a man also held for his academic pursuits; through his continual coming-to-grips with the phenomenon of Stefan George, both Gundolf and his work gained in depth and import. It is to George that he owes his system of coordinates. In his notebooks from the years 1918-25 appear the revealing sentences: "With regard to Stefan George: specific points of view can thrive only in a specific spiritual climate; diet and hygiene of the mind; his severity, even to the point of asceticism. Concentration; do not admit too much that dilutes and dissipates. . . . Don't waste, but preserve silence. The value of ritual: 'Difficult tasks to be faced daily.'[21] The essence of things in themselves. No analogy."[22] Stefan George's sense of order, of "the standard set for height and depths,"[23] clearly remained an axis in Gundolf's ever-revolving system of thought.

By his writing and teaching, Gundolf repaid George in rich measure. Long after their separation, George

---

[20] Gundolf, *Gedichte* (Berlin, 1930).
[21] Quotation from Goethe, *West-Östlicher Divan*, "Vermächtnis altpersischen Glaubens."
[22] Gundolf Archives.
[23] George, *Gesamt-Ausgabe*, 6-7: 128; *Works*, p. 206.

spoke of him in his circle of friends with praise: "He was the most gifted of the lot of you. Ideas! He had them by the thousand; they'd have stretched from here to the sea! They came to him as soon as he woke. He had hardly pulled on a sock before he would be sitting at his table writing. From then on he was up to his elbows in ink." And one of the friends added significantly: "The opposite of what Goethe said of Friedrich Schlegel is true of Gundolf: 'To be versed in the highest spiritual matters and at the same time to pursue a purpose with regard to these is vulgar.' He never pursued a purpose."[24] Curtius notes rightly: "No disciple of George did so much to spread the new vision."

In what did Gundolf's own particular achievement consist, as it confronts us in his books on Caesar, Paracelsus, Shakespeare, Goethe, Kleist, and the Romantics; in his essays on Hutten, Klopstock, Hölderlin, Arndt, Grillparzer, Stifter, and Wedekind; and in his lectures on the Age of the Reformation and the Baroque?[25] Although he had passed through the strict schooling of Erich Schmidt in Berlin, his spiritual point of departure lay outside academic learning. His close friendship with the poet, his own artistic inclination, his ready response to the possibilities of the German language led him to a level of attainment associated in the

[24] R. Boehringer, *Ewiger Augenblick* (Aarau, 1945), pp. 30f; new edn. (Munich-Düsseldorf, 1965).

[25] See Gundolf, *Hutten, Klopstock, Arndt* (Heidelberg, 1924); *Hölderlins Archipelagus* (Heidelberg, 1911); "Franz Grillparzer," *Jahrbuch des Freien Deutschen Hochstifts* (Frankfurt, 1931); *Adalbert Stifter* (Halle, 1931); and "Frank Wedekind," *Trivium* 6 (Zurich, 1948; new edn., Munich, 1954). For courses of lectures see C. V. Bock, "First Report on the Gundolf Papers," *German Life and Letters* 15 (1961): 16ff. One course, "Von Luther bis Lessing," is currently being prepared for publication by Dr. V. A. Schmitz. Reference to Gundolf's books is made elsewhere in these notes.

history of German criticism with Wilhelm von Humboldt's essay on Schiller, August Wilhelm Schlegel's studies of Dante and Shakespeare, and above all Friedrich Schlegel's review of Goethe's *Wilhelm Meister.* Gundolf did not stretch his poets on a Procrustean bed of abstract thought or examine them for their philosophical or political ideas, nor did he subject them to a psychological examination or inspect them from the standpoint of influences or biographical presuppositions. In his notebooks, he quotes the following guiding principle from Carl Justi's *Winkelmann* (Leipzig, 1866): "A work of art is what it is, not what it appears to be in relation to others. We want to see what it contains in itself, and not just compare it with several others in order to be able to speak about what it is not, what it is not yet, or what it is no longer."

Gundolf's vibrating, receptive mind pored passionately over the texts of the poets and listened to their pulse in order to search out the "heart of the matter" from which the form develops organically. The evaluative criterion he derived from the work itself. He presupposed a highly comprehensive knowledge of the text, together with a subtle feeling for the specific weight of its language and an intimate understanding of how a writer lives in his work. In his notebooks, he defines the "business of the history of ideas" as "exploration, i.e., tracing the development and the nature of literature," and "evocation, i.e., showing its meaning and import in present-day life. For any given work does not have the same significance for all epochs, each new day gives a new importance to and insight into what has gone before, and the meaning of exploration and scholarship itself undergoes changes from time to time. . . ." All this assumes a certainty in one's standard of evaluation, such as can only be obtained through long association with poets of the first order. The critic must know "by what means the original poets, the Masters, have distinguished themselves at all times from the epigones, the artists of the second order."[26]

Gundolf is a distinguished representative of "Geisteswissenschaft" as inaugurated by Wilhelm Dilthey (1833-1911), under whom Gundolf had studied at Berlin. The approach itself had already been established by Herder and Goethe as morphology, and was then significantly advanced by Nietzsche and by Bergson in his conception of creative development; it has since opened up new paths to perception in the most diverse disciplines, in the histories of art and civilization, in sociology, ethnology, and anthropology. Through the emigration of German scholars in the 1930's, this approach has also borne fruit in the Anglo-Saxon and Romance countries.

For Gundolf, the study of literature started with the basic question: What can we today gain from a preoccupation with the past as it is handed down to us in poetry and prose? The Humanists had begun to examine enthusiastically but critically the authenticity and meaning of extant texts, but it was not until the eighteenth and nineteenth centuries that self-consciousness became so powerfully directed towards the past that one could speak of an historical approach. The then still open question of the uses and drawbacks of "historicism" was posed with great force by Nietzsche in his *Unzeitgemässe Betrachtungen*. Nietzsche inquired for the first time into spiritual and psychological motives and thus into the significance and the "point" of historical research for contemporary life. He distinguished between critical, antiquarian, and monumental types of historical writing. The latter he placed highest, since

[26] George, "Über Dichtung," *Gesamt-Ausgabe*, 18: 85.

it seizes on the more fruitful moments of the past as an intensification of the present. Gundolf's manner of observation and thought may differ in many respects from Nietzsche's, and it is possible that for his own part he would have objected to the notion of a "monumental" type of historical writing; but this is undoubtedly a concept fundamental to his researches. Like Nietzsche, Gundolf held that an approach that claimed to be "unrelated, . . . unconditioned or free from any evaluation, is, in so many words, without justification."[27] Inquiries of this kind seemed to him to be scholarship for scholarship's sake, that is, pointless.

On one occasion, Gundolf formulated the point of departure for his studies in this way: "The Ideas of Plato, the Heavenly Kingdom of Christ, the Hellenism of Alexander, the Empire of Caesar, Dante's *Divine Comedy*, etc. are original visions transmuted and realised in works, deeds or forms of conduct. What these men have done is to externalise their vision and experience of the Divine. For us there is neither vision nor experience outside their works. We have no more immediate revelations of the Divine than those revealed to us in records of creative and heroic heights."[28]

If one reads these sentences closely, one can understand the position occupied in Gundolf's scheme of things by the "great man," the genius. The great are endowed with the greatest of inner tensions; they receive inspiration from an absolute objective reality, and manage to bear such inspiration by transforming it into their work and their wisdom. Thus they create new life, which bursts asunder old orders and empty forms, and once more place the world under a law. This is

[27] Gundolf, *Caesar im Neunzehnten Jahrhundert* (Berlin, 1926), p. 12.
[28] Notebook, Gundolf Archives.

probably what Goethe, too, was indicating when he remarked, in beguilingly simple terms, "Where subject and object meet, there is life."

Gundolf is acting as an out-and-out Platonist when he starts his studies from the *a priori* of a scale of values which culminates in the "whole man" ("der Gesamtmensch"). He once said: "I have written about Caesar and Shakespeare, Goethe and Stefan George because I needed them as handles to the cup of beauty and truth." We are familiar with the cult of the personality in art and politics, learning and theatre, sport and film, and may as a consequence find it difficult to distinguish the "strong man" from the "whole man." Gundolf, however, was concerned with tracing and presenting the condition and significance of genuine greatness. In his preface to *Caesar* (Berlin, 1924), he allots to the historian the chief office of serving as a custodian of culture, especially at a time when false Caesarian claims and counterclaims are being staked by industrial giants and a rabid mob. "For the sake of the dignity of man and for our own humility's sake, the memory of the great figures of the past must be kept alive."

Leopold von Ranke (1795-1886) and his historical writings were a model for Gundolf; he admired Ranke's critical penetration, which surpassed mere description, together with his respect for facts, for the individual and unique nature of what happened and how it came to pass.[29] In Gundolf's own domain of literary history, however, one is not dealing with chronicles, registers, edicts, and other records which form the raw material of history, but with language already perceptively moulded. A note of Gundolf's on the nature of poetry runs like this: "Verse preserves the memory of the unity of sound and meaning, restores the connection between

[29] *Gundolf-Curtius Briefwechsel*, p. 196.

the individual and the rhythm of the universe, and denotes not so much design as a soul caught up in the primary rhythms of the world."[30]

If, like Gundolf, one wishes to perceive whether and in what way "the individual and the rhythm of the world" connect in any one poetic work, then the first methodological point must be to establish the criterion of such perception. Then, precisely what is the criterion of authenticity? Authenticity is that scarcely definable yet unmistakable quality which enables an expert to distinguish the original masterpiece from a copy however well produced. The genuineness of any work can only be judged from its form. If this were not so, it would be difficult to see why so much of what has been said through the ages in verse or prose about ultimate problems should have fallen into oblivion. As Gundolf put it in a letter, the work of a genuine artist survives as "the adequate symbol of his immortality," but "whatever is expressed in an incongruous form becomes historical, antiquated, withered."

Gundolf's style may be judged to be verbose. But his aim is not that of recapturing subjective impressions in all their opalescence. On the contrary, he is driven by the desire of the phenomenologist to define the object in front of him as exactly as possible. It is as if he had to give a name to unknown fauna or flora. He strives for a highly differentiated terminology and employs his wealth of vocabulary to bring home to the reader exactly what he has seen. He refers to this process of inner appropriation when he writes at one point that he is plunging deeper into Goethe and making himself "the hollow mould of this image."[31]

Gundolf needed a differentiated language, almost,

---

[30] Notebook, Gundolf Archives.
[31] *Gundolf-Curtius Briefwechsel*, p. 230.

indeed, a poetic form of expression all his own, in order to present in the sustained medium of his style widely different authors and works. Only with such a language could he hope to avoid falling into hackneyed abstractions and technical jargon.

The most important thing he wanted to develop in his students was the capacity to recognize from the form —i.e., from tone, rhythms, and imagery—what distinguishes an authentic work from a peripheral one. The latter might possess in high measure one single quality, be it mental agility, sensitivity, imagination, or sensuousness, but it is the inimitable fusion of qualities that distinguishes the former. In this light it is easy to understand Gundolf's oft-repeated warning joke: "You may say, 'I don't like elephants,'—but you must never say that an elephant is a mouse."

On the occasion of a study about his method, Gundolf wrote in reply: "Since my 'method' is that part of my work which I know least about, a mirror of the kind you provide is instructive . . . , although I am always afraid that it may distort human beings by focussing upon the 'approach' to them . . . , and that the applicability of concepts and mental tools may be tested at the expense of the perceptions and insights which have to be gained anew each time."[32] And on another occasion he wrote: "Methodological ado—audible clattering with the tools of the trade."[33] On the other hand, however, Gundolf rendered himself a very strict account of the presuppositions of his work, as sketched in the following entry in one of his notebooks: "Most scholars believe themselves free of presuppositions because they do not know their own norms, their ultimate values—

[32] Gundolf Archives.
[33] Notebook, Gundolf Archives; see also Gundolf, *Romantiker* 1, "Vorwort."

they merely take over from their predecessors. It is a part of academic integrity and thoroughness that one should be clear in one's own mind and express oneself clearly about the reason, the principle for the sake of which one is investigating. . . . Responsibility, obligation, no small-talk—speak freely. The most important formulation: 'Though tens of thousands be the forms of things, / you shall give voice to one alone: my own.' "[34] In a letter of 1930 he points to his collection of essays, *Dichter und Helden* (Heidelberg, 1921), as providing "the best survey of my mode of thinking." However, elucidation of his method is scattered throughout his books and letters. To these may be added the following extract from the unpublished introduction to a lecture on Grimmelshausen, written in 1923. Gundolf begins by saying that a writer's achievements are at the same time the best commentary on his life and characteristics. Then he continues: "A poet's biography has to be deduced from his work, not vice versa; we are concerned with soil only for the fruit it bears. *Faust* throws more light on Goethe's life than his life throws on *Faust*, or, rather, *Faust* tells the authentic story of Goethe's life, better than all his letters, annals and anecdotes."[35]

In order to see how Gundolf's conceptions of the "Gesamtmensch," of the great poet and what he called "Urerlebnis" (primary experiences) and "Bildungserlebnis" (more intellectual, secondary, experiences) may function in practice in literary history, it is perhaps best to go to his book *Shakespeare und der deutsche Geist* (Berlin, 1911). In this work he traces what happens when a poet of the first order invades a foreign literature. Gundolf's history of the reception of Shakespeare in

---

[34] Notebook, Gundolf Archives. Quotation from George, *Gesamt-Ausgabe*, 5: 21; *Works*, p. 122.

[35] Gundolf Archives.

Germany becomes a successive grading of German writing itself. It is an instructive example of his method and of his ability to apply it. Half a generation later, he attempted a more ambitious outline of European thought, taking Caesar as the geometric centre. Both times he surveys tradition the way an astronomer sees the sky, with systems of suns, constellations, large and smaller planets, fixed stars, and tailed comets, revolving around powerful centres.

In a letter of April, 1911, George commented on the Shakespeare book. His praise and criticism show very clearly what he expected from Gundolf and which sources of danger he had warned him against. He writes: "It is conceived with a competence that is quite extraordinary, and contains latent merits above and beyond the often daring assertions. Often indeed the 'Older Generation' must wonder: 'What gives this young "scholar" the right to talk like this?' They do not possess your orientation, your sense of a 'centre.' And at this point, my dear and best friend, even your Master must allow himself a comment: one must never tell all one knows. You have not overstepped the bounds of moderation to a dangerous extent, but you must still beware of imagining that 'intellectual diffusion amounts to mastering the essence.' In just a very few places even in the section on Goethe, a somewhat greater degree of MODESTY would have been desirable in your mode of expression. You castigate so severely the shortcomings of literary critics, and yet even you would not have escaped errors merely through the SYSTEM of your thinking, but you have escaped them thanks to your mode of feeling. Otherwise, I am full of praise and admiration. Do you follow?"[36]

A younger friend of George's, also commenting on

[36] *George-Gundolf Briefwechsel,* p. 224.

Gundolf's *Shakespeare und der deutsche Geist,* con-
veys something of the climate of the Circle and affords
a sense of the keen, clear wind of criticism which blew
through all the reverent admiration. On March 5,
1911, Ernst Morwitz wrote to Gundolf: "I have read
your book in proof, with the exception of the chapter
on Lessing. I like the factual clarity with which it is written. You have obviously stripped your former ornate
manner which seems to me to be a very good thing.
For even if you yourself never overdid this, you only
need to take one look at the writings of those who consider this to be the chief thing and who have imitated
you. What point is there in inventing verbal conglomer-
ations when the same thing can be said better and more
decently in concise, understandable sentences? I cannot tell you how happy I am that you yourself have now
dealt a mortal blow to these aberrations. The section on
Voltaire is quite splendid! In just a few sentences you
have captured there what is probably the premise of
your whole undertaking, namely to try and see the lesser lights against one that outshines them, thus placing
the minor poets in terms of their relative proximity to
a major one."[37]

In the last years of his life, Gundolf gave a hint during a conversation with a student as to where he would
place himself in the history of criticism: "My books tell
you what is important for you out of the past and what
you can leave alone. No one will need to or be able
to repeat what I have done. I represent a transition;
I am the first of a new outlook and the last of a declining one which still thinks in historical terms."

It is, perhaps, too early to estimate Gundolf's position in the history of the German mind in general and

[37] Gundolf Archives; with the kind permission of E. Morwitz,
New York.

that of literary studies in particular. Certainly he may
be regarded as the final stage in a process of development. Today it would scarcely be possible to continue
in a direct line from his manner of presentation. Even
Max Kommerell (1902-1944), who came after all from
the same background and discipleship, and whose work
would be unthinkable without Gundolf as a predeces-
sor, had to strike a different course in his very first book
Der Dichter als Führer in der deutschen Klassik (Berlin,
1928).

It has often been noted that works of literary interpretation enjoy but a short-term influence. Their approach and their concepts are linked to the time in
which they are formed and are directed towards their
contemporaries. One or two generations later they will
be out-of-date. Gundolf himself felt this "dating" in
his own books. Thus he expressed the opinion that the
level established by his monograph on Goethe had become the common standard for studies of this kind.
Certain of his coinages like "Urerlebnis" and "Bildungserlebnis" were absorbed into the vocabulary of
criticism. Really, he maintained, he ought now to write
a completely new book on Goethe. But the name of
Gundolf marks a moment in the history of literary
criticism which, precisely because it will never return,
ensures for his books a lasting significance. This significance does not lie in the results of his research, nor does
it depend on whether and how far his views and evaluations have had to be revised. It lies in what might be
called his "existential situation," a rough indication of
which follows.

At the turn of the century, a young man coming from
a South German Jewish background, endowed with
poetic talent, educated in the classical tradition, and
marked out by an extraordinary ability to understand

and interpret, falls under a powerful spell and entrusts his spiritual well-being to the guidance of a poet who re-orientates him and flings him into a new freedom. Such, in very crude terms, were the circumstances of Gundolf's existence. In the end, the make-up of his own character hampered him and brought him into a state of conflict between what he loved, understood, and desired on the one hand, and what his nature and strength would permit him, on the other. It is with this limitation in mind that one must regard his work. It provides both a record of his joy in the fullness of his experiences and, at the same time, marks the boundary across which he could not pass. The final conflict with George merely brought to light a crack in the foundation which had been there all the time. Ironically enough, what linked Gundolf with his time and ensured his success was perhaps precisely that part of his make-up that did not come from George and was indeed foreign to the latter's nature.

Through Gundolf's books, George for the first time exerted on the contemporary scene an influence which was not due directly to either his poetry or his own personality. Gundolf's mode of interpreting, effectively employed in his books on Shakespeare and Goethe, was now to be put to the test on a living poet. Even the panegyric character of his book on George (Berlin, 1920) was accepted since its author had proved himself as a literary historian. Previous writings on George by Hofmannsthal,[38] Georg Simmel,[39] Ludwig Klages[40] and

[38] Hugo von Hofmannsthal, "Gedichte von Stefan George" (1896), *Prosa I* (Frankfurt, 1950), pp. 282ff.; "Über Gedichte" (1904), *Prosa II* (1951), pp. 94ff.

[39] Georg Simmel, "Stefan George. Eine kunstphilosophische Studie" (1901), *Zur Philosophie der Kunst* (Potsdam, 1922), pp. 29ff.

[40] Ludwig Klages, *Stefan George* (Berlin, 1902).

Friedrich Wolters[41] had been noted, but Gundolf's book influenced a wider public—above all, the younger generation.

In this process, however, something happened which did not correspond to George's idea of what the essence and effect of poetry should be. Excellent and incisive as the picture that his nearest pupil sketched of him may have been, it bore, even so, the imprint of a well-tried professional manner. George designated such books— books whose task might be that of breaking down the wall of prejudice and misunderstanding in order to rouse the contemporary reader out of his small-minded indifference—as "political." In this context, then, "political" means that George considered works of scholarship—as distinct from poetry—as *engagés*; that is, he regarded them as purposebound. He warned emphatically against the "lie of shallow interpretation" and claimed that this was the modern form of shrugging off the exhortations of the poets and "revelers, whom once murder removed more gently."[42]

Gundolf's books were successful, even though they were not easy reading, did not sketch out exciting biographies, did not attract the reader through any psychological interpretations and, what is more, presupposed a reasonably good knowledge of the texts under discussion. By 1931 his first publication, *Shakespeare und der deutsche Geist* (1911), had sold almost thirty thousand copies. His lengthy study of *Goethe*, published in 1916, had sold over forty-five thousand by 1932. But more important than these figures are the reactions which accompanied his publications. Wilhelm Dilthey, the Nestor of the history of ideas, had professed in 1911, the year of his death, that *Shakespeare und der*

---

[41] Friedrich Wolters, *Herrschaft und Dienst* (Berlin, 1909).
[42] George, *Gesamt-Ausgabe*, 18: 73.

deutsche Geist had opened up to him a view "from the mountain into a Promised Land."[43] And Eberhard Gothein, another scholar of the older generation, and one of Jakob Burckhardt's students, commented on the same book: "This is really something! . . . I have hardly ever read an essay in literary history that is so much of a work of art in itself. What comes through is a strong personality and at the same time a quite solid but never boastful scholar. . . . The way he combines detailed descriptiveness with a delineation of the overall historical links is absolutely wonderful. . . . With just one step he has placed himself among the major historians of ideas."[44] To the voices of these scholars may be added the testimony of a poet. Rainer Maria Rilke wrote to Norbert von Hellingrath on July 24, 1914, that the reading of Gundolf's *Goethe* had been "of the utmost significance" for him since its "sure structure, raised on such extensive foundations, offered me a wide and completely new mental prospect" which would have on him "effect upon effect for a long time to come."

Early in his career older scholars saluted Gundolf's new promise; at the end of his life young Germanists were recognizing him as an outstanding representative of their discipline. Richard Alewyn has written: "Gundolf's impressive number of studies assures him of a place among literary historians of the first order. . . . His last work, *Shakespeare. Sein Wesen und Werk* . . . is profound and rounded . . . as a piece of interpretation . . . , it displays mastery in both its language and its structure but, apart from all this, it stands as the record of a man who has matured . . . through difficult

---

[43] Quoted by Edgar Salin, *Um Stefan George*, 2nd enlarged edn. (Munich-Düsseldorf, 1954), p. 63.

[44] Marie-Luise Gothein, *Eberhard Gothein. Ein Lebensbild* (Stuttgart, 1931), pp. 199f.

experiences and become wise and generous." A measure of the esteem in which Gundolf came to be held are the obituaries which appeared in the newspapers of many countries of the world.[45] Tributes were paid to him not only in the press of neighboring German-speaking countries but also in English, French, Italian, and even in Polish, Greek, Spanish, and Japanese newspapers and periodicals. In many of these one can sense a personal note which transcends the public acknowledgment usual on such occasions.

Gundolf was to have delivered the memorial lecture at the Sorbonne on the hundredth anniversary of Goethe's death in 1932. He had already written down his address a year prior to the lecture and three months before his death. Its appearance as a booklet in Berlin in 1932 marks the last time that any new publication by Gundolf appeared on the German market until 1954, when his essay on *Frank Wedekind* (first published in *Trivium*, Zurich 1948), was reprinted in book form by a Munich publisher. All other posthumous publications, like *Rainer Maria Rilke* (Vienna 1937), *Anfänge deutscher Geschichtschreibung* (Amsterdam 1938), and *Friedrich des Grossen Schrift über die deutsche Literatur* (Zurich 1947), appeared abroad.

Times had changed. The first inscription above the entrance to the new Heidelberg University building was suggested by Gundolf and read, as it does again today: "To the live spirit." But in 1933, just two years after his death, this was considered to express a "Jewish mode of thinking" and was consequently perverted into its very opposite: "To the German spirit." Gundolf's books disappeared from the shop windows and were allowed to go out of print. An article in the *Völkischer Beobachter* prescribed how Gundolf was to be judged

[45] Gundolf Archives.

in Germany from now on; the article spoke of "the fad-
ing dazzle of a delusion" and "a typical case of Jewish
intellectualism." As for George, at first the authorities
showed a certain reticence, but when they were forced
to realise that the poet was not going to be severed from
his Jewish friends, the wind quickly changed.

Not until after the war was Gundolf reprinted in
Germany. As early as 1947, *Shakespeare und der
deutsche Geist* reappeared under the imprint of Küpper Verlag. But the aura surrounding Gundolf's name
had faded in the dark years that had passed. Under the
Nazis he had been attacked as a Jew who lacked a feeling for Teutonic values; after the war he was warned
against as being the founder of a "typically German"
cult of the hero in literature and history. He was now
accused of presenting Caesar, Shakespeare and Goethe,
Kleist and George as absolutes in isolation, and of pay-
ing too little attention to their functioning in the over-
all political, social, and economic situation.

There was another important factor in Gundolf's fall
from popularity. Post-war students had first of all to ac-
quire elementary knowledge. They needed books which
imparted facts, treated texts from a strictly analytical
standpoint, supplied bibliographical references, and
taught the methods of literary criticism. Justifiably,
mistrust was felt for works which were based upon "insight" or which advanced a sweepingly comprehensive
picture. A "monumental" way of writing history was
not what was required. There was a desire to get to the
bottom of the sociological and psychological motivations of literature. At the centre of interest stood the
empirical Self: man, cast into life, laden with the burden
of his inheritance, and giving expression to his fear
and despair. In this climate, Gundolf's books were
thought to be too differentiated, too rich in their mode

of expression, too apodictic in their judgments, and—above all—far too greatly determined by a preconceived system of values. An interpreter, it was now maintained, should step back; he should just simply lead the reader quietly to the text and refrain from passing judgment.

In his seminars, Gundolf emphasized again and again that the task of scholarly works—other than reference books, grammars and the like—was to show results in an impeccable form. He jokingly compared them with a meal which, after decent preparation, should be put on the table in a way pleasing to the eye. One would not place the ingredients in front of one's guests or urge them into the kitchen in order to demonstrate. But, after the Second World War, students of literature were concerned with learning just that—the ingredients and how to prepare them.

One can understand the reasons for such a turning away from Gundolf's work, while recognizing that they fail to do justice to him and his type of interpretation. Elsewhere, eminent *hommes de lettres* possessing both scholarly and poetic talents have carried the examination and evaluation of literature from one generation to the next. Through the wealth of their own minds, no less than through their erudition and command of language, they have proven themselves well qualified to assess the famous and the neglected, and to link the present with the past. One may think here of Dryden, Samuel Johnson, Coleridge, Walter Pater and T. S. Eliot, Sainte Beuve and Valéry.

Otto Regenbogen recognized this point in the memorial address he gave for his former colleague Friedrich Gundolf in the Great Hall of the University of Heidelberg in November, 1931. He remarked that the concept of the German university rested on three dis-

tinct activities which, although separate, would nevertheless fuse from time to time—namely on teaching, research, and interpretation. The task of the teacher is
to transmit in a lively way what is already known and
what has already been achieved. The researcher must
forge ahead in order to bring new knowledge to light.
But it is the interpretative critic who prevents the fullness of knowledge from becoming sterile; he links
things together to give a fresh picture. "This ability to
integrate supported by passionate enthusiasm as much
as by a keen mind has been Friedrich Gundolf's
most important contribution to the academic life of
Germany."[46]

Gundolf was, perhaps, not much of a University teacher in the current sense of the word. His lectures were
really only readings aloud, in that he confined himself
to reading out his carefully worded manuscripts in a
somewhat detached manner. It sometimes happened
that he would break off at the bell in the middle of a
sentence and retreat in haste from the overcrowded
lecture hall. The way to profit from his lecture courses
was to have studied beforehand the author he was going to talk about and then after the lecture to write
down from memory the essence of what had been said.
This was clearly something for advanced students.
Nevertheless, undergraduates and students from other
faculties would flock to attend, and it is only fair to say
that students at Heidelberg had plenty of choice. The
university boasted an unusual number of distinguished
scholars. Ludwig Curtius, Eberhard Gothein, Karl
Jaspers, Carl Neumann, the brothers Alfred and Max
Weber, Heinrich Zimmer, are but a few of those of
high standing and renown who taught there.

[46] Otto Regenbogen, *Friedrich Gundolf zum Gedächtnis* (Heidelberg, 1931), p. 22.

Today it is difficult to say precisely in what the fascination with Gundolf lay. Was it in his blend of pride and almost embarrassed modesty, in the vaguely romantic remoteness enveloping the keen edge of his intellect, or in the interplay of melancholy and wit, of reserve and effervescence? Whatever it was, his audience felt that this man had a convincing rapport with poetry and poets. Gundolf is said to have once remarked during a conversation that Goethe shook his hand but that Shakespeare had embraced him. The remark was not meant to seem conceited; he wanted to convey that the great writers he studied and wrote about had taken hold of him and had never let go.

It would be rash to assume that Gundolf had done nothing but treat the history of literature and ideas according to the principles instilled in him by his Master. He had gained from his close friendship with Stefan George neither dogmas nor doctrines but an experience of both happiness and conflict. It was this experience which endowed everything that he said or wrote with immediacy. Scholarship, expertise, good sense—all these were to be found to a very high degree in other university teachers, too. But Gundolf was, as it were, the burnt child that did *not* dread the fire but believed that man could infer the laws of life from the lives and works of the poets.

In spite of his being elected a member of the Heidelberg Academy of Sciences in 1929 and awarded the city of Hamburg's first Lessing Prize in 1930, a shadow fell over the last years of Gundolf's life, first owing to his separation from Stefan George, then, in 1927, to a serious operation. Nevertheless, he brought to conclusion the two volumes of *Shakespeare. Sein Wesen und Werk*, which was to be his last major work. A letter from Ernst Morwitz, dated December 12, 1928, may show how an old friend of George's received this publication. Morwitz writes: "I admire the clarity of thought and style, and what you say about Shakespeare's presentation of youth (Vol. 1, pp. 43-49) I found extraordinarily good and illuminating. Despite its breadth, the book is never tiring or tortured in expression. One feels that you wanted— as you always said—to make this your life's work and that you have achieved it."[47]

In the summer of 1931 Gundolf, having just passed his fiftieth birthday, died unexpectedly in Heidelberg after a short illness. He died on the twelfth of July, Stefan George's birthday.

[47] Gundolf Archives; with the kind permission of E. Morwitz, New York.

Ernst Robert Curtius

By Arthur R. Evans, Jr.

BORN into the *noblesse de robe* of German gentry, officialdom, and scholarship, Ernst Robert Curtius seemed predestined, by right and obligation of ancestry, to play a leading role in Germany's national life. The Curtius family came from the coast of the Baltic sea, Ernst Robert's great-great-grandfather, Carl Werner (1735-95), having emigrated as a medical doctor from the present Estonian port city of Narva to Lübeck, the prosperous emporium at the west end of the Baltic and formerly the capital of the Hanseatic league. His son, Carl Georg (1771-1857), whose life spanned the golden age of German literature and thought, typified, as a devout and humane burgher, that enlightened commitment to religion, culture, and politics which characterizes the history of the family. Carl Georg's attachment to culture is exemplified in his befriending the Romanized German leader of the Nazarite school of painters, Johann Friedrich Overbeck, a patronly gesture which was to be repeated years later by a younger member of the family when Friedrich Curtius, Ernst Robert's father, provided lodging and support for the Strasbourg organist and theology student, Albert Schweitzer.[1]

The most illustrious member of the family was Carl Georg's next to youngest of four sons, the Nestor of German Hellenists, renowned historian and archaeologist, Ernst Curtius (1814-96), whose idealized features and poetic gaze, as sculpted by Friedrich Schaper, once proudly faced his grandson's writing desk in Bonn.[2] Ernst Curtius led the diggings at Olympia in the era of imperialist excavations and, in addition to reconstructing the exact proportions of the temple of Olympian Zeus, discovered the Hermes of Praxiteles. Recalling Curtius' lectures, which he attended in Berlin in the autumn of 1895, the British historian G. P. Gooch remarked that "to pass from the lecture room of

[1] Although the family had left Lübeck by the end of the nineteenth century, Ernst Robert Curtius' younger brother, Friedrich (b. 1896), has returned since the last war to the city of his forebears where he is at present the head of a clinic for internal medicine. See Friedrich Curtius, "Über 30 Jahre Arzt," in *Therapie der Gegenwart* 102 (October, 1963): 1181f. A brief perusal of his book, *Individuum und Krankheit* (Berlin-Heidelberg-Göttingen, 1959), reveals an intimate familiarity with modern German philosophical and humanistic literature. There are close affinities in scientific outlook and approach between Friedrich Curtius and his brother-in-law, the well-known professor of medicine at Heidelberg, Victor von Weizäcker (d. 1957). For Albert Schweitzer and the Curtius family, see Werner Picht, *The Life and Thought of Albert Schweitzer*, trans. (New York and Evanston, 1964), p. 182. Picht, a cultural historian, is the husband of E. R. Curtius' younger of two sisters, Greda who was, herself, a music student of Schweitzer's. It was Albert Schweitzer who introduced Curtius to Romain Rolland's *Jean Christophe*.

[2] Actually there are two Schaper busts of the grandfather: the other is in the vestibule of the Museum at Olympia. Schaper is perhaps best known for his "Goethe-Denkmal" (1872-80) in the Berlin *Tiergarten*.

Treitschke to that of Curtius was like taking the train from Potsdam to Weimar."[3] Between the years 1857 and 1867 this "schönste Greis" composed a three-volume *Geschichte Griechenlands*, a work of *haute vulgarisation* intended to accompany Mommsen's history of Rome (1854-56), and a work which was to serve for years as the indispensable introduction to Greek culture. Because of its popular appeal, the study provoked a storm of protest among the *vieux grognons* of German classical scholarship, much the same way that the first books of Ernst Robert Curtius, with their avowed modernity and their appeal to a literate public of nonspecialists, were to rankle the composure of German Romance academicians.[4]

Ernst Curtius was for a short time the tutor of Prince

[3] "Recollections of German Historians," *The Listener* 55 (April 5, 1956): 351. For Ernst Curtius, see Hilde Hermann, "Die drei Familien Curtius," *Neue Deutsche Hefte* 1 (June, 1954): 209f.; and Thomas Hodgkin, "Ernst Curtius," *Proceedings of the British Academy* 2 (1905): 31f.

[4] For the reception by his colleagues of Ernst Robert's early work, *Die literarischen Wegbereiter des neuen Frankreich*, in contrast to its reception by the serious public at large, see Curtius, "Rückblick 1952," *Französischer Geist im zwanzigsten Jahrhundert*, hereinafter referred to as *Französischer Geist* (Bern-Munich, 1965), pp. 523-24; and for the general attitude of Curtius' professional associates toward his work, see the amusing remarks of Albert Béguin, "E. R. Curtius en Allemagne et à Paris," in "Hommage à Ernst Robert Curtius," *Allemagne d'aujourd'hui*, Sept.-Oct., 1956, pp. 11-12. From the start, Curtius associated himself enthusiastically with the controversial, far-reaching reforms introduced by the Weimar educational minister, Carl Heinrich Becker, into the Prussian university curriculum. These included the acceptance of modern literature as a subject worthy of scholarly study. See Leo Spitzer, "L'Etat actuel des études romanes en Allemagne," *Revue d'Allemagne* 6 (1932): 572f.; and Werner Richter, "Carl Heinrich Becker, Bildungsminister der ersten deutschen Republik," in *Freundesgabe für Ernst Robert Curtius zum 14. April 1956*, ed. Max Rychner and Walter Boehlich (Bern-Munich, 1956), pp. 191f.

Friedrich-Wilhelm of Prussia (1831-88), the urbane and liberal eldest child of the first German emperor, Kaiser Wilhelm I; the prince, as Kaiser Friedrich, mounted the throne only to die, his period of rule being fated to last for just ninety-nine days. At the mid-point of the century, Curtius accompanied his charge to the University of Bonn, the *Rheinische* Friedrich-Wilhelms-Universität (so named for the prince's grandfather), the palatial central building of which formerly housed the archbishops of Cologne and was constructed out of materials from the fortifications of the old Roman *Castra Bonnensia*. It was at Bonn where Friedrich Diez, the founder of Romance philology, taught from 1821 to 1876[5] and where in 1929, some eighty years after his grandfather's tour of duty, Ernst Robert, whose devotion to Germany's Roman past plays such a profound and decisive role in his life-work, came to succeed Meyer-Lübke in the chair of Romance studies.[6] Prince Friedrich-Wilhelm's sister, Luise von Baden, was the godmother of Ernst Robert Curtius' mother, the bilingual countess Erlach-Hindelbank, who was born into a patrician Bern family which, on the Erlach side, had settled in the city in the late thirteenth century and could count among its ancestors one mayor and one close confidant of Frederick the Great. When Ernst Curtius' first wife died, he married his sister-in-law, Clara Reichelm; the two had a daughter, Dora, who married the son of Karl Richard Lepsius (1810-84), the

[5] See Curtius' memorial essay, "Bonner Gedenkworte auf Friedrich Diez," in *Gesammelte Aufsätze zur romanischen Philologie* (Bern-Munich, 1960), pp. 412f.

[6] In his recollections of Stefan George, Curtius speaks of visits that he made as a young man to the poet's home in Bingen: "Ein Wegweiser besagte dort: 'Achtzig Wegstunden nach Bonn.' Das war mir wie ein geheimnisvoller Ruf . . . ," *Kritische Essays zur europäischen Literatur* (Bern, 1954), p. 107.

Egyptologist. Dora was thus the sister-in-law of the late impressionist painter Reinhold Lepsius and his wife, Sabine, whose home on the Kastanien-Allee in Berlin's smart Westend was a meeting place for Germany's intellectual elite in the years before World War I. It was here that Ernst Robert Curtius first met Georg Simmel and became acquainted with Stefan George, Friedrich Gundolf, and Charles Du Bos.[7]

Though lacking Ernst Curtius' worldly connections and social prestige, Georg Curtius (1820-1885), his older brother and namesake of his father, enjoyed an importance in German academic life nearly equal to that of Ernst's. A classical philologist, he edited the *Leipziger Studien zur Classischen Philologie* for years, and his *Griechische Schulgrammatik*, first published in 1852, became a standard work in the field, occupying a position in classical philology somewhat comparable to his brother's *History* in humane studies.

Ernst Robert was born in 1886 in Thann, north of Mulhouse, in German-occupied Alsace where his father, Friedrich (1851-1931), the son of Ernst Curtius by his first marriage and the step-brother of Dora Lepsius, had been sent as a civil functionary. After a brief stay in Colmar, the family moved to Strasbourg where from 1903 to the outbreak of the Great War, Friedrich Curtius served with distinction as the executive director of the Augsburg Confessional Church, a position demanding great tact and practical intelligence as it involved overseeing the fortunes of the German Lutheran Church amidst a preponderantly French Catholic pop-

---

[7] It was through Reinhold Lepsius that Rilke was introduced to Rodin. According to Charles Dédéyan, a painting by Lepsius of Ernst Curtius hangs in the National Gallery in Berlin. See *Le Cosmopolitisme littéraire de Charles Du Bos* (Paris, 1965), 1: 179.

ulation. In the still highly readable book of reminiscences which he wrote for his children, Friedrich Curtius liked to point to the striking juxtaposition in the
center of Strasbourg of the great Münster and the
Palais des Rohan, the German gothic and French neo-
classical monuments which were the architectural symbols of Alsace's dual national and cultural heritage.[8] Ever
since the partition of Charlemagne's legacy and the persistent reduction of Lothaire's share following the
Treaty of Verdun in the ninth century, the area of Alsace has been fair game for its giant neighbors to either
side. As one Alsatian has ruefully put it, in commenting upon his homeland as the theatre for an endless history of Franco-German power struggles, "Our only
advantage lies in the fact that whatever be the out-
come of the war we're sure to find ourselves on the side
of the winner."[9] It was Friedrich Curtius' hope, elo-
quently expressed in the closing pages of his memoirs,
that Alsace, sharing intimately in the culture of the
two peoples, be an instrument for peace and amity in
the evolution of their future relationships.[10] The spirit
which animates the great output of Ernst Robert's writings in the decade after World War I is a response to
this summons, an act of filial piety to his father's
lifework.

In Ernst Robert's youth, thanks to the work of the
Strasbourg poet, Ernst Stadler, who translated Péguy
and whose own verse shows the strong influence of
Claudel, and owing to such journals as the *Musée
alsacien* and the *Cahiers alsaciens*, which kept a literate
public informed of the latest trends in French intellec-

[8] *Deutsche Briefe und Elsässische Erinnerungen* (Frauenfeld,
1920), p. 241.
[9] Cited in Michel Legris, "L'Alsace entre deux langues," *Le
Monde*, Sept. 13-14, 1964.
[10] *Deutsche Briefe*, p. 249.

tual life, the Alsatian garden became a refuge of peace, a point where contacts between the two cultures could be made and differences reconciled. The Kaiser's pan-Germanism was as emphatically rejected as was the ardent nationalism of Maurice Barrès.[11] Curtius and his friends read the newly-founded *La Nouvelle Revue française* with its professed internationalism and cultural relativism, and Stefan George's *Blätter für die Kunst* which eschewed topical issues and deliberately turned away from all that had an immediate political relevance. At the outbreak of hostilities in 1914, Friedrich Curtius incurred the disfavor of his superiors by refusing to carry out the local German military commander's orders forbidding the use of the vernacular in sermons at mass in the French-speaking quarters of Strasbourg and the surrounding towns. As a high governmental official put it to Curtius: "For me the true church is that one whose *summus episcopus* is the King of Prussia."[12] Faced with such an attitude, Curtius took a position of *non serviam*, resigned his post, and at the end of the war returned to Germany, making his home in Heidelberg where six years later, in 1924, Ernst Robert was appointed to the University's chair of Romance Philology.

[11] See Curtius' preface to his *Maurice Barrès und die geistigen Grundlagen des französischen Nationalismus* (Bonn, 1921). There is now a new, unchanged, edition of this work, published at Hildesheim in 1962.

[12] See the art historian Werner Weisbach's *Geist und Gewalt* (Vienna, 1956), p. 138. This was not the first time that Friedrich Curtius found himself at odds with the higher echelons of power. In 1906 he undertook the publication of the memoirs of the Prince of Hohenlohe-Schillingsfürst, who was from 1885 to 1894 the enlightened governor of Alsace and Lorraine. The appearance of the *Denkwürdigkeiten*, with their outspoken criticism of Wilhelm the II's treatment of Bismarck, provoked a strong reaction in government circles, and for a time Curtius was decidedly out of favor.

Ernst Robert had studied at Strasbourg under Gustav Gröber (1844-1911) for whom he retained a life-long fondness and admiration. Not only were his doctor's thesis, an edition of a twelfth century text, *Li Quatre Livre des Reis* (1911) and his *Habilitation-schrift* on Ferdinand Brunetière (1914) dedicated to Gröber, which could have been more or less expected, but also his *magnum opus*, written at the end of a long and varied scholarly career, *Europäische Literatur und lateinisches Mittelalter* (1948), bears an "In Memoriam" to the Strasbourg master.[13] Along with his intense absorption in medieval literature, which bore fruit in the monumental *Grundriss* and in the founding and editing of the *Zeitschrift für romanische Philologie*, Gröber took a lively interest in modern French literature and literary criticism. These two sides of his scholarly activity are reflected in Curtius' first writings: on the

[13] As well as to Aby Warburg, about whom we shall speak later. On the occasion of Gröber's death, Curtius wrote a moving obituary in the *Strassburger Post*, Nov. 11, 1911; and in 1952 a long appreciative essay, "Gustav Gröber und die romanische Philologie," now collected in *Gesammelte Aufsätze*, pp. 428f., in which he stresses his indebtednesss to his former teacher: "Unter seiner Leitung hatte ich noch meine Studien abschliessen können. Keiner der Nekrologe, die ihm damals gewidmet wurden, befriedigte mich. Sie sprachen das nicht aus, worin ich seine wissenschaftliche und menschliche Grösse sah. Wenn ich versuche, es heute darzulegen, löse ich eine Dankesschuld ein, die fast ein halbes Jahrhundert umfasst. . . . Seine Werke werden—sehr zu Unrecht— nicht mehr gelesen. Nach mir wird so bald nicht mehr jemand kommen, der über ihn schreibt" (p. 428). Professor Yakov Malkiel kindly informs me that "it is little known, but definitely relevant, that G. G.'s *Grundriss*, at least in its original design, was to contain chapters on Romance cultural history, including painting, sculpture, music, philosophy, and sciences. This blueprint shows the breadth and sweep of G. G.'s thinking. See K. Völlmoller's *Krit. Jb.*, VI (1903), on the enforced tightening of the original design." I wish to take this opportunity to acknowledge my warmest thanks to Prof. Malkiel for his painstaking reading of my essay.

one hand, his choice of a doctoral dissertation and his critique of G. Bourgin's edition of Guibert de Nogent's *De Vita sua* (1913) and, on the other, his book on Brunetière and his youthful enthusiasm for the *NRF* group. This enthusiasm was to crystallize and find, immediately after the war, a commanding form in *Die literarischen Wegbereiter des neuen Frankreich* (1919), with its essays on Gide, Rolland, Claudel, Suarès, and Péguy.[14]

But we can trace a direct line of succession back from Curtius to beyond Gröber. For the latter was a student of Adolf Ebert (1820-90), the first among modern philologists to develop critically and systematically the concept of medieval literature as a unity dependent for its growth and refinement upon the continuity of Latin literature as it evolved from late antiquity. His ideas were put down in the three-volume work, *Allgemeine Geschichte der Literatur des Mittelalters im Abendlande* (1874-89), but this historical survey went only as far as the end of the tenth century and hence stopped before those periods of greatest and most significant output. Gröber then continued Ebert's efforts by writing a history of medieval Latin literature which reaches well into the High Middle Ages; his *Übersicht über die lateinische Literatur von der Mitte des 6. Jahrhunderts bis ca. 1350* (1902) forms a part of the second volume of the *Grundriss* and, in scope and intention, is a work wholly without precedent. Gröber wanted to show how late antique and medieval Latin literature influenced the incipient Romance literatures in their choice of theme, subject and technique, but his energies were spent in the descriptive and chronological part of his study, and he never lived to pursue analytically, in detail and

[14] The notes to the edition of Guibert's *De Vita sua* are now reprinted in *Gesammelte Aufsätze*, pp. 54f.

breadth, the actual workings of medieval Latin upon the vernaculars. It fell then to Curtius to take up this aspect of the general problem. Hence the lines of research initiated by Gröber's teacher were brought to a brilliant completion in one of the masterpieces of modern scholarship, his student's *Europäische Literatur und lateinisches Mittelalter*. However, the common scholarly concern which links together these three generations of Romance philologists reaches even farther back, striking its roots in the soil of Germany's golden age of historical research, for Gröber and Ebert are indebted to the pioneering work of Diez, and the latter's is inspired by the philosophical presuppositions of German Romanticism and, most particularly, by Goethe's concept of world literature. Thus an ideal curve of development runs from Goethe to Curtius, characterized by a broadening and deepening of the field of literary study for the purpose of determining the genesis, continuity, and transformation of forms, motifs, themes, and styles.

Of decisive importance for Curtius' spiritual formation was his friendship with Friedrich Gundolf, a bond which lasted some ten years and led to episodic associations between the young Romance professor and Stefan George. We have a record of this friendship in the exchange of letters published by Castrum Peregrini of Amsterdam, one of the last outposts of the esoteric and once influential *Georgekreis*.[15] Six years Gundolf's junior and for a time his colleague at Heidelberg,[16]

[15] Friedrich Gundolf, *Briefwechsel mit Herbert Steiner und Ernst Robert Curtius*, ed. with an intro. by Lothar Helbing and Claus Victor Bock (Amsterdam, 1963).
[16] The University of Heidelberg, in the late twenties, counted among its professors some of the most distinguished minds in Germany: Max and Alfred Weber; the archaeologist and classical

Curtius wrote to him, "When I reflect upon my intellectual and moral growth and my present outlook, then it becomes ever more clear how much you have influenced me."[17] The nature of the relationship with Gundolf points to a central and recurring experience in Curtius' life: his search among his contemporaries and the masters of the past for a spiritual leader, a *praeceptor patriae*. Present in all his writings, even the most scholarly, is a strong moral passion for renewal and a persistent urge to counsel, reprove and exhort. It is the spiritual life of Germany within the greater cultural and religious ambit of Europe that is his abiding concern. In Curtius the faith and hope of the humanist make constant appeal to a secular canon of saints consisting of poets and thinkers who have shaped a vision of life which is morally liberating and aesthetically enhancing. Gundolf was a commanding figure, strikingly handsome and possessed of a superior and outwardly forceful mind. In the fervent tone and lofty idealism of many of the letters exchanged between the two, we sense the same kind of warm spiritual fraternity that once existed among the young Romantics of Jena and Heidelberg. The correspondence began in 1908 when Curtius was twenty-two years old, at a time when Stefan George, in Curtius' words, counted as the "great formative influence in my life."[18] Until their rift in the late twenties, Gundolf was the poet's favorite and most

---

scholar Ludwig Curtius (no relation); Karl Jaspers; the philosopher Heinrich Rickert; and the specialist on Indian art and thought Heinrich Zimmer, whose daughter married Hugo von Hofmannsthal. See Arnold Bergstraesser, *Politik in Wissenschaft und Bildung* (Freiburg, 1961), pp. 91-92.

[17] *Briefwechsel*, p. 222.

[18] *Ibid.*, p. 131. Cf. the ecstatic letter from the young Curtius to George, dated May 30, 1910, as cited in *Castrum Peregrini*, 60 (1963): 49-50.

gifted disciple—and the way to George lay through Gundolf. Curtius hoped that the poet would intercede on his behalf to have the manuscript of his fledgling work, the *Wegbereiter*, printed and distributed by George's publisher, Georg Bondi in Berlin. The book would then bear George's imprimatur, and its author would be numbered among those few who had met the stern requirements of "contemporary Germany's most important figure."[19] But no such patronage was forthcoming. The Master was scornful of Curtius' book and rejected it out of hand, as the recent publication of the George-Gundolf correspondence makes abundantly clear. The work is not only roundly condemned, but most of those chosen as French *Wegbereiter* are contemptuously treated. In a letter of 1916 to Gundolf, the poet wrote: "He [Curtius] ought to choose topics of a very different sort . . . for C.'s mind is as opposed to ours as it's possible to be."[20] Curtius, presumably unaware of the harshness of George's reaction, confines himself in his retrospective essay on his conversations with the poet to this rather anodyne report of the affair: "I admired certain contemporary French authors and planned to write about them. For this I hoped to get George's backing; I never got it. In a note dictated to Gundolf, he tried to dissuade me from my project; it read, 'What do those "Frenchies" understand about poetry.' On the margin, in George's own hand: 'and yet *with much affection, St. G.*' "[21]

[19] The words are Gundolf's, cited in *Kritische Essays*, p. 107.

[20] *Stefan George–Friedrich Gundolf. Briefwechsel* (Munich-Düsseldorf, 1962), pp. 288, 286. In Edith Landmann's *Gespräche mit Stefan George* (Munich-Düsseldorf, 1963), she reports the poet as saying to her in 1920, in reference to the young Curtius's book: "Das ist so schief, dass es von einem Franzosen sein könnte" (p. 95).

[21] *Kritische Essays*, p. 112. The italics are Curtius'.

This refusal must have come as a keen disappointment to the young scholar since the *Wegbereiter* was so manifestly written under the influence of George and his Circle. When in 1918 Curtius wrote in his Preface to the first edition: "This book is offered to the youth of our country, and proclaims our ardent belief in the spiritual rebirth of Germany,"[22] he was giving expression to sentiments which recur constantly in the letters he wrote at this time to Gundolf.[23] The George movement and the contemporary direction of French literature represented by the aesthetic doctrines of the *Nouvelle Revue française* were linked in young Curtius' mind by a common concern for spiritual renewal. Each, in its way, stood for a rejection of *fin-de-siècle* skepticism, cultural vulgarity, and aesthetic decadence, and were united in a will toward intellectual and moral integrity through the discriminating, disciplined striving for form. The watch words of the *NRF—mesure, profondeur, rigueur*—could be applied equally well to the *Georgekreis*. The artistic and cultural ambitions of both groups pointed to the likelihood of a new Europeanism dedicated to overcoming encumbering traditions and complacent, nationalist ideologies. It was a

[22] *Französischer Geist,* p. 5.
[23] E. g., "So wollen wir in frommem Bunde in den neuen Tag hineinschreiten und am Werke bauen" (*Briefwechsel,* p. 242). The point of the poet's influence upon his first book is made quite explicit in a letter of 1916: "So ist mir die Arbeit unter den Händen zu einer Auseinandersetzung zwischen zweien meiner Geistesinhalte: französischer Geist und georgischer staatswille, geworden. Im Buch kann und darf das natürlich nicht in der form der diskussion herauskommen. Es wird aber, hoff ich, für den eingeweihten hie und da fühlbar sein" (*ibid.,* p. 251). And in the "Rückblick" appended in 1952 to *Französischer Geist,* Curtius writes: "Eine politische Forderung war es . . . , die zwischen den zeilen der *Wegbereiter* stand" (p. 520).

time when, as George put it, "greatness again became great."[24]

But both movements were to disappoint Curtius' expectations. George retired into proud isolation, the *Kreis* kept changing its members, and the Master's authoritarianism provoked the alienation of nearly all those who had once been close to him.[25] Curtius' last contact with the poet came in 1919, a year after the publication of the *Wegbereiter*.[26] Though respectful of George's neo-paganism and his cult of Greek virtues, Curtius was by birth and habit too much of a Christian to feel at home in the exclusive religion of aesthetic and ethical ritualism. What he was striving for at this time was a conciliation between *Griechentum* and *Christentum*, a Christian Orphism in which the world would be

[24] "Der Dichter in Zeiten der Wirren," *Das Neue Reich*, in *Werke* I (Munich-Düsseldorf, 1958), p. 416.

[25] Curtius records his disillusionment in these lines written in 1931, two years before the poet's death, and incorporated a year later into his book, *Deutscher Geist in Gefahr*: "Nachdem sich die einst so hoffnungsvoll wie ein neuer Geistesfrühling einsetzende Bewegung des Stefan George-Kreises in der phrasenhaften Dogmatik von seltenförmigen Gebilden totgelaufen hatte, war Hugo von Hofmannsthal der letzte befugte Verkünder einer neuen Einheit von Nation und Sendung" (p. 19). These lines first appeared in the article "Abbau der Bildung," *Die Neue Rundschau*, Sept., 1931. They are of further interest in that they point up, at a relatively early date, the now familiar George-Hofmannsthal polarity, an opposition which will be sharpened and given epigrammatic expression a few years later in the opening pages of Curtius' essay, "George, Hofmannsthal und Calderon," first published in 1934, and later made a part of his collected essays on European literature. It is interesting to follow, in the letters to Gundolf, Curtius' change of feeling toward George's Austrian rival. In the early correspondence he joins Gundolf in belittling Hofmannsthal; then gradually, and grudgingly, he yields to the attraction of an art and imaginative outlook which were ultimately to exercise such a profound influence upon his own writings.

[26] *Kritische Essays*, pp. 114f.

redeemed through the revelation of beauty and suffering. "Your notion," he wrote to Gundolf, "that the Greek ideal and Christianity do not exclude each other is precisely the basis upon which I have ordered my life."[27] Disenchantment with his French trailblazers came shortly afterwards, for the common ideals and energies which had animated pre-war literature in France began to wane after the armistice. Péguy had been killed in battle; Suarés, embittered and misanthropic, had already produced his best; Romain Rolland, disillusioned by what had come of his efforts to rise above the enmities which had devastated Europe, turned to the East and became enamoured of "Bolshevism" and the Soviet experiment, a shift in allegiance which Curtius could only deplore; finally, Gide and Claudel were to follow radically different paths and, after 1925, the date which ends their fascinating correspondence, the two became sworn enemies. Proust, whom Curtius joined to the list of *Wegbereiter* and introduced to German readers in his dazzling essay of 1925, had died prematurely some three years previously.[28] The much hoped-for French-German *rapprochement* became impossible after the ominous political events of 1923, marked by the occupation of the Ruhr, inflation, separatist agitation in the Rhineland, and the entrance of Hitler into German public life with the November *Putsch*. The hopes that accompanied *Die*

[27] *Briefwechsel*, p. 262.

[28] This study, along with those on Paul Valéry and Valery Larbaud, formed part of the volume entitled *Französischer Geist im neuen Europa* (Stuttgart, 1925), and should be considered a sequel to his earlier book on modern French literature. These essays together with those of the *Wegbereiter* and the addition of previously published pieces on Maritain and Abbé Bremond now make up the volume, *Französischer Geist im Zwanzigsten Jahrhundert*.

literarischen Wegbereiter were still-born: the work was never translated into French and its final edition appeared, significantly, in this same year of 1923.[29] After that there was no responsive audience for a book which thus far had enjoyed a lively if limited reception by the younger generation in Germany and by foreign critics. Curtius, commenting much later, in retrospect, upon the configuration of historical forces and creative talent propitious to the French cultural renascence in the early decades of the century, invokes a law of conception, growth, and decay which presides over every spiritual phenomenon, the phases of which he defines as: "Origins, growth, differentiation, dissolution." It

[29] In this regard, see Victor Klemperer, "Das neue Deutsche Frankreichbild (1914-1933), ein historischer Überblick II," in *Beiträge zur romanischen Philologie* 2 (1963): 70, note 1. In his essay, "The Crisis of Comparative Literature," René Wellek, discussing the political motivations behind the writing of the *Wegbereiter*, states that "Curtius had defined his conception of the good European"; then cites, as his definition, a passage from *Französischer Geist* (p. 237) which begins: " 'Ich weiss nur eine Art, ein guter Europäer zu sein: mit Macht die Seele seiner Nation haben . . . ' "; and adds, in commentary, "a cultural power politics is recommended: everything serves only the strength of one's nation." (*Concepts of Criticism*, New Haven, 1963, p. 288.) But our eminent literary historian has read too hastily: the citation is not from Curtius himself, as it is clearly purported to be, but from André Suarès! Nor can it be said to be quoted by Curtius in support of his own views; rather it is drawn from the section, "Zum Bilde Frankreichs" (pp. 223-42), in which the German critic surveys objectively, largely through quotation, the different conceptions of their own country held by the authors treated in the main part of the *Wegbereiter*. It is further misleading to juxtapose as comparable—in the one case a German reacting to France, in the other a Frenchman's attitudes toward Germany—Curtius' subsequent disillusionment with the modern movement in France and the morbid, doctrinaire views of Jean-Marie Carré in *Les Ecrivains français et le mirage allemand* (Paris, 1947). Though at times shaken, Curtius' loyalty to France remained constant to the end of his life.

was so with the Jena school of Romantics, with the George Circle—and with the *Wegbereiter*.[30]

Curtius' efforts as an interpreter of contemporary French culture brought him to the attention of the internationally-minded Mayrisch family at Colpach in Luxembourg. A socially prominent and highly cultivated industrial magnate, chairman of the Aciéries Réunies Burbach-Esch-Dudelange, Émile Mayrisch had, with his wife, Aline, established at their summer estate a center for European amity, a "petit noyau de la future Europe."[31] There, where chestnut trees shaded bronzes by Bourdelle and Maillol, Despiau and Kolbe, eminent German and French businessmen, scholars, and artists convened to exchange views. For Curtius it was a "Prospero's island in the Ardennes forest,"[32] where one could hobnob with Walter Rathenau and Annette Kolb, and where in 1921 he first made the acquaintance of André Gide and Jacques Rivière. From Colpach the way led naturally to Pontigny and its celebrated *décades*, or ten-day summer meetings, under the tutelage of Paul Desjardins (1859-1940).[33] It was at the invitation of Gide

[30] See *Französischer Geist*, p. 520.

[31] Jean Schlumberger, citing Paul Desjardins, in *Œuvres* 5 (*1934-40*) (Paris, 1960), pp. 340-41. Mme Mayrisch, under the pseudonym of Alain Desportes, had favorably reviewed the *literarische Wegbereiter* in the pages of the *NRF* 15 (1920): 626f. See the memorial volume, *Colpach*, edited by a group of friends from Colpach under the auspices of the Luxembourg Red Cross (Luxembourg, 1957).

[32] Curtius, "T. S. Eliot und Deutschland," *Der Monat* 1 (December, 1948): 72.

[33] For the history of Pontigny and its *décades*, see Anne Heurgon-Desjardins, *Paul Desjardins et les Décades de Pontigny* (Paris, 1964). These summer meetings, in the tradition of Pontigny, have been resumed since the last war. Arnold Toynbee writes in the Preface to his *Reconsiderations*: "In July 1958, at Mme Heurgon-Desjardins's invitation, I had the pleasure of tak-

that Curtius took part in the summer session of 1922,
and again in 1924 he participated, this time at the be-
hest of Charles Du Bos with whom he thus renewed a
contact made some eighteen years earlier in Berlin.
There, in the great Burgundian abbey church—a prize
example of Cistercian architectural zeal dating back to
the early twelfth century but secularized in 1905 on the
occasion of the separation of church and state and the
suppression of the religious orders—scholars and artists
from the four corners of Europe gathered to minister
to the rites of *la sainte religion des lettres*. For Curtius
the lectures, the long afternoon promenades, the evening discussions, and the sports and games meant a direct and intimate contact with France's intellectual
élite.[34] Curtius has defined for us the singular appeal
of Du Bos in a vivid impression which is as revealing
of the German critic himself as it is of his French friend:
"I was at that time continually in search of a France
which would share in the common spiritual concerns
of a regenerated Europe. In this respect I was delighted
to find that Gide could not live without Goethe,
Shakespeare or Dostoyevsky . . . that Larbaud knew intimately Whitman's and Joyce's work. But neither Gide
nor Roger Martin du Gard nor Jacques Rivière . . .
had an innate sympathy for what I would call, to put
it briefly, 'Metaphysics,' which is an essential element
of the German awareness of life. Du Bos had this. For
him Novalis was more interesting than Laclos and
Meister Eckhart more challenging than Stendhal. To
discover this was for me, at the time, very exciting; but

---

ing part in a 'décade,' held at Cerisy-la Salle in Normandy, at
which my work was the subject of discussion" (*A Study of History*, vol. 12, London, 1961).

[34] See Curtius' letter to Marcel Proust, cited in Huergon-Des-
jardins, *Paul Desjardins*, p. 401.

I soon noticed that no one at Pontigny saw Du Bos as I did."[35] A common preoccupation on the part of the two critics with religion and the spiritual life added a new element, then, to Curtius' dialogue with France. Accompanying Curtius to Pontigny on his second visit was Max Scheler (1874-1928), then at the height of a brilliant career which was to be tragically cut off four years later when the philosopher was only in his mid-fifties. Scheler was for Curtius Germany's greatest and most comprehensive thinker since Nietzsche;[36] and if Curtius owed the inspiration for his *Wegbereiter* book to George and Gundolf, then it was from Scheler that he derived the methodological basis and ideational categories for his later essay on French civilization, "Die französische Kultur." The studies appearing in Scheler's *Nation und Weltanschauung,* particularly "Über die Nationalideen der Grossen Nationen," form the model for the kind of thematic and structural analysis of French cultural life which Curtius undertook.[37]

[35] *Kritische Essays,* p. 228. In 1930, in the fifth series of his *Approximations* (Paris, 1948), pp. 109f. Du Bos devotes to Curtius a study which remains the finest assessment to date of the German critic's preoccupation with French literature.

[36] See the essay "Friedrich Gundolf," in *Nya Dagligt Allehanda,* Stockholm, Oct. 18, 1931.

[37] These studies appear now in Scheler's *Gesammelte Werke,* vol. 6 (Bern, 1963); for "Über die Nationalideen der grossen Naitonen," see pp. 121-30. The essay first made its appearance in the volume *Krieg und Aufbau,* 1916. In Scheler, just as in the example of the *Georgekreis,* Curtius sought a guide, the personal embodiment of an ethical and spiritual ideal. This is quite evident in the funeral oration which he pronounced at the grave of the philosopher on May 23, 1928: "Er ist vielen nicht nur ein Freund, nicht nur ein Lehrer, sondern auch ein Helfer und ein Arzt geworden . . . Jeder empfing von ihm seine Bestätigung, und wurde dadurch angespornt und erhöht . . . Wenn wir von ihm gingen, schauten wir das Leben mit neuen Augen, wir waren herausgerissen aus der Enge unserer Gewohnheit und Beschränkung, hinausgeführt in die Weite und Fülle des Daseins, etc."

It was through Scheler, too, that he came to know of Ortega y Gasset's work, and soon Spain's voice was added to the European concert of nations with a succession of essays on Ortega, Unamuno, and Pérez de Ayala.[38] It appears evident from his early correspondence with Ortega that Curtius planned a group of studies on modern Spanish writers, eventually to appear in book form, which would parallel his earlier books on contemporary French authors.

A preoccupation with Spain and her heritage was to be Curtius' long way around to a fresh look at Hofmannsthal, a reappraisal which had a profound effect upon the direction and justification of Curtius' later studies. "A continental line of communication ran from Madrid to the Vienna of the Hapsburgs. Standing guard on this line was Hofmannsthal. . . ."[39] The youthful Curtius, very much under the influence of Gundolf,

---

Cited from a typescript of the oration kindly sent to the author by Frau Märit Furtwängler-Scheler. This search for a guide to the understanding of Europe's destiny and the rôle which he and his generation were to play in its unfolding, occurs again in the case of Albert Thibaudet (1874-1936), whom Curtius met in Heidelberg at a time nearly contemporary with Scheler's death. Among modern interpreters of French letters, he took pride of place, and Curtius considered him the successor to Sainte-Beuve. "Lecteur de Thibaudet dès la première heure, je fus aussitôt conquis par lui. A son insu, il devint mon maître: il m'expliqua la France" (NRF 47 [1936]: 62).

[38] "Durch meinen verehrten Freund Max Scheler, den ich kürzlich in Cöln besuchte, hatte ich Gelegenheit, die Revista de Occidente kennen zu lernen." From a letter by Curtius to Ortega, dated December 10, 1923, in "Ernst-Robert Curtius–José Ortega y Gasset: Ein Briefwechsel," Merkur 10-11 (October-November, 1964): 903. The studies on the Spanish authors have been reprinted in Kritische Essays, with the addition of a second essay on Ortega, written in 1949, which appeared in translation in Partisan Review a year later.

[39] Kritische Essays, p. 7.

dismissed George's Viennese rival and predicted that he would "end up as the author of romantic melodramas. It's curious to see the affinities with Rostand!"[40] As he gradually worked himself free from George and his group, Curtius came to an awareness of Hofmannsthal's exceptional gifts, more particularly his universalism of outlook, and eventually recognized that, through his concern to relate individual and national expression to a common European tradition, Hofmannsthal might serve as a guide to the realization of his own deeply-felt convictions. Descended by way of his mother from Austrian peasantry and related through his father to Italian nobility, with Bohemian and Jewish blood as an admixture—a younger contemporary of Freud and Schnitzler yet buried in the habit of a Franciscan tertiary—Hofmannsthal bore in his person those diverse elements, attitudes, and aspirations which the Austro-Hungarian empire strove to master. Situated at the meeting point of east and west, north and south, imperial Austria was a vast political amalgam of Roman, German, and Slav. Hofmannsthal saw it as his mission to be the interpreter of Austria's destiny, to explain her special role in the history of Europe as a mediator of cultures, assimilating and harmonizing conflicting habits of mind. What Curtius most admired in Hofmannsthal was what he called his integrating imagination—*integrierende Phantasie*[41]—that ability to draw upon the

---

[40] *Gundolf-Curtius. Briefwechsel*, p. 147. It is amusing to contrast these remarks which would have shocked the older Curtius, with the observation he made much later, in the essay on George, that it was the German poet's habit contemptuously to excommunicate from his circle any followers who had compromised the ideals expected of them, adding, in a wry thrust at George: "Hofmannsthal als Librettist!" (*Kritische Essays*, p. 110). Here irony is used in defense of the Austrian.

[41] *Kritische Essays*, p. 138. The first of the essays on Hofmanns-

entire spiritual substance of the past and to give it new and relevant forms. In this respect he was in the direct line of the great poets of European literature: Virgil, Dante, and Goethe. In the Austrian's plays and essays, Curtius saw splendidly illustrated the thesis which he came ever more insistently to promote and defend, that of the continuity of Western culture. Hofmannsthal's major theatre, in its dependence upon Calderón's *comedias* and *autos sacramentales*, builds a bridge to the full and variegated world of the Spanish baroque, which has its traditions deeply rooted in the popular and ecclesiastical piety of the Middle Ages and which Curtius will, in his later years, come to prefer to the norms and ideals of French classicism.

The years of concern with Hofmannsthal coincided with Curtius' turn to modern English literature and his occasional contributions to T. S. Eliot's *Criterion*. He introduced Eliot to Germany, first in 1927, through his translation of *The Wasteland* ("He is the creator of a new mood which it will be impossible in the future to forget."), and then through a long critical piece in which he defined Eliot as a *poeta doctus*, a learned, syncretistic artist of the Alexandrian type. In his essay on Joyce, which appeared two years later, the emphasis on thematic design and recurring pattern continues the approach first used in the studies on Balzac (1923) and Proust and adumbrates methods of analysis adopted in the late period of Curtius' work.[42]

---

thal appeared in 1929. For the above characterization of the Austrian poet, see H. A. Hammelmann, *Hugo von Hofmannsthal* (New Haven, 1957), pp. 50-51.

[42] Curtius' regard for Eliot was reciprocated by the poet. The latter spoke of the essay "Humanismus als Initiative" (later incorporated, as chap. 5, into the volume *Deutscher Geist in Gefahr*) as "one of the best and most reasonable expositions of a 'humanist' attitude that I have ever read" (*The Criterion* 12 [1932]: 74).

Curtius opened the new decade with one of his finest and most widely accepted achievements, a book on French civilization, *Die französische Kultur*, which summarizes the experience of twenty years of intense preoccupation with French cultural life.[43] By resorting to a comparative approach which points up crucial and abiding differences between French and German attitudes, he could bring out objectively, in sharp relief, the dominating traits and ideals of the two cultures, their unique and complementary destinies within the larger frame of European history. In its efforts to identify the *Strukturmerkmale einer Volksindividualität*,[44] an idea which reaches back in origin to Herder and the beginnings of Romanticism, the work is situated

---

See also Eliot's letter in the collection *Freundesgabe für Ernst Robert Curtius*, pp. 25f. In addition to his wide familiarity with English letters, Curtius was also an avid reader of American literature. His friend, Willy Haas, the director of *Europäische Revue*, writes: "Er kannte die zeitgenössische amerikanische Literatur wie kaum ein anderer" (*Die literarische Welt, Erinnerungen* [Munich, 1958], p. 279). He published an essay on Emerson in 1924 (now included in *Kritische Essays*); knew Walt Whitman and the New England writers, including Henry Adams; and after World War II, translated, in a gesture of considerable generosity and remarkable imaginative empathy, the highly poetic and strongly regional novel, *The House of Breath*, by the Texas writer, William Goyen. For a list of Curtius' translations which include, *inter alia*, works by Valéry, Góngora, and Jorge Manrique as well as the late latin *Pervigilium Veneris*, see *Freundesgabe für Ernst Robert Curtius*, pp. 233-4.

[43] Stuttgart, 1930. "Ein besonderer Vorzug dieses Bandes, der fraglos . . . *das reichste deutsche Frankreichbild enthält, das bisher geschaffen wurde*, . . . liegt darin, dass C. dem Riesenthema gegenüber nirgends in fachliche Enge und nirgends in Dilettantismus verfällt." Klemperer, "Das neue deutsche Frankreichbild (1914-1933)," p. 90, italics ours. This is the verdict of a Marxist critic who, in many respects, is hostile to Curtius' outlook.

[44] The expression is drawn from Curtius' article, "Probleme der französischen Kulturkunde," in *Neue Jahrbücher für Wissenschaft und Jugendbildung* 1 (1925): 649.

very much within the tradition of German *Geistesge-schichte*. Its guiding principle, giving the book his-torical continuity and perspective, is a study of the in-fluence exerted on the two nations by Rome. France is seen as the heir to Rome's universalist tendencies in the sense that she conceives of her civilization as having an absolute validity and serving as a model to all; France submitted to the Roman imperium, whereas Germany resisted it, and in her submission, she shared with Rome, from the time of the Frankish hegemony on, some five centuries of her history. France received from her conquerors her language, religion, and po-litical sophistication; she was the beneficiary of Roman norms of reason and civility, authority and justice, and partook of the Latin delight in clarity and rationality of expression. But the *génie latin* formed a part, too, of the German heritage, a fact too often overlooked. "For those of us of German heritage," Curtius wrote on an earlier occasion, "the universal history of the human spirit is not bordered by the Tiber and the Seine. The Rhine and the Danube, the Main and the Neckar are no less affected by Rome.... We shall never let ourselves be shunted off into a vague Central European waste-land. The West is more than its western and southern European border states; the West is the imperium of Charlemagne."[45] Curtius is fond of pointing to the profound links which bind Goethe and George, both Rhine-Frankish poets, to Rome and her history. Goethe felt at times that he had once lived under Hadrian, while for George the vinecovered banks of the Rhine near his native Bingen, celebrated in such poems as "Ursprünge" and "Rhein I-IV," called up memories of Germany's Latinity. In her dialogue with

[45] From the article, "Paul Valéry, *Rhumbs*," in *Europäische Revue* 2 (1926): 405.

France, Curtius argued, Germany must learn the way to recover this Latin element, which is an essential part of Goethean humanism and can serve as a shaping and stabilizing force in those daemonic adventures of the German mind to push back the frontiers of art and thought. The polarity which Curtius once formulated schematically as "Prussia-Austria, Berlin-Vienna, Kant-Mozart, Döblin-Hofmannsthal," finally resolving itself in "the tension between the Roman-German southwest and the Slavic-German northeast," is one of the great obstacles preventing Germany from achieving a unified cohesive culture.[46] The example of France is at the other antipode and hence eminently deserving of study.

In 1932, with his essay on "Friedrich Schlegel und Frankreich," Curtius brought to a close the modernist phase of his life's work, the period stretching back to World War I and concerned primarily with defining the role of French civilization in the formation of a new Europe. With his linguistic gifts, ranging curiosity, and informed sympathies, he had become Germany's *arbiter elegantiarum*, the interpreter of new trends, and a leading participant in the cultural diplomacy of the twenties intent upon fostering a truly vital and serious intellectual life. The study on Schlegel, coming as it did at a crucial moment in Curtius' spiritual development, was exemplary and symbolic, for in describing the French education of one of the heroes of German Romanticism, he was, in fact, recounting his own story. The history of Schlegel's efforts to arrive at a proper understanding of French culture reveals in its basic, underlying pattern the way that must be followed by every young German who wishes to come to terms with France—and with Europe. Schlegel found in

[46] See *Deutscher Geist in Gefahr*, p. 23.

France the key to a European way of thinking, and an important consequence of his stay in Paris was his founding and editing of the review *Europa*, dedicated to the promotion of a broad, irenic view in the study of national literatures. "That a leading German writer while living in Paris and through contact with France, is led to reflect upon the concept of 'Europe,' a concept given such a profound significance in Novalis, is a fact of paramount historical importance."[47] These words, used to summarize Schlegel's achievement, apply with equal force to Curtius' encounters with France. But the case of Schlegel is paradigmatic in another regard as well. His research into the poetry of the Middle Ages and his Vienna lectures of 1815, published as the *Geschichte der alten und neuen Literatur*, with their survey of medieval literature and assessment of its place and relevance within the total context of European *belles-lettres*, anticipate the labors of the later period of Curtius' critical activities.[48]

The publication of the Schlegel study took place the same year as Hitler's ominous challenge to Hindenburg for the presidency of the Reich. Curtius' response to the gathering storm was his hortatory essay *Deutscher Geist in Gefahr* (1932), in which he pleaded for Ger-

[47] *Kritische Essays*, p. 91.

[48] In this connection, Curtius writes: "Gerade darin, dass er Mittelalter und neue Zeit, Ältestes und Aktuelles gleichzeitig aufzunehmen und zu verarbeiten wusste, sehe ich seine Besonderheit und seine Bedeutung. Es gibt kaum ein Gebiet der Romania, auf dem Friedrich Schlegel nicht einmal gearbeitet hat" (*Ibid.*, p. 87). Schlegel's example anticipates another direction, too, in Curtius' scholarship, namely his interest in mystico-theosophical literature. The older scholar's esteem for the French illuminist, Saint-Martin, is paralleled, a century later, by the younger Romanist's sketches of the philosopher, Franz Baader. See the collection of journalistic articles written by Curtius in his late years, *Büchertagebuch* (Bern, 1960), pp. 88f.

many to recover and build upon the ideals of Goethean humanism. In the course of his studies of French culture and now in his alarm over the national crisis in Germany, he had steadily become convinced of the need for understanding the various national literatures of the West in their common origin and development. We can trace this process by calling to mind again the inspiring figures and profound lessons which acted upon his imagination in the period *entre les deux guerres*. France and Germany, each in its own way and in varying degrees, were seen to have been profoundly affected by their Roman past; Hofmannsthal was admired as the overseer of a cultural heritage whose axis ran from Madrid to Vienna, and Eliot esteemed as the defender of classicism in art and traditionalism in politics and religion; Gide, Du Bos, and Larbaud were admired as the spokesmen for "Europeanism" in a nation long used to considering itself the sole arbiter of cultural values; while Ortega acted as the herald of a reinvigorated Spain integrated with the European community and Stefan George's poetry stood as proof of the vitality of Germany's classicism. But in the chaos of the ensuing decade these figures became obscured and their lessons inoperative. Hitlerism meant the crude and hectic revivalism of a nordic, gothic Germany severed in spirit from its greater European whole. His advent to power was followed shortly by the Spanish Civil War, and in the whirlwind the ripe fruit seeded by the *Regeneradores* of 1898 fell to the ground: Unamuno was silenced and Ortega went into exile.[49] The fall of France came only three years later.

[49] Four writers who exerted a decisive influence on Curtius' thought died prematurely: Hofmannsthal at fifty-five, Scheler at fifty-four, Proust and Gundolf at fifty-one.

Curtius was fond of quoting a favorite saying of
Jakob Burckhardt's: "Bene vixit qui bene latuit."[50]
This *Lieblingsspruch* characterizes the physical and
spiritual conditions in which Curtius spent the second
period of his life's work. With his program of teaching
drastically curtailed and a free participation in the cultural life of the nation made impossible, he retired to
the seclusion of the library, there to devote himself to a
prolonged and comprehensive study of the basis and
evolution of Europe's literary tradition. Forced retirement gave him the leisure to act upon the convictions
of middle age. A second world war was imminent and
would spell the end of nineteenth-century nationalism;
just as, in the realm of the spirit, historical and literary
studies pursued along narrowly specialist lines were
obsolete. To be sure, specialization and the unchal-
lenged orthodoxy which tended to limit manageable
fields of study in accordance with the political map or
in terms of a now outdated periodization had made possible exacting methods and tools of research and, in the
process, had created rigorous standards of analysis and
verification. Now, however, the scope must be extended
so as to comprehend a broad European survey, and
within this much wider focus a comparative view of
literary phenomena must be worked out toward the
end of perceiving, across the ages, a coincidence of experience and expression, parallel patterns executing some
grand design in materials often widely separate in time
and place. These are the scholarly premises underlying
the long series of research essays, composed in the thirties
and forties, on the continuity of Western literature

[50] See for example, his *Literarische Kritik in Deutschland*
(Hamburg, 1950), p. 19. The citation is slightly misquoted:
"(Crede mihi), bene qui latuit, bene vixit," Ovid, *Tristia* 3, 4,
25. Cf. *Deutscher Geist in Gefahr*, p. 27.

which, recast, would constitute *Europäische Literatur und lateinisches Mittelalter.* But the grounds for this project lay much deeper. During the long night of German barbarity when Europe was fighting for its survival, Curtius wished by his monumental labor to affirm the permanence of Europe's humane tradition. Transferred now to the plane of *Philologie,* Curtius' wartime studies were a series of *Streitschriften,* the inevitable sequel to his *Deutscher Geist in Gefahr.* His ivory tower was in reality a command post from which he defended the values of a way of life and thought which reach back to antiquity. The special focus of his studies was the Latin and Romance literatures of the Middle Ages, the cultural complex of medieval *Romania* which stretched from the Black Sea to the Atlantic and owed its inception and growth to the Germanic invasions, the Roman imperium, and the Latin Church: Christianity, Rome, and Germania—that European trinity which inspired the deepest loyalties and struck the most responsive chords in Curtius' thought. The Latin Middle Ages are a neglected yet crucial period for the understanding of the survival of antiquity and the growth of the modern vernacular literatures: "It is the crumbling Roman road leading from the antique to the modern world."[51] However, the antique poetry and thought which survived into the Middle Ages was not principally that of the classical authors but, owing to the senescence which overtook the Latin world in the third

---

[51] *Europäische Literatur und lateinisches Mittelalter,* p. 29. The term, "Latin Middle Ages," is Curtius' own formula. By this he meant the inheritance of the Roman idea of world mission in the making of the Middle Ages; as an historical reality it begins with Charlemagne who invokes Rome's claim to universalism. "Ich bezeichne damit den Anteil Roms, seiner Staatsidee, seiner Kirche, seiner Kultur und der Prägung des gesamten Mittelalters, also ein viel umfassenderes Phänomen als das Fortleben der lateinischen Sprache und Literatur" (*ibid.,* p. 37).

century A.D., that of the decadent Latinity of late classicism.[52] The medieval period received its notions of classicism from writers like Macrobius, Symmachus, Claudianus, and Ausonius, not from the authors of the Augustan age who, though known, exercised no right of priority. The former "diverge as much from Classicism as the sculpture of the Arch of Constantine does from the art works of the *Ara pacis Augustae.*"[53]

The medieval interpretation of history is governed by the concept of *renovatio,* the *translatio imperii*: that is, the contemporary moment is conceived of as a renewal of the old and derives its validity through its approximation to a period of time in the past (Roman antiquity loosely and vaguely understood) considered as an absolute norm.[54] This idea, when applied to literature, means that all medieval poetry is school poetry based upon an imitation of models chosen indiscriminately from the Latin authors of the Golden Age, from the period of decadence, and from early Christianity. To savor and assess medieval poetry, then, we must read the *auctores* who were then a part of the curriculum and not those read today in the European Gymnasium. Furthermore, schooling in the critical appreciation and correct composition of poetry was dependent exclusively upon rhetoric, the tradition of poetics inherited from antiquity. What links together classical and medieval literature, pagan and Christian expression, is rhetorical convention. "All late Roman and medieval

[52] Curtius, "Zur Literarästhetik des Mittelalters III," *Zeitschrift für romanische Philologie* 58 (1938): 440f.; and *Europäische Literatur,* p. 396.

[53] *Gesammelte Aufsätze,* p. 111.

[54] See "Zur Literarästhetik des Mittelalters II," *Zeitschrift für romanische Philologie* 58 (1938): 133, for the examples cited in support of this concept.

Latin poetry is more or less rhetorical."[55] With the "rebirth of antiquity" in the Italian Renaissance, the study of rhetoric became even more intense, though it now appertained to a canon of authors more truly representative of Greco-Latin classicism. Hence a knowledge of the rhetorical tradition becomes the key to an understanding of the progress of Western literary life as it spans the more than fifteen hundred years separating Constantine (d. 337) from the Romanticism of the mid-eighteenth century. Herein lies the possibility of writing a genuine history of European literature which, independent of criteria and categories drawn from the historical disciplines, would remain faithful to the autonomous structure of its subject, aware that, though sensitive to all the pressures of the past and present, artistic verbal expression boasts its own laws and course of development.

However, a truly inclusive survey of the Western literary tradition, presupposing as it would a contact with and mastery of all the significant texts and sources, is manifestly an impossibility. Besides, how could we give to this mass of fact and commentary a readable, digestible form? "One would have to be everywhere at the same time. As a substitute for such an impossible ubiquity, methodological expedients will have to be found: the systematic presentation of numerous topographic observations taken from the most varied points of view and under the most varied circumstances."[56]

---

[55] *Ibid.*, p. 137.
[56] "Zur Literarästhetik des Mittelalters III," *ibid.*, p. 433. For Curtius' decisive rejection of conventional literary history ("Eine erzählende und aufzählende Geschichte gibt immer nur katalogartiges Tatsachenwissen. Sie lässt den Stoff in seiner zufälligen Gestalt bestehen."), see *Europäische Literatur*, p. 25. Cf. the interesting observations by Erich Auerbach in "Philologie der Weltliteratur," *Weltliteratur, Festgabe für Fritz Strich zum 70.*

The problem then is one of method and we can trace
Curtius' discovery of a solution if we go back in time to
a few lines which he wrote in the introduction to his
Proust essay of the mid-twenties: "It is the presupposi-
tion of all criticism that certain things will strike the
critic's attention. . . . Reception is the basis of perception, and this, in turn, leads to conception."[57] This
critical principle is, itself, based upon the approach
Proust used in his study of Ruskin, in which he strove
to determine the singular characteristics of the English writer's narrative art in order to present "les traits
essentiels du génie de l'écrivain." Projected by Curtius
upon a much larger scale, the method will serve to delin-
eate the salient features of an entire literary tradition.
He always insisted upon the fact that he began his readings of late antique and medieval writers without any
preconceived notions, in a random, unsystematic way,
simply trusting in the experience of years of alert and
sensitive reading to guide him as to what was significant

Geburtstag (Bern, 1952). Curtius took great pains to see to it
that in reducing his extensive series of philological studies to
book form he give the material a pleasing, readable appearance.
One of the epigraphs to his book is a sentence from Ortega:
"Un libro de ciencia tiene que ser de ciencia, pero también tiene
que ser un libro." For a list of the studies, see *Europäische
Literatur*, pp. 565-66.

[57] *Französischer Geist*, pp. 278-79. Such a formula, and its
application, call to mind the celebrated "philological circle" of
Curtius' great contemporary, Leo Spitzer. See the latter's *Linguistics and Literary History* (Princeton, 1948), p. 19, where he
establishes the philosophical and theological basis for his method
in the *Zirkel im Verstehen* of Dilthey and Schleiermacher. Of
special interest in our case is the fact which Spitzer points out
further on in the same essay: "For the students in Romance,
Gröber formulated the idea of the philological circle (without
mentioning the 'circle' itself) in . . . [the] *Grundriss* 1/3
(1888) . . ." (p. 35).

in his new line of research.[58] And so it happened that certain rhetorical devices, formulae and common places, themes and stylistic mannerisms, metaphors, tropes, and conceits would strike his attention; awaken resonances; call to mind a train of associations; and begin to cohere and crystallize. To pursue historically a recurring theme or figure of speech in its origin, elaboration, and transformation—say, that of the "ideal landscape" or the "book as metaphor"—was to obtain a view of the inner workings, the economy and continuity of European literature.

Chief among the heuristic devices that Curtius used, and which, thanks to him, has gained wide favor in contemporary scholarship, is the *topos* or rhetorical common place—any theme, conceptual motif, image, or stylistic pattern which occurs repeatedly in varying forms at different periods.[59] By studying the persistence

[58] See "Zur Literarästhetik des Mittelalters II," p. 198; "Die Musen im Mittelalter," *ZRPh* 59 (1939): 129; and *Europäische Literatur*, pp. 386-87.

[59] *Topoi* originate with Aristotle's *Rhetorica* and in the subsequent history of antique rhetoric come to mean conceptual or sentimental commonplaces, stock formulations, used by orators in preparing speeches and addresses ("Locos appello . . . sedes argumentorum, in quibus latent, ex quibus sunt petenda." Quintilian, *Institutionis Oratoria* V, 10, 20). See "Zur Literarästhetik des Mittelalters II," pp. 135f.; *Europäische Literatur*, pp. 79f. and 92; and *Gesammelte Aufsätze*, pp. 7-8. With the decline of the Greek *polis* and, later, the Roman republic, the two most important kinds of oratory—political and judicial—disappear from the public scene and take refuge in the schools where they exercise a strong influence on pedagogical theory and practice. Necessarily, the *topoi* become an important part of the rhetorical curriculum which, as we have seen, includes literary studies, i.e., the critical study of texts as well as the learning of rules for the composition of literary works. However, the process can work the other way around, with certain *topoi* originating in the mythopoetic imagination and then being appropriated by rhetoric, e.g., Elysium, the Golden Age, *puer senex*, etc.

In recent studies dealing with *topos* and its meaning, Curtius

of rhetorical *topoi*, we can follow clearly discernible lines of continuation, *Stilkontinuitäten*, which run from Statius to Calderón and beyond to Goethe. This Curtius calls a *historische Topik* which, owing to the abandonment of neo-classical aesthetics and to our much more highly developed historical awareness, would replace the older normative rhetoric as the proper approach to the study of literature.[60] Nuances in the meaning of a given *topos* and its frequency of occurrence can and will change depending upon historical setting. Therefore our *Nova Rhetorica*, moving as it does backward and forward in time and cutting across linguistic boundaries, could study its *topoi* as reflections of a change in sensibility and world-view, and so lead, because controlled by empirical evidence—the direct

---

has been criticized for a vagueness in terminology and for illegitimately stretching the term to include any kind of recurring formula, ideational or stylistic, in support of his general thesis of literary continuity. Indeed he relates certain of his poetic *topoi* to Jungian archetypes and his loosely-defined theory of topics makes frequent appeal to the analyst's theory of the collective unconscious. See *Europäische Literatur*, pp. 92 and 115. For recent studies treating of Curtius and topology, see María Rosa Lida de Malkiel, "Perduración de la literatura antigua en Occidente," *Romance Philology* 5 (1951-52): 99f.; Dámaso Alonso, "Tradition or Polygenesis?" *Modern Humanities Research Bulletin*, no. 32 (Nov., 1960), pp. 17f.; Edgar Mertner, "Topos und Commonplace," *Strena Anglica*, Festschrift für Otto Ritter zum 80. Geburtstag (Halle, 1956); Walter Veit, "Toposforschung," *Deutsche Vierteljahrschrift für Literaturwissenschaft und Geistesgeschichte* 37 (1963): 120f.; and Otto Pöggeler, "Dichtungstheorie und Toposforschung," *Jahrbuch für Aesthetik und Allgemeine Kunstwissenschaft* 5 (1960): 89-201.

[60] Curtius cites Valery Larbaud: "Un ouvrage de critique vraiment 'scientifique' dont le manque se fait sentir, c'est une sorte de Répertoire des thèmes que nous rencontrons si souvent chez les Lyriques modernes à partir de Pétrarque" (*Gesammelte Aufsätze*, p. 7). Cf. Gottfried Benn's penetrating remarks on *Europäische Literatur* in his *Doppelleben* (Wiesbaden, 1958), pp. 165-66.

citation of text—to a solid and rigorous "Geistes-
und Formengeschichte der europäischen Literatur."[61]
Hence Curtius' "science of literature" could be made
to serve a greatly broadened compass of interest and yet,
within its domain, adhere to methods of analysis proper
to literary study *ex propriis principiis* and not imported
from outside. An awareness of the evolution of literary
constants can give us a clearer idea of the interplay between tradition and individual talent, the vital exchange
between the old and the new which in later years became the ultimate concern of Curtius' writings. So, for
example, he will show us how, in the magnificent last
canto of the *Paradiso* (lines 94ff.), Dante incorporates and
transforms into *terzine* of matchless beauty three dis-
parate motifs from the varied history of the Argo legend, drawn successively from Apollonius, Catullus, and
the *Roman de la Rose*. Through such a transmutation
and command of tradition on Dante's part, literary
reminiscences are restored to life by fusion with a new
and greater whole, while, in its turn, the new creation
gains immeasurably in gravity and resonance by recalling past treatments of the myth.[62]

A topic is in fact the literary counterpart of the art
historian's motif, and *Toposforschung* can be thought
of as an equivalent to "an art history without names,"
a literary iconography.[63] Curtius, therefore, set out to

[61] "Zur Literarästhetik des Mittelalters II," p. 138. "Man kann
an der Geschichte rhetorischer Formeln ein Stück Kulturgeschichte ablesen," *ibid.*, p. 141.
[62] See "Das Schiff der Argonauten," *Kritische Essays*, pp. 428f.
Curtius had earlier intended to entitle his *magnum opus, Lateinisches und Romanisches Mittelalter,* adding the programmatic
subtitle, *Untersuchungen zur literarischen Tradition Europas.* See
the letter to K. E. Gass, dated June 30, 1944, in Karl Eugen Gass,
Pisaner Tagebuch (1961), p. 414.
[63] "Zur Literarästhetik des Mittelalters II," p. 139.

do for literary history what Aby Warburg, Saxl, and
Panofsky had been doing for more than twenty years
in art history, and it is with this intention in mind that
he dedicated his *Europäische Literatur* to the memory
of Warburg (as well as to Gustav Gröber).[64] When Fritz
Saxl states that "the problem which the Warburg Library has set for itself is the question of the extent and
nature of the influence which classical antiquity has
exercised upon later cultures,"[65] we can see that for both
Warburg and Curtius the historical problem was essentially the same, namely an inquiry into the restorative and normative value of tradition, *de Thesauro*.
Each in his way was intent upon studying the survival
of figurative expressions which, by translating universal
human feelings with aptness, force, and distinction,
transcend the merely personal and pass into the social
memory.[66] Analogies might also be drawn, though of a

[64] See Curtius' essay, "Antike Pathosformeln in der Literatur
des Mittelalters," in *Estudios dedicados a Menéndez Pidal* I
(Madrid 1950), pp. 257f. (now reprinted in *Gesammelte Aufsätze*, pp. 23f.), where he applies Warburg's coinage, "Pathosformeln," to an analysis of Lucan's influence on the Old French epic.
The formula appears first in Warburg's early study, "Dürer und
die italienische Antike" (1905)—now in *Gesammelte Schriften*
(Leipzig-Berlin, 1932), pp. 445f.—in which he demonstrates the
dependence of early Renaissance Italian artists on devices and
motifs of late antique statuary, vases, etc., for the intensifying of
emotion.

[65] "Die Bibliothek Warburg und ihr Ziel," *Vorträge der Bibliothek Warburg 1921-22* (Leipzig-Berlin, 1923), p. 1. Cf. G. Bing,
"A. M. Warburg," *Journal of the Warburg and Courtauld Institutes* 28 (1965): 299f.

[66] A further parallel between Curtius' investigation into late
antique and medieval Latin rhetoric and the iconographical research of the previous generation of German art historians is
indicated in this interesting note by Gertrud Bing in which she
is discussing the achievement of Alois Riegl and his contemporaries: "Riegl (his *Spätrömische Kunstindustrie* appears in 1901)
and Wickhoff had established the claim of the arts of '*decadent*'
and *transitional periods*, like *Latin Antiquity* and *Early Chris-*

looser sort, between Curtius' views and André Malraux's concept of "le musée imaginaire" which reveals, through dramatic juxtaposition, elective affinities between art objects of widely different periods and places. When Malraux writes: "The museum [as such] separates the art work from the 'profane' world and brings it into relationship with other works of opposing or rival styles. It is a confrontation of metamorphoses," he is adopting a view of history akin to Curtius'.[67]

If Warburg's iconographical investigations and Gröber's philological concern with medieval Latin stand as precedents and inspirational models for Curtius' methodology and field of concentration, then his guide

---

tianity, to fair consideration on their own merits, irrespective of the aesthetic appeal which they may seem to lack or possess, and iconographical interpretation was given as much attention as formal analysis" ("Fritz Saxl [1890-1948]: A Memoir," in *Fritz Saxl, A Volume of Memorial Essays from his friends in England*, ed. D. J. Gordon [Edinburgh, 1957], p. 3, our italics). In view of Curtius' awareness of a close correspondence between the philosophical and methodological presuppositions of his own work and those of a prevailing trend in art history, his harsh strictures against *Kunstgeschichte* appearing in the opening chapter of *Europäische Literatur* and, later, in *Büchertagebuch* must appear somewhat paradoxical. The apparent inconsistency can be explained, I believe, if we bear in mind that his reservations center on two points: 1) the criteria of stylistic analysis of Wölfflin and his disciples have exerted an exaggerated influence upon literary history ("Ist am Ende Goethes *Faust* offen, der Valérys geschlossen?" *Europäische Literatur*, p. 21); and 2) in our day art history threatens to replace *belles lettres* in the formation of a culturally educated elite ("Die Kunstgeschichte . . . war u. ist zum Teil noch heute das geistige Existenzminimum der 'Gebildeten,'" *Büchertagebuch*, pp. 37-38).

[67] André Malraux, *Les Voix du silence* (Paris, 1951), p. 12. Curtius devotes a brief article to Malraux in his *Büchertagebuch*, pp. 98f. No similarities are drawn between his own research and Malraux's, but he does situate certain of the philosophic discussions in the novel *Les Noyers de l'Altenburg* within the tradition of German historicism. See p. 99.

to a comprehensive mastery of the whole of European literature as an "intelligible field of study" is Toynbee's *A Study of History*. For Curtius, Toynbee is the outstanding contemporary heir to the patrimony of German historical thinking—heir to Hegel, Ranke, Burckhardt, and Troeltsch—intent upon explaining, in terms of the dialectic of history,[68] political and social change, philosophical systems and theological speculation, moral assumptions and alternations in styles of life. Toynbee's unparalleled historical awareness is due chiefly to a traditional British empiricism, evident in his scrutiny and control of an enormous quantity and diversity of fact, coupled with a philosophic quest for ultimate meaning as exemplified by the sovereign ability with which he discovers meaningful patterns and regularities in the flow of events. The English historian's eschewal of conventional historiography, both with respect to

[68] Curtius reports that when the first three volumes of Toynbee's *Study* appeared in 1934, they went completely unnoticed in German intellectual reviews, and that later on it was much the same story with volumes 4 to 6 published in 1939. See *Kritische Essays*, p. 379, note 1. Curtius himself, who just after World War II contributed an analysis of the historian's work entitled "Toynbees Geschichtslehre" to *Merkur*, 2 (1948): 498f. (now reprinted in *Kritische Essays*, pp. 356f.), was familiar with Toynbee's work at least as early as 1937, for he cites Toynbee in his critique of W. F. Patterson's *Three Centuries of French Poetic Theory*, appearing in *Literaturblatt für germanische und romanische Philologie*, nos. 5-6 (1937), p. 186. He also serves as a *point d'appui* in Curtius' essay of 1944, "Über die altfranzösische Epik I," *ZRPh*, 64 (1944): 257 (now in *Gesammelte Aufsätze*, p. 127). See also *Europäische Literatur*, p. 387, where the German critic appropriates Toynbee's term, "intelligible field of study," to define the province of his own research. On the other hand, Toynbee knew of Curtius' *Deutscher Geist in Gefahr* which he quotes in vols. 6 and 9 (pp. 387 and 144f., respectively, of *A Study of History*, paperback edn., New York, 1962-63), as well as the previously cited estimate of his work, "Toynbees Geschichtslehre," which he alludes to in defense of his theories (*Study*, vol. 12: *Reconsiderations*, s.v. 1964).

chronological narration and period specialization, and his reliance upon historical constants and models, "laws" and examples, match the German critic's impatience with traditional literary history and his search for a new methodology and narrative art. "The structure is determined," Curtius writes in characterizing the composition of his *Europäische Literatur*, "not by logical order but by thematic continuity."[69] Thanks to heuristic principles discernible in the unfolding of the historical process itself—such as challenge-and-response, withdrawal-and-return, the movement of schism and palingenesia, and the stories and archetypes of mythology and world religions, all comparable in their way (though used on a much vaster scale) to Curtius' rhetorical devices and poetic *topoi*—Toynbee succeeds in reducing world history to an intelligible order, in giving to momentous events and personages a symbolic weight. Like Toynbee who, in writing the latter portions of his *Study* during the upheavals of World War II, invoked as a model, *toutes proportions gardées*, the memory of Saint Augustine undertaking his *De Civitate Dei* during the time of Alaric's sack of Rome,[70] Curtius was conscious that his historical reconstruction of the European literary tradition had been forged in answer to the crises of our time and that, supported by a conception of history such as Toynbee's, his work affirmed the truth that meaningful advances in historical thinking have come about under the stimulus of catastrophic or portentous happenings.[71] Both men see themselves as

[69] *Europäische Literatur*, p. 385.
[70] See *Study*, vol. 4, "Preface," pp. vi-vii.
[71] *Europäische Literatur*, pp. 13-14, and the proud but noble words of the Preface to the second edition: "Mein Buch ist nicht aus rein wissenschaftlichen Zwecken erwachsen, sondern aus Sorge für die Bewahrung der westlichen Kultur. Es macht den Versuch, die Einheit dieser Tradition in Raum und Zeit mit neuen

humanists of authentic mold doing battle for a way of life that is threatened with extinction. In a recently published essay of reminiscences, a student and disciple of Curtius calls *Europäische Literatur und lateinisches Mittelalter* "the most objective and, at the same time, the most personal scholarly accomplishment to appear in our time."[72] Indeed the imposing *apparat* of philological erudition cannot hide the pathos, the deeply confessional nature of the work. The book is a *credo* in which all of the major themes, central preoccupations, and dominant influences in the lifetime of a great modern German cosmopolitan are brought together, integrated, and affirmed anew in a vibrant, monumental whole: antiquity and Christianity; Virgil, Dante, and Goethe; Bergson, Scheler, George, and Hofmannsthal; Gröber and Toynbee; Germany and *Romania*; and, finally, philosophy, history, and poetry. Ripeness is all . . .

Curtius' response to the poetry of places was intense and absorbing. He took keen pleasure in Rhineland excursions and afternoon promenades in French and Italian towns where the gardens, architecture, and old streets would delight the aesthetic sense and free the mind to muse. Among such pilgrimage centers, Rome took pride of place. Ever since his decisive visit to the Eternal City in the spring of 1912, when he was twenty-five years old, *Römerpietät* steadily assumed in his life the proportions of a myth. A letter to Gundolf describes

---

Methoden zu beleuchten. Im geistigen Chaos der Gegenwart ist es nötig, aber auch möglich geworden, diese Einheit zu demonstrieren. Das kann aber nur von einem universalen Standpunkt aus geschehen" (p. 9).

[72] K. A. Horst, "Ein Lehrmeister europäischer Bildung," *Zeitwende, Die neue Furche* 31 (1960): 668. Cf. "Anhang," *Kritische Essays*, p. 439.

the soul-shattering experience of his first contact with antique Rome:

> What can I tell you about Rome! All of the slowly formed layers of my education have been shaken, dug up, split apart. The whole field of my soul plowed and newly seeded. Rome has done all this to me. Everything in me is in a turmoil and I don't know yet what will happen. You can be sure that I will never again experience such a revelation, such a shift of gravity.[73]

Rome in her universalism was the revelation of historical continuity and permanence, the many-storied living symbol of harmony and that peculiarly German *Alleinheitsgefühl* which throbs at the center of all of Curtius' writings. By his annual visits to the city, he renewed the Goethean adventure of the *Drang nach Rom.* "Roman sun, Roman spring."[74] Rome discovered and revisited was the inspiration for a lifetime devoted to the cultivation of a universalist outlook and the search for ideals, themes, and norms by which divergent cultures and different historical epochs could be characterized, compared, and ultimately united in a grand, compelling synthesis. Curtius relates that as a student he took a boat trip down the Rhine to Cologne, and

[73] *Briefwechsel*, pp. 208-209. Cf. the letter from Romain Rolland to Curtius, "Cette ville [Rome] qui a eu, dites-vous, sur votre vie une action décisive . . . ," cited in "Rückblick 1952," *Französischer Geist*, p. 515. See the fine but all too brief remarks of Jacques Heurgon, "Curtius et Rome," in *Allemagne d'aujourd'hui*, pp. 18f., written, unfortunately, before the publication of the correspondence with Gundolf; and the penetrating observations of Otto Pöggeler, "Dichtungstheorie und Toposforschung," pp. 192-93. Willy Haas reports that in Curtius' study in his home at Bonn there hung "eine seltsame allegorische Vision betitelt Rom, ein Gemälde der französischen Renaissance" (*Die literarische Welt*, p. 279).

[74] *Gundolf-Curtius. Briefwechsel*, p. 209.

that from the bend in the river at the entry to the city
he could see the church of *Maria in Capitol*. Here in
name and fact was the perfect harmony—"Christentum
und Römertum"—of the two profound realities of his
being.[75] The magic stillness and composure of the Roman landscape, its suggestion of the paradise garden
—fountain, cypress, statuary, and cerulean sky suffused
in tender light and weighted with memories—became
a permanent reminder of civilized, tranquil order and a
reflection of the humanist ideal of *otium*.[76] He confesses
in a letter to Gundolf that in his university days a verse
from one of Virgil's eclogues—"Mille meae Siculis in
montibus agnae"—acted upon him like a revelation of
beauty and something to be longed for.[77] Virgil, who
inherited the Greek epic tradition and was familiar
with Oriental esoteric learning; who glorified the Roman imperium in peace and war and celebrated the
eternally human pursuits of pastoral pleasure; labor of
the fields and martial virtue ("cecini pascua, rura,
duces"); who in the unsurpassed plasticity and harmony
of his verse served as a standard for European poetry in

[75] *Kritische Essays*, p. 108. The river and church form the components of George's *Rheinmythos*: see "Anhang," *ibid.*, p. 439;
and *Europäische Literatur*, p. 20.

[76] "Wenn ich mich prüfe," Curtius once wrote, "ist ein schöner
Garten unter allen menschlichen Werken doch das, was mir das
reinste Glück gewährt"—"Italienische Eindrücke," *Luxemburger
Zeitung*, May 22, 1924. Cf. the essay on Virgil in *Kritische Essays*,
pp. 16-17. The chapter, "Die Ideallandschaft," in *Europäische
Literatur*, pp. 191f., is an excellent example of the way in which
Curtius transmutes deeply personal feelings into strict, objective
scholarship. We would recall here the importance of the *garden*
as setting and symbol in George's poetry.

[77] *Briefwechsel*, Feb. 9, 1912, p. 201 (the verse in the letter is
slightly misquoted). Thirty-nine years later in a broadcast over
the BBC, during a moment of personal reminiscence, Curtius
again cited this Virgilian line as peculiarly evocative ("Diese Worte
berührten mich wie ein Zauber"). See *Kritische Essays*, p. 23.

the same way that Raphael's art acted as the model for European painting; and whose arcane prophecies were eagerly received and piously transformed by the Christian West—Virgil, Dante's "savio duca," was Curtius' preferred poet, too, and his spiritual guide on the Via Sacra leading to a mastery of the two-thousand-year-old European literary tradition. Citing, in an article of the twenties, lines from the first of Virgil's *Bucolics* ("fortunate senex, hic inter flumina nota / et fontis sacros frigus captabis opacum"), Curtius goes on to comment: "This 'inter flumina nota' is a key to the soul and art of Virgil. Its opposite is Faust's 'Werd' ich zum Augenblicke sagen. . . .' The Virgilian and the Faustian soul can never understand each other."[78] Everywhere the note struck by Virgilian Rome is the same: *monumentum aere perennius,* a grandness of vision and the promise of an ordered, fruitful, uninterrupted peace.[79]

[78] "Literarische Unsterblichkeit," *Neue Schweizer Rundschau* 29 (1926): 1070. It is interesting to note that each of the five chapters of *Deutscher Geist in Gefahr*—that book aimed, in effect, at Germany's Faustian excesses—bears an epigraph from the *Aeneid.*

[79] In a letter written in the autumn of 1923 to the classicist Jacques Heurgon, Curtius says: "Rome est un monde à part, ce n'est plus la douceur italienne, c'est la grandeur et la sérénité des choses éternelles et des pensées éternelles. Il y a quelque chose de cela déjà dans l'Enéide que je relis actuellement pour la dixième fois peut-être" ("Curtius et Rome," p. 18). Gide, his lifelong friend, shared with him this same reverence for Virgil. Contributing to the special number of the *Nouvelle Revue française,* "Hommage à André Gide" (Nov., 1951), Curtius, writing in French, presents a moving *document humain* which touches upon the appeal of simplicity and permanence, felt equally by the two men, in Virgil's poetry. On a visit to the scholar's home in 1947, the French writer pointed out to him a passage from the *Aeneid* which had particularly caught his attention; the German, too, had noted these lines. "Nous avions admiré les mêmes vers, à l'insu l'un de l'autre. Il était émouvant de se rencontrer à travers Virgile et de trouver en lui une résonance aux deuils qui accablaient cette Europe trempée de sang. La belle voix grave de

It is the combination, complementary and mutually
reinvigorating, of a German Protestant ethical idealism
and an innate affinity with the Latin instinct for sensuous beauty and clarity of form, a romantic nostalgia
purified by classic discipline, that gives to Curtius' work
its enhancing humaneness, its vital strength, plenitude,
and resonance. German to the core and at the same
time *ein guter Europäer*, he might well have applied to
himself Goethe's words: "I am a citizen of the world, I
am from Weimar" ("Ich bin Weltbewohner, bin Wei-
maraner"). With the exception of Goethe, Germany's
literature, unlike its philosophy or music, has not become an integral part of our Western heritage. Different from the Latin and Romance literatures which seek
to give a new and permanent form to a perennial fund
of ideas and emotions, the German way lies rather in ex- `
ploration, in the search for the profound, elemental
sources of being—a "Drang nach den Urmächten."[80]

Gide faisait ressortir la majesté des vers latins" ("Rückblick 1952,"
Französischer Geist, p. 518). Gide's *Supplément à l'Ecole des
femmes* (1929) was dedicated to Curtius. A colleague writes: "It
may interest you—and your future readers—to learn that C[ur-
tius] demanded, as a prerequisite for entrance into his Seminar
. . . an excellent translation into German of a difficult passage
from Virgil." (Letter from Y.M.)

[80] In lines which recall Hofmannsthal's characterization, in
"Das Schrifttum als geistiger Raum der Nation" (1927), of the
contrasting ways that literature takes in France and Germany as
one of *Geselligkeit* vs. *Originalität*, Friedrich Sieburg writes: "Es
(Deutschland) findet sich lieber in tieferen Schichten wieder,
dort, wo das fliessende Element noch kein Verlangen nach Gestalt
spürt, keinesfalls dort, wo Gesittung und Universalität vom Geiste
untrennbar sind. Immer noch gilt die dunkle Geburt mehr als die
freigewordene Gestalt" ("Lorbeer für E. R. Curtius," *Die Zeit*,
April 12, 1956). Cf. the penetrating observations of Charles Du Bos
on the German language in *Journal III* (Paris, 1949), Jan. 16,
1926: p. 22. Hofmannsthal's famous essay may have been influenced to some extent by similar ideas put forth by Curtius a
year earlier in the article already cited, "Literarische Unsterblichkeit"; by that time the two men were in close contact.

The German poet is a seer intent upon divining the un-
fathomable and inexpressible, and the work of each
new master, a Hölderlin, Nietzsche, or George, is a
fresh departure and a new discovery. He works in an
opposite way to the Latin and Romance poet, a Virgil
or Valéry, who re-creates within a fixed and universally
valid tradition. It was Goethe's achievement and, to a
lesser extent, Hofmannsthal's that they succeeded in
bridging the two ways, and it is to this line of succession that Curtius' lifework belongs.

Curtius' cultural conservatism, ethical bent, and flair
for perceiving significant trends in contemporary literature and scholarship make for a marked tendency to ad-
monition and exhortation. The temptation is always
there to assume the mantle of *praeceptor Germaniae*.
Rarely in his writings does he refrain from making some
adjuration or call to order:

> This should be the attitude of those who today bring
> their homage to Goethe; . . . I consider it the obliga-
> tion of a German intellectual to receive this
> legacy [Goethe's] with respect and to interpret it with
> an ever deepening understanding; . . . Dante schol-
> arship will be doing something useful when it. . . .
> Philology as knowledge—that is what I suddenly un-
> derstood at that moment; and ever since then I have
> always asked the question of both my own work and
> that of others: "What has this accomplished for the
> cause of knowledge?"[81]

[81] See respectively, for the above series of quotations, *Kritische
Essays*, p. 85; *Die Tat*, June 2, 1949; *Europäische Literatur*, p.
371; and *Gesammelte Aufsätze*, p. 455. With age and the catastrophes that befell Germany, Curtius became increasingly pessi-
mistic about the future of German culture. In the late essays there
occasionally creeps in a tone of bitter disappointment with and
reproach toward his countrymen. Willy Haas writes of him
in the war years: "Er war in all den bösen Jahren ein bitterer

This hortatory impulse stems from deeply held moral and aesthetic convictions which find their justification in Curtius' concern for the preservation and unity of Europe's cultural heritage. Such articles of faith are variously expressed, as we have seen, in his search for regeneration through the poet-seer George and discovery of the vitality of tradition in the example of Hofmannsthal; in his celebration of Rome and the myth of the Rhine. Those who would promote conflicting views are dealt with harshly. These are the contemporary false prophets, the most prominent of whom are Maurice Barrès whose anti-Germanism Curtius denounced just after World War I and, Curtius *dixit*, Karl Jaspers whom he savagely attacked at the end of World War II because of the philosopher's presumed lack of respect for Goethe. Barrès' unregenerate nationalism and the charismatic power he wielded as a *maître de jeunesse* stood squarely in the way of a realization of Curtius' dream of a reconciled France and Germany.[82] The antithesis of Barrès was Gide and the writers of the *NRF*, and indeed the salutary mission of the *Wegbereiter* lay precisely in rescuing France from the moral scepticism, overheated aestheticism, and hysterical exaltation of the national genius so characteristic of the previous generation of writers, of whom Barrès was the most conspicuous example. It was Curtius, the modernist, the champion of cultural cosmopolitanism, who

---

und sarkastischer Mann geworden—fesselnd und grossartig in seiner Bitterkeit" (*Die literarische Welt*, p. 279). Cf. also the closing pages of Renée B. Lang's paper, "Le Cosmopolitisme d'André Gide," *Actes du IVᵉ Congrès de l'Association Internationale de Littérature Comparée* (Fribourg, 1964), pp. 63-64.

[82] *Maurice Barrès und die geistigen Grundlagen des französischen Nationalismus*. The book, though overlong in places, is a model of exposition: Barrès' ideology is systematically and objectively analyzed, and only in the final chapter, when all the evidence is in, does Curtius begin his demolition work.

broke lances with Barrès; whereas the broadside directed against Karl Jaspers was delivered by Curtius, the traditionalist, in defense of Germany's sacred past.[83] In his address on the occasion of receiving in 1949 Frankfurt's Goethe prize, Jaspers, in an effort to de-mythologize the master, tried to determine what was still living and what was dead in Goethe's work, whereupon Curtius in a testy rebuttal accused the philosopher of narrowness, prejudice, and ignorance:[84] to use our con-

[83] In some remarkable pages in the Barrès book (211-14) devoted to the type of reflective, socio-literary critic—"der schöpferische Kritiker"—that is produced in France (Stendhal, Sainte-Beuve, Taine, Renan, or Barrès himself), Curtius points to a seemingly inevitable turn in the intellectual evolution of such a critic: having begun as an innovator, he ends as a defender of traditional values, e.g., Taine, who in his early years contemptuously rejected the official philosophy of the day, the spiritualism of Cousin and his disciples, will, in the aftermath of the Franco-Prussian war, write his conservative-minded *Origines de la France contemporaine*. It is piquant to note that the truth of these observations made in 1921 by the then thirty-five-year-old Curtius will repeat itself in his own case. The discoverer of the French *Wegbereiter* later on becomes the commentator of medieval Latin literature. "Man schreibt mit 63 anders als mit 39," as he says in a letter to Ortega ("Ein Briefwechsel," p. 914).

[84] Jaspers' paper, entitled "Unsere Zukunft und Goethe," appeared in *Die Wandlung* 2 (1947): 559f.; Curtius' reply, "Goethe oder Jaspers," was first published in the Zürich newspaper, *Die Tat*, April 2, 1949, and later in the Hamburg weekly, *Die Zeit*, April 28, 1949. The literary scholar's angry dissent from Jaspers' views provoked a storm of controversy which raged in the German press for over two weeks, and vied for attention with the American airlift over Berlin! In the *Rhein-Neckar Zeitung* of May 7, 1949, seven Heidelberg professors (including Curtius' friend, Alfred Weber) issued a proclamation defending Karl Jaspers and expressing regret over the provocative tone of Curtius' article. The latter answered them in the same newspaper on May 17, which contained also a brief comment by the Basel philosopher, and added his final remarks to the whole affair in *Die Zeit*, June 2, 1949. For an excellent evaluation of the controversy, which seeks to understand and appreciate the views of both sides, see Werner Milch, "Goethe, Curtius, Jaspers und die Öffentlich-

temporary age as the ultimate measure of Goethe's accomplishment is to reveal a parochial, anti-historical bias and an exaggerated notion of the importance of the present moment. The issues raised and the differences revealed in the Curtius-Jaspers quarrel bring out in sharp relief the contrast between Existentialism and Idealism, post-Nietzschean philosophy and the legacy of German historicism.[85]

Commenting in a youthful letter to Gundolf on the Goethe-Schiller correspondence, Curtius remarks, "In this exchange I find Goethe, for the most part, quite uncongenial."[86] If he was reticent and disapproving

keit," in *Archiv der Hessischen Nachrichten*, June 3, 1949. Cf. also Leo Spitzer, "Zum Goethekult," *Die Wandlung* 4 (1949): 518f., which contains a harsh indictment of Curtius' position.

[85] The defender of Goethe would subscribe heartily to these words by another champion of tradition, Sainte-Beuve: "Tout en parlant notre langue, en subissant les conditions des âges où nous sommes jetés et où nous puisons notre force comme nos défauts, demandons-nous de temps en temps, le front levé vers les collines et les yeux attachés aux groupes de mortels révérés: *Que diraient-ils de nous?*" ("Qu'est-ce qu'un classique?" *Causeries de lundi* III [Paris, n.d.], p. 54). The italics are Sainte-Beuve's. It is not without interest to note that Curtius, writing at the time of the centenary of Goethe's death in 1932 and looking forward to the bicentenary of the poet's birth in 1949, had already stated that "entre ces deux dates . . . quelques Européens auront peut-être su maintenir vivantes en eux l'image et l'action de Goethe: fidélité qui serait lourde de sens pour notre proche avenir" ("Goethe ou le classique allemand," *La Nouvelle Revue française* 38 [1932]: 330. The original article, "Goethe oder der deutsche Klassiker," appeared in the *Deutschfranzösische Rundschau*, 1932, pp. 169f.

[86] Frühjahr, 1911, *Briefwechsel*, p. 188; cf. also pp. 191-92. Curtius' change of heart toward Goethe is paralleled, as we have seen, by a like change of feeling toward Hofmannsthal. His memory is less than faithful when he says in the Preface to the *Kritische Essays*, "Hofmannsthal, der mir seit je Höchstes bedeutete" (p. 7). The same is true with Rudolf Borchardt who early incurred the contemptuous wrath of George and his Circle because of the former's criticism of the Master. The sentiments expressed in Curtius'

in his early years, his attitude toward Goethe changed in time, owing at first, perhaps, to the new edition in 1922 of Gundolf's important literary biography of the poet which Curtius reviewed the next year for the *Luxemburger Zeitung.* His increasing concern with the concept of European literature is naturally related, as stated earlier, to Goethe's idea of world literature, and in the fateful years of National Socialism and the war it was inevitable that the sage of Weimar should be invoked as a model of civilized virtues and a source of strength. His Rhine-Frankish origins point to Germany's physical and cultural bond with the Roman imperium, and the prominence which Rome holds in the poet's life and work makes of his devotion an inspiring precedent to Curtius' own private cult. It is in the order of things that Goethe's olympian pose, his classicism, and his role as *Volkserzieher* would exercise an especially strong appeal upon the late Curtius. Germany's greatest literary genius is at the same time the author most indebted to Europe's literary past, and it is this solidarity with all that has gone before him which makes of Goethe something other and more than a major German poet. The ancient and modern, innovation and continuity, the two poles about which Curtius' writings constantly revolve, are consummately embodied in the poet's work. Goethe belongs to the happy few who merit the critic's highest praise, those in whom the past is fulfilled and raised harmoniously to a higher level of integration.[87] Curtius' preoccupation with Goethe

---

BBC lecture of 1951, now reprinted as "Rudolf Borchardt über Virgil," in *Kritische Essays* (pp. 23-30), are very different from what he says about him in his letters to Gundolf. See *Briefwechsel,* pp. 152 and 188-89.

[87] In writing of another of his favorites, Balzac, he mentions characteristic of the novelist, his *Integrationserlebnis.* See *Kritische Essays,* p. 174. Three separate pieces in the *Essays,* all

at the end of his life meant a return homeward after all the years spent with Romance and Latin literatures, just as did his brief but warmly appreciative essay in *Büchertagebuch* on the nineteenth-century German Catholic theosophist, Franz von Baader (1765-1841), whom Curtius had previously mentioned in his early book on Balzac. From this essay and a previous one (1951) in the same collection on theosophy in the eighteenth century, we get the strong impression that, had he lived longer, Curtius would have done something much more substantial with Baader. If this is true, then at the end of his life he was going back again to his early interest in mysticism and esoteric theories of world-harmony, which formed the basis of his studies on Balzac and Emerson (1924), as well as to German Romanticism and Novalis for whom he always had a special affection, and, finally and perhaps most importantly, to the idealistic and religious piety of his youth and family circle. This great cosmopolitan remained then at heart very German, and in a profound and only seemingly paradoxical sense we can say that the source and strength of his Europeanism came from a deeply rooted attachment to national traditions and ideals.[88]

---

belonging to the last years of Curtius' activity, and the same number of journalistic essays ("entries")—there are twenty-three in all—in the posthumous *Büchertagebuch*, are devoted to Goethe. In the latter collection, he writes with pride: "Als Achtzehnjähriger wurde ich 1904 in Weimar dem achtundsiebzigjährigen Fräulein Krackow vorgestellt, die als Kind noch in Goethes Garten gespielt hatte. So habe ich doch noch einen Menschen gekannt, der Goethe gesehen hat" (p. 55). Cf. "Goethe ou le classique allemand," p. 331.

[88] It is interesting to note that Curtius, the Romance scholar, wrote his first study of any length and importance (apart from his academic dissertation) on Kant—"Das Schematismuskapitel in der *Kritik der reinen Vernunft*," *Kant-Studien* 19 (1914): 338f.— and that the last thing he published were some notes on Hof-

Curtius' entire critical activity was concerned with raising problems, opening perspectives, and breaking new paths. He did not aim at definitive or exhaustive interpretations, or at anything like the tendency in modern criticism to what Eliot has called "lemon squeezing." Exemplary in this regard is what he writes in his book on medieval Latin literature: "Here as elsewhere, our task is to point out and to stimulate, not to be exhaustive."[89] His brisk, elegant style, which owes nothing to traditional academic German but seems modeled upon modern French prose, delights in aphoristic résumés, incisive formulations, and choice reminiscences from a wide range of reading. Even when dealing with the driest philological topic, his prose exhibits grace and artistry along with precision. Yet only rarely, and then mostly in his youthful writings, does he show a studied attempt at fine expression or evocative effects. His thought is too mobile and energetic, his temperament too nervous and ironic to allow him to fall easily into the mandarin prose rhythms of the professional *homme de lettres*;[90] moreover, the healthy positivism of the

---

mannsthal—"Glosse zu Hofmannsthal," *Die Neue Rundschau* 65 (1954): 535f.

[89] *Europäische Literatur*, p. 147. See also "Rückblick," *Französischer Geist*, where he characterizes his criticism as "eine Gipfelwanderung," and adds: "Weglassen scheint mir ein oberstes Gebot literarischer Kritik" (p. 526). Eliot's phrase comes from his address, "The Frontiers of Criticism," The Gideon Seymour Memorial Lecture Series (University of Minnesota, Minneapolis, 1956), p. 14.

[90] There are mannerisms in Curtius' style, however, the chief of which is a rather too artful use of dashes. He will also, on occasion, resort to facile, journalistic devices. His essay on Hesse (1947) begins like this: "November neunzehnhundert achtzehn . . . Bleierne Trostlosigkeit liegt über den Menschen." Three years later in his study on George, he repeats the same dramatic opening: "Berlin, Winter neunzehnhundertsechs auf sieben . . ." (*Kritische Essays*, pp. 152 and 100, respectively).

scholar-teacher acts as a makeweight to the aestheticism of the critic and connoisseur. The phrase by which he once defined Barrès fits him as well: "ein Künstler der Reflexion."[91] The formal, technical analysis of a single literary work in order to determine the essential relationship and ultimate aesthetic unity of its form and content, the type of literary study fostered by Crocean aesthetics and promoted by Anglo-American New Criticism or German *Stilforschung*, had little appeal for Curtius.[92] The very few examples of "close reading" which we find scattered through his writings, such as the *explication de texte* applied to Proust's style or the comments on Dante's art of composing *terzine* (in the chapter on the Argonauts in *Kritische Essays*) are, to be sure, masterfully done, but are only incidental to a much freer and more comprehensive critical ambition. For Curtius' way does not lie in arriving at a synthesis of an author's *oeuvre* through a detailed, cumulative analysis of individual works but rather in attempting a characterization, psychologically nuanced, urbane, and rich in allusion, by means of a discussion of major themes set off against a broad background of literary and historical reference. For him literary works exist

[91] *Maurice Barrès*, p. 211. Cf. the passage on Ortega as prose artist in *Kritische Essays*, p. 258; Curtius shares the Spaniard's *amor intellectualis* and felicity of expression. We could as well say of him as he does of Ortega: "Denn [er] ist ein Stilist von blendender Eleganz . . . seine Sätze schnellen ab wie Pfeile und treffen mitten ins Ziel" (*ibid.*, p. 272).

[92] Though as European minds they had much in common, Curtius, unlike Karl Vossler or Leo Spitzer, did not care for Croce's theories. See the Curtius-Ortega *Briefwechsel*, p. 904; K. A. Horst, "Ein Lehrmeister europäischer Bildung," p. 666; and *Europäische Literatur*, p. 25. He knew the *Estetica* and cites from it in his book on Brunetière, p. 31, note 1. Croce reciprocated these feelings: see his sarcastic rejection of Curtius' *magnum opus* in *Quaderni della Critica* 6 (1950): 118f.

not in isolation, not first and foremost as the products of a private sensibility, but in continuum and central to the play of a variety of social and cultural forces. He was the first in Germany, for example, to understand the importance of Bergson's philosophy as well as the impact of the Dreyfuss case as incentives for a new generation of writers, his *Wegbereiter*, to break with the past in search of new ideals.[93] Such criticism inherits the literary culture, sensitivity to values, and *esprit de finesse* of the tradition of Sainte-Beuve while at the same time belonging, by reason of its historicism, to the mainstream of German *Geistesgeschichte*, and as such is, broadly speaking, philosophical in temper and moral in purpose. An alert sensibility, guided by tact and intuitive sense, sorts out the decisive themes, symbols, and stylistic constants peculiar to a writer's work, tests their quality by the intensity of resonance and range of association which they awaken in the mind—words like *Grundrhythmus, Resonanzboden,* and *Klangvolumen* recur time and again in Curtius' writings—and relates them to the broader whole of Western literature wherein they find their validation and enrichment. Thus Hofmannsthal is revealed as the "magical brother" of Novalis, and Ortega's philosophical essay is shown to be the Hispanic variant of a genre cultivated in France and brought to its definitive expression in Barrès and Maurras; Cocteau's art continues that of the medieval *jongleur* while Joyce's late work falls very much within the tradition of European mannerism. "Genuine criticism," Curtius contends, "will never seek to prove but to point out. Its metaphysical basis is the conviction that the spiritual world is arranged according to a system of

[93] See Victor Klemperer, "Das neue deutsche Frankreichbild," p. 71.

affinities."[94] The varied elements of an author's imaginative life and compositional art—"die seelischen Formelemente"—represents centers of force which are drawn together by the critic into what he calls a system of coordinates so that a thematic pattern emerges, a firmly contoured silhouette which seizes the essential features of an author and situates him within the larger frame of European literature. Perception, penetration, integration—this is the rhythm that commands the critical act. Hence a study of the *idées-forces* in Balzac's work, comparing them to earlier concepts in Renaissance philosophy, in Leibniz, and in illuminist theories of the eighteenth century, enabled Curtius to move far beyond earlier interpretations of the French novelist and gave us the "Balzac visionnaire" which to this day is still valid and fruitful for modern criticism. Likewise, in what must have been one of the earliest essays anywhere devoted to Eliot—we know that it was the first in Germany—he interprets his English contemporary in terms of the concept of *Alexandrianism* (with no pejorative meaning attached), as one who within the total cultural heritage reconsiders, recombines, and invents anew, thus pointing to an artistic phenomenon typical of our age.[95]

But, as we have seen, the same intuitive discovery of

---

[94] *Kritische Essays,* p. 317. Our description of Curtius' "method" draws upon the essays on Proust and Larbaud in *Französischer Geist,* pp. 278 and 407 respectively; the pieces on Hesse and Eliot in *Kritische Essays,* pp. 160, and 316-17 respectively; and *Europäische Literatur,* pp. 386-87. Cf. K. A. Horst, "Zur Methode von Ernst Robert Curtius," *Merkur* 10 (1956): 303f., and the brief note by Claude David, "Thématique de Curtius," in *Allemagne d'aujourd'hui,* pp. 12-13.

[95] See in this connection Gustav René Hocke, *Das europäische Tagebuch* (Wiesbaden, 1963), pp. 362f., and Frank Wood, "Rilke and Eliot: Tradition and Poetry," *The Germanic Review* 27 (1952): 246f.

significant facts over a broad field of inquiry—"Der
liebe Gott steckt im Detail" (Warburg)—and the subsequent search for interrelationships among them are at
the basis of Curtius' years of research into the medieval
foundations of Europe's literary tradition. Here the patterns are woven from an infinitely greater number of
strands than before, but the craft is the same: *Europäische Literatur und lateinisches Mittelalter* is an inventory of themes and motifs, archetypes and images,
which are central to the outlook of the Western literary
mind. Its artistic design, composed loosely in the manner of a symphonic work, permits us to see, stretching
out over two millennia, the inner connections of European literature. "The arrangement of the presentation
and succession of the chapters," he writes in defining
the organization of his book, "is such that it results in
a step-by-step progress and a spiral ascent. . . . The interweaving of threads, the reappearance of persons and
motifs in different designs, reflects their interconnected
historical relations."[96] Even the myth of Rome, that
geographical symbol for Curtius' *Alleinheitsgefühl* and
his will to the mastery of the memory of the West
through a comprehensive knowledge of its literature,
can be understood in much the same terms as have been
used to describe his philological approach. In a letter
to a friend, he tells of his recent return home from a stay
in the Italian capital and of his regret upon having to
leave it: "I left Rome heartbroken, and my sadness has
only increased in the first days home after my return. . . .
All the beauties and grandeur of Rome are but the aspects of her soul to which I am attached by a love which
defies all analysis."[97] The expression, "les aspects de

[96] *Europäische Literatur*, pp. 384-85.
[97] See Jacques Heurgon, "Curtius et Rome," p. 19, my italics.
Cf. Otto Pöggeler, "Dichtungstheorie und Toposforschung," p.

son âme," is the direct equivalent, on the plane of
sentiment, of Curtius' literary formula: "die seelischen
Formelemente."

Curtius as a European critic, in his self-imposed task
of standing sentinel over Europe's cultural heritage,
shared in the Alexandrianism of his artist contemporaries. Indeed his enormous critical and scholarly output, exhibiting as it does a keen sense for beauty, a sovereign command of many languages and literatures,
an exceptional talent for opening historical perspectives, for comparing and relating across time and space
broad areas of knowledge, may be thought of as a kind
of modern *museion*, a cult offering to Mnemosyne, goddess of memory and mother of the Muses. In a revealing
passage, his student, Karl Horst, notes how delighted
Curtius was, years after reading Proust, to discover in
the name of the heroine, Oriane, of the Spanish chivalric romance, *Amadis de Gaula* (1508), the first name
of the Duchesse de Germantes.[98] The tendency, becoming progressively stronger in his late years, was to
look at literature as though through a stereoscope: details seen from different points of view blend into a single image so that the impression received is one of fullness and relief. Yet often in reading *Europäische Literatur und lateinisches Mittelalter* and the late essays treating of *topoi* and metaphor, we feel that the synoptic
view has been won by ignoring changes of outlook and

---

193. Curtius' sociological essay on French civilization is likewise
undertaken on the same premises as his literary criticism. The
book is not intended to be a compendium of French cultural life
but instead to offer a characterization of national values and com-
peting systems of ideology, to disengage those vital elements which
go to make up the French mind—"nicht Deskription also, sondern
Strukturanalyse" (*Die Französische Kultur, Eine Einführung*,
"Vorwort," p. vii).

98 "Ein Lehrmeister europäischer Bildung," p. 660.

taste in different periods, and by minimizing the fact that the differing aesthetic intentions of individual creative poets can affect or alter meanings accruing to the same figure or motif. Beyond the indisputable importance of the fact and demonstration of the unbroken use of the "book as metaphor" in Western literature (*Europäische Literatur*, chapter XVI), we should also wish to know, in more detail and with greater speculative acumen as to the historical factors involved, the individual and varying uses of this particular metaphor when resorted to by different authors. Through a radical, one-sided stress on the rhetorical tradition in European literature at the expense of individual creativity and innovation, fruitful though it undoubtedly is as a necessary corrective to romantic theories of artistic genius, Curtius, the youthful discoverer of Joyce, Proust, and Claudel, ends up by adopting a position comparable in its way to a Tainean or Marxist criticism. *Les extrêmes se touchent*, for it is simply a new kind of determinism, albeit more subtle, in which he substitutes an aesthetic for a socio-historical causality. Speaking of Dante's many-sided indebtedness to Virgil, he can say of their meeting in the *Commedia*, though more than a thousand years separate the two poets in time: "All history is lifted to the plane of simultaneity."[99] In a

[99] *Kritische Essays*, p. 434. "Eine Spannung von dreizehn Jahrhunderten trennt ihn [Dante] von Virgil, aber sie wird überbrückt durch die Begegnung" (*loc.cit.*). In his review article of *Europäische Literatur*, Hugo Friedrich shrewdly remarks: "Der eigentliche Gegenstand des Buches sind nicht die Autoren, oft nicht die Literaturen, sondern es ist die Kontinuität. Sie bilden ein Credo, und die *Topoi* sind die liturgischen Formeln dieses Credo" (*Schweizer Monatshefte* 29 [1948]: 505. There are, to be sure, the splendid pages on poetic creativity at the very conclusion of the work, in the section, "Nachahmung und Schöfung" (p. 400f.), but in the book as a whole, it is the first of these terms that by far predominates. Cf. also Curtius' remarks on the "law"

way analogous to the perspectivism of the modern novel
since Joyce, Curtius' view of literature tends to see past
and present as occupying the same temporal and spatial
planes. All time seems to occur simultaneously. "The
'timeless present' which is an essential characteristic of
literature means that the literature of the past can always
be active in that of the present. So Homer in Virgil, Virgil in Dante, Plutarch and Seneca in Shakespeare...."[100]
But history is process, and means change as well as
permanence. It is figured as much by Heraclitus' cosmic fire as by his cosmic ground. Curtius, whose early
criticism, particularly his essay on French civilization,
showed a mastery of German historical consciousness,
a singular awareness of artistic creation as being responsive to new directions in styles of life, and whose late
work is so intent upon establishing a truly historical

---

of *Diskontinuität* in the life of the spirit, in *Gesammelte Aufsätze*,
p. 171.

Mention should be made of Erich Auerbach's rich and nuanced
critique of Curtius' masterwork in *Romanische Forschungen* 62
(1950): 237f (now reprinted in *Gesammelte Aufsätze zur romanischen Philologie*, Bern-Munich, 1967, pp. 330f). It is disappointing to have to report Curtius' acerbic reaction to this fine and, for
the most part, admiring assessment of his book; it is to be found
in an extended aside buried in a footnote to his previously mentioned essay on Gröber (1952), in *Gesammelte Aufsätze* (p. 445).
Three years later, Curtius elaborates on the gist of his note in an
effort to discredit Auerbach's use of the classical theory of "Stilt-
rennung" as a basis for his conception of realism in *Mimesis*;
see "Die Lehre von den drei Stillen in Altertum u. Mittelalter,"
Romanische Forschungen 64 (1952): 57f (omitted, perhaps wisely,
from his *Gesammelte Aufsätze*). In the closing pages to "Epilego-
mena zu *Mimesis*," Auerbach, serenely and it would seem con-
vincingly, rejects Curtius' ill-spirited arguments. See *Romanische
Forschungen* 65 (1953): 5-13.

[100] *Europäische Literatur*, p. 25. Cf. the observations on Constantine Kavafis' poetry in *Büchertagebuch*, p. 42. Our above
strictures have been in part anticipated, though expressed quite
differently, by Leo Spitzer in his review of *Europäische Literatur*;
see *American Journal of Philology* 70 (1949): 428-31.

Literaturwissenschaft, seems at the end, ironically, to have negated history.

Peculiarities of time, place, and individual artistic temperament recede into the background and the poetic masterpieces of the past, with their tropes and devices, stand out grouped alongside each other in a timeless present—a myriad of constellations shining in a Platonic heaven obedient to the pull of Rhetoric. Here perhaps we come to the heart of the matter. Beneath the severe, imposing exterior of the philologist with his canons of scientific objectivity, lie the pathos and nostalgia of the artist who would seek to fold the past into the present so as to make it yield, in one grand, fundamental accord, its accumulated beauty and wisdom. The scholar's research finds its initial impulse and ultimate justification in the wonderment of the *promeneur solitaire* responsive to the memories evoked by Roman streets:

> How often in the past have I peered over all these foundations and inscriptions, wandered through the streets and interrogated the ruins; it is only now that I begin to perceive in them all a unique, grand and solemn chord which is like the soul tone of the Eternal City. And all my ways have as their only goal to be more deeply attentive to this sound, for it brings together the art and the history of all epochs into a marvelous unity.[101]

Upon recalling a birthday visit that he made to the aged Gide, Curtius once wrote: "It is always interesting to learn under what circumstances an important per-

[101] "Italienischer Herbst," in *Luxemburger Zeitung*, Dec. 30, 1924. Cf. the question posed in *Kritische Essays*, p. 442, to which our study has tried to find an answer: "Wie hängen Leben und Werk eines Forschers zusammen?"

son dies.''[102] In the spring of 1956, five days after he had reached his seventieth year, Ernst Robert Curtius died in Rome.

Among modern men of letters, Curtius stands apart. A luminary among that great constellation of German Romance scholars and teachers, Vossler, Spitzer, Olschki, and Auerbach, he was at the same time a critic of culture, a brilliant literary essayist deeply engaged in discerning, assessing, and indeed taking a part in shaping the aims and standards of the modernist phase of European literature arising out of the catastrophe of World War I. In urbanity of style and outlook, range of interest, volatile curiosity, and intensity of historical consciousness, only such patricians of the mind as Croce or Edmund Wilson are his equals. And though they share with Curtius the same pride in national and family traditions and the same sense of being called to act as arbiters in the formation of public taste, the American Plutarch is without the broad solid base of Curtius' classical education and lacks that sheer weight of Teutonic learning which confronts and intimidates us in his late writings on European literature, while the great Italian's aggressive feelings toward modern poetry and thought, and his serene life-long reliance upon the liberal bourgeois humanism of his heroes of the *Risorgimento,* make for an attitude of mind which often seems curiously remote from the upheavals of our time which are better reflected in the tension, restlessness, and problematical urgency in the work of his German contemporary and near-counterpart.

Looked at now from the distance of a decade or so since his death in the aftermath of World War II, Curtius can be seen as the last great representative of what

[102] See *Büchertagebuch,* p. 77.

is virtually an extinct breed. In this the "second twentieth century," the demise of the encyclopaedic European humanist goes its way with the passing of the Old World statesman of authoritarian bearing and breadth of vision. The material and spiritual circumstances of life no longer provide the basis for a humane, individualist culture, for that free, disinterested pursuit of "self-improvement" without which the style of life and scholarly output of a Curtius are unthinkable.[103] It is probable, in the world of tomorrow, that literary humanism as it has traditionally been conceived, a *paideia* and version of order fostered by an oligarchy of poets and thinkers, and based upon a respect for the inheritance of the past, style in life and art, and honor and decorum in conduct, will play only a small role in the development of an ecumenical culture. In the end, Curtius, with his customary percipience, seemed to be aware of this. That is what fills him with a fearless contempt for the public scene about him and gives to his last writings their harsh and lofty tone. They are the anguished valedictory of a giant going down to defeat.

[103] He was fond of quoting Baudelaire's words from *Mon Coeur mis à nu*: "Qu'est-ce que l'homme supérieur? Ce n'est pas le spécialiste. C'est l'homme de loisir et d'éducation générale. Être riche et aimer le travail." See, for example, *Französischer Geist*, p. 405.

Ernst H. Kantorowicz

By Yakov Malkiel

MY CREDENTIALS for writing an essay on Ernst H. Kantorowicz must be carefully qualified. During the nine years or so that his teaching and research activities on the Berkeley campus overlapped with my own (1942-51) I met him quite regularly in the stacks of our University Library and at the homes of mutual friends; was occasionally invited to his place; attended several semipublic lectures of his and had the satisfaction of seeing him in the audience at a few of my own academic performances. Equally important, I quite often heard him take part, with unusual gusto, even ardor, yet with characteristic fairness, in the thorough discussion of lectures given by fellow scholars on (to use Goethe's label) "westöstlich" themes, before Berkeley's then flourishing *Colloquium Orientologicum*. Also, I was fully aware of the courageous stand—in a slightly ironic context—he was taking at the height of the Loyalty Oath Controversy, which, as is well known, left a deep scar on the University of California, especially on its oldest campus.

All this treasure of cherished memories does not make me a sophisticated medievalist, art historian, numismatist, connoisseur of Dante scholarship, or Byzantine expert capable of an authoritative assessment of Kantorowicz's difficult, diversified, and highly original writ-ings. If I nevertheless muster the courage to supple-ment an earlier necrology of my former senior col-league, a piece which was geared almost exclusively to his Berkeley activities,[1] with the present broader-gauged

[1] See "Ernst H. Kantorowicz," *Romance Philology* 18 (1964-65): 1-15. I have profited from some oral or epistolary comments made on that occasion by Harold Cherniss, Michael Cherniavsky, Otto J. Maenchen, and others. Certain factual errors in my necrol-ogy I can now correct. As a child, Kantorowicz learned English from the lips of a governess. No attempt to lure him away from Berkeley was made by the Princeton Institute prior to California's Loyalty Oath Controversy.

Perhaps the keenest retrospective analysis of Kantorowicz's total performance—a panoramic view based on forty years of personal friendship and academic camaraderie—was contributed by Fried-rich Baethgen: "Ernst Hartwig Kantorowicz," in *Deutsches Archiv für Erforschung des Mittelalters* 21 (1964): 1-14. It absorbed most of the information poured out by Edgar Salin in his formal necrology, *Historische Zeitschrift* 199 (1964): 551-57, and, on a more generous scale and with a more intimate bias, in a privately distributed pamphlet, to which I have had no access. Salin, more than ten years senior to Kantorowicz, is sympathetic to the plight of his fellow-exile, whose meteoric rise to fame he once observed with an unjaundiced eye; but his own peaceful if enforced trans-fer from Heidelberg to nearby Basel hardly resembles the crazy quilt of Kantorowicz's peregrinations. Baethgen's obituary con-tains a summary and an appraisal, admirably substantial in their succinctness, of Kantorowicz's three book-length ventures. It is followed (pp. 14-17) by H. M. Schaller's Bibliography, running to 45 items, a piece which has not been entirely superseded by the scholar's Autobibliography—somewhat fuller (60 items), but still less than exhaustive—published posthumously in his *Selected Studies*, ed. Michael Cherniavsky and Ralph E. Giesey (Locust Valley, N.Y.: J. J. Augustin, 1965), pp. xi-xiv. For a short memo-rial notice sharply silhouetting Kantorowicz's Princeton period and enumerating the many honors he then received see Gaines Post, Erwin Panofsky, and Joseph R. Strayer, *Speculum* 39 (1964): 596f; Panofsky's share in this moving tribute clearly involves the precise identification of Kantorowicz's discoveries in art history.

The Editors' Preface to the *Selected Studies* offers no informa-tion on the whereabouts of Kantorowicz's scholarly legacy, includ-ing the text of such unpublished lectures as he himself hinted at

essay, it must be clearly understood that I am for once acting as a layman, with the modest authority conferred by such a humble status. My sources of information will be shreds of personal recollections; casual interviews with a few of Kantorowicz's friends still stationed on the West Coast;[2] the reading of searching appraisals of his work by real specialists; a measure of

---

in later writings. Carefully catalogued, though incomplete, collections of reprints of his articles are preserved in Berkeley's "Archives" and among the holdings of London's Warburg Institute, a stone's throw from University College. Has there been compiled a formal list of those projects of his that failed to mature, not a few of them mentioned incidentally in his last book, *The King's Two Bodies?*

I have not yet succeeded in taking cognizance of certain collections of possibly relevant material assembled on the occasion of the one hundredth anniversary of Stefan George's birthday. The Schiller-Nationalmuseum organized an exhibition on that occasion, the catalogue for which was compiled by Bernard Zeller (*Stefan George 1868-1968. Der Dichter und sein Kreis. Eine Ausstellung des Deutschen Literaturarchivs im Schiller-Nationalmuseum Marbach a.N.*, Catalogue No. 19 [Munich: Kosel, 1968]); I know it obliquely through A. Fratzscher's detailed review, "Der seltsame grosse Mensch: zum hundertsten Geburtstag Stefan Georges," *Börsenblatt für den Deutschen Buchhandel—Frankfurter Ausgabe*, No. 8 (January 28, 1969), cols. 254a-56a. The reviewer also mentions G. P. Landmann's anthology of "Georgians": *Der George-Kreis; eine Auswahl aus seinen Schriften* (Cologne: Kiepenheuer & Witsch), as well as a new translation into German of Claude David's famous monograph, all of which may contain slivers of information on Kantorowicz's formative years.

[2] To Käte (Mrs. Leonardo) Olschki I owe several bits of information which have helped me to re-create the atmosphere that prevailed in Heidelberg in the 1920's, in Berlin in the 1930's, in New York around 1939, and in Berkeley throughout the 1940's. I am likewise indebted to Professors Kurt Baldinger (Heidelberg), Arthur R. Evans, Jr. and Percival B. Fay, for a variety of attentions; and to my Assistants Margaret Sinclair Breslin, Kathleen Connors, and Louise Pescetta for their intelligent help and unswerving loyalty. Some excellent last-minute improvements on my occasionally clumsy wording are due to Sarah George of Princeton University Press.

familiarity with a fairly new crop of books devoted, by observers and participants alike, to the Stefan George Circle to which Kantorowicz belonged (and which so notably molded the content and style of his research);[3]

[3] As a rule these writings contain but a few shreds of information, which are not particularly candid or revealing, at that—a state of affairs from which it is safe to conclude that a discreet and far-sighted Kantorowicz, despite his unwavering personal loyalty to the poet, made it a point to stay out of most of the "goings-on" (including crises, fits of jealousy, quarrels, frictions, intrigues, maneuvers) that marked and marred the history of the Circle. This is a tribute to his intelligence and a measure of his ability to see things in due perspective. See Robert Boehringer, *Mein Bild von Stefan George: Text, Tafeln* (Munich and Düsseldorf: Helmut Küpper [formerly Georg Bondi], 1951; rev. 2nd edn. ["For the 1968 Centennial"], 2 vols., 1968), pp. 94, 175, 180; 2nd edn., pp. 87, 168, 296. See also Kurt Hildebrandt, *Das Werk Stefan Georges* (Hamburg: Dr. Ernst Hauswedell, 1960), pp. 126, 150, 160, 232, 239, 278; Edith Landmann, *Gespräche mit Stefan George* [completed in July 1942], ed. G. P. Landmann (Munich and Düsseldorf: Helmut Küpper, 1963), pp. 166, 173f; Edgar Salin, *Um Stefan George. Erinnerung und Zeugnis* (Munich and Düsseldorf: Helmut Küpper, 1948; rev. 2nd edn., 1954), rev. edn., pp. 55, 58, 159, 308, 310f, 326; Ludwig Thormaehlen, *Erinnerungen an Stefan George*, ed. Walther Greisdell (Hamburg: Dr. Ernst Hauswedell, 1962), pp. 90, 182, 210f, 227f, 251, 253, 256, 262, 290. The iconographic section of Boehringer's book contains a striking photograph of a very young, already intense Kantorowicz (T 135 top; undated, but traced to his Munich period); the frontispiece of *Selected Studies* shows the historian in his old age. A tool of limited usefulness (see p. 271) for the probing of Kantorowicz's *œuvre*, but one of great importance for any inquiry into his environment, is G. P. Landmann's meticulous and comprehensive bibliography, *Stefan George und sein Kreis: eine Bibliographie* (Hamburg: Dr. Ernst Hauswedell, 1960).

Friedrich Wolters' controversial attempt—hailed by K. Wolfskehl but repudiated by F. Gundolf—at an "officially" sanctioned history of the Circle, *Stefan George und die "Blätter für die Kunst"; deutsche Geistesgeschichte seit 1890* (Berlin: Georg Bondi, 1930), contains some relevant crumbs of information (provocatively, unindexed; but cf. p. 493), but stands apart in tone and intention. Though it appeared in 1930, the year of its author's death, in 1915 there was an ill-timed public announce-

and the remnants of my general first-hand knowledge of German culture acquired during almost nineteen long years (August 1921–February 1940) of practically uninterrupted residence in Berlin.

The name of Ernst Kantorowicz (he used no middle initial in Europe) came to my attention shortly after I discovered the existence of modern German poetry, at the age of fourteen. The back pages in the slim volumes of Stefan George and in the heavier tomes of his friends' scholarly writings contained discreet clues to a major new book on Emperor Frederick the Second, that imaginative, enlightened German ruler who, intriguingly, had purposely spent almost his entire life in Southern Italy, thus temporarily moving the center of German culture to the heart of the Mediterranean. On my late-afternoon strolls along West Berlin's fashionable main artery, the Kurfürstendamm, I admired the exhibits of recent books, placed in the show windows on account of their beautiful printing and binding and in anticipation of their appeal to cultivated laymen rather than to narrow specialists. Technical monographs in history and philology (of which there was no dearth in Germany between the wars) were consistently excluded from these displays. I later learned that they had a separate market in select academic bookstores scattered over the downtown university district; yet Kantorowicz's temptingly attractive book was on sale both in the austere Center and in the elegant West. My interest in the George movement was sustained by the thrill that I experienced, at the age of sixteen or so, in literally devouring Gundolf's no longer new Goethe book, a real classic; but my exposure to Wolters' quasi-

---

ment of the imminent publication of what, in the end, turned out to be but a preliminary draft.

official report on George and his Circle—a report visibly biased and pompous, also disquietingly pretentious— alerted me to the darker aspects of the movement. At that time, I learned, most opportunely, from my cousin Dr. Raïssa Bloch—a student of Albert Brackmann's, a poet in her own right, and in every way a delightful young woman, who became something of a mentor for me—that she knew Kantorowicz very well indeed from almost daily contacts at the headquarters of the Monumenta Germaniae Historica (where they both worked). She described him as a witty, charming, many-sided conversationalist, completely lacking in that stiffness which vitiated the work and twisted the personality of some of his friends.

Meanwhile, Gundolf died and I clearly remember that the news of his demise was prominently carried on the front page of most German dailies—a rare distinction for a professor of humanities, even in 1931. Hitler, in those years, was literally *ante portas*.

I passed the oral part of my Matura examination on March 3, 1933—two days before the "German Revolution"—and was tentatively admitted to the Friedrich-Wilhelm University. Although the subjects that attracted me were in the fields of Latin and Romance, I could not resist the temptation of directly observing a genuine George disciple. A lecture course by the psychiatrist-philosopher Kurt Hildebrandt was all that I found, and it proved to be acutely disappointing. The lectures, delivered in a monotonous drawl, were downright soporific, and the occasional sly anti-Jewish innuendoes, which might otherwise have involved at least an element of dubious piquancy, were simply revolting amidst the Nazi orgy. George, self-exiled to Switzerland, died in December, and I shortly thereafter attended the memorial for him in Berlin's Lessing

Hochschule, an occasion on which the poet's older friend Melchior Lechter recited a selection of his verse in the prescribed ritualistic manner. Kantorowicz, then shuttling between Berlin and Frankfurt, doubtless attended that ceremony. Meanwhile, the braintrust of the Nazi government, searching frantically for prestigious forerunners and harbingers of the movement (most of whom it later repudiated, as in the case of Oswald Spengler), invited as a visiting professor a quite unconventional "loner," Ludwig Klages, the Bachofen disciple and creator of characterology who in his Munich days had taken part in the George movement. My attendance at his lectures thus rounded out my observation, at first hand, of the kind of people who had gathered around George and had helped him launch that legendary journal, the *Blätter für die Kunst*.

After 1934 my academic interests developed in a radically different direction, toward philology and linguistics—in large part, I must confess, because it then seemed to me that these "objective" disciplines could not be so easily corrupted and perverted as could history and literary criticism, on account of the latter's ineradicably subjective slant. To be honest, I almost made it a point to lose sight of some of the persons and some of the things whose mere mention had excited me during my adolescence. (I made an exception in favor of Karl Wolfskehl's *Die Stimme spricht*, whose two editions I reviewed in the Berlin weekly, *Die Jüdische Rundschau*, in 1934 and 1936, respectively.) Then, upon reaching Berkeley in July 1942, after a long odyssey, I met, among the European exiles, Kantorowicz, who had arrived on the West Coast three years ahead of me. It was this totally unexpected personal encounter that reawakened some dormant lines of my earlier curiosity.

While any uprooting is bound to be an excruciatingly painful experience for heavily committed intellectuals, there were in the case of Kantorowicz special circumstances—central to his *engagement* as a scholar —which singularly aggravated the difficulty. These supervenient ingredients were contributed, in part by certain conditions surrounding his academic work or inherent in it; in part, by his general attitude toward life and his fellowmen, including his broader and narrower environment. The prime determinants of that attitude were his background and upbringing; his early scholastic involvements; his first, not yet sharply focused, exposure to university affairs, with special attention to certain favorite teachers and disciplines; and, above all, the lessons he learned during his ten years or so of close association with the George Circle; to say nothing of the disarray that followed upon the demise of that close-knit group's central figure, the aged symbolist poet and Socratic sage, George.

It is known that during their years of active service in World War I numerous young German soldiers and officers of romantically intellectual leanings tucked away slim volumes of esoteric poetry in their back rolls. Some would read the Hellenizing verse of the newly rediscovered classic Hölderlin; others would turn to some modern bard. For those in search of a virile, chastened style, a sacerdotal mood, an aristocratic tone, and the expression of some genuine, tangible meaning in their precariously circumscribed lives, Stefan George offered a powerful challenge and provided clear-cut, unequivocal answers. To some readers the doctrine radiating from his magic poems seemed to amount to a kind of religiously permeated world view.

I wonder whether Kantorowicz, at the time he volunteered for service in a regiment of field artillery rather

than waiting for his conscription, was already familiar
at first hand with the writings of George, who by 1914
had published the five most influential collections of
his verse: *Die Bücher der Hirten*, delicately classicist;
Das Jahr der Seele, enchantingly romantic; the ornate
Der Teppich des Lebens; Der Siebente Ring, mystic,
hermetic, and haunting; and, above all, *Der Stern des
Bundes*, an inflammatory rallying cry to the phalanx
of his loyal followers. It is very likely that he did, because
his cousin Gertrud Kantorowicz, also born in Posen
but his senior by a margin of nineteen years, was an
early contributor to George's exclusive *Blätter für die
Kunst*.[4] His actual contact with the Circle was established in Heidelberg—at that juncture, its principal cita-
del—around 1920, a moment which thus became a turning point in the life of the budding historian.

Ernst Kantorowicz was born in 1895 into a wealthy
Jewish merchant family, nationally famous as distillers
of exquisite cordials. The family's original headquarters
was Posen (now again known as Poznań), the capital
of a Prussian province carved from a dismembered
Poland. Among Kantorowicz's many, and sometimes
conflicting, loyalties and lines of curiosity, even the
closest inspection does not uncover the slightest affectionate concern for Slavs, in general, or for Poles, in
particular. In this respect he differed from Rainer Maria
Rilke, that Prague-born Austrian poet who developed

---

[4] On Gertrud Kantorowicz's impressively wide range of interests and skills (original poetry, translation of H. Bergson, Introduction to a posthumous collection of her lifelong friend G.
Simmels' articles, studies in Greek and Italian Renaissance art)
and on the circumstances surrounding her tragic end, see Boehringer, *Mein Bild von Stefan George*, pp. 94f; G. P. Landmann,
Stefan George und sein Kreis, p. 272; L. Curtius, "In memoriam
Theresienstadt," *Merkur* 2 (1948): 474f. The Czech motion picture *Transport to Paradise* evokes the climate of Theresienstadt—
down to the grim, not to say grisly, details.

an early tenderness for Czechs and later, through them, for Russians. The talented younger generation of the many-pronged Kantorowicz family clearly gravitated toward Berlin rather than toward Warsaw; it was here that Ernst attended an excellent humanistic or classical secondary school, the Kaiserin Augusta-Viktoria Gymnasium, which offered an exacting nine-year curriculum emphasizing such subjects as Greek, Latin, and history.[5] As the scion of an affluent family, Kantorowicz could then, upon entering the Berlin University, afford to experiment for a while with diverse subjects under the aegis of the Faculty of Philosophy. The accurate record of what he accomplished there in barely two semesters is currently unavailable, but it would be a surprise to learn some day that he kept aloof from the local representatives of "klassische Altertumswissenschaft"—essentially, a combination or integration of archeological, historical, literary, and philological studies—which, through the efforts of U. Wilamowitz-Möllendorf and, in his wake, Eduard Norden, had become a widely admired hallmark of metropolitan scholarship.

[5] In reading Latin aloud, Kantorowicz never rid himself of the (mis)pronunciation that for centuries had been inculcated into German *Gymnasiasten*. His excuse—if he ever proffered one— might have been that in dealing with Late and medieval Latin, his real specialty, such an accent was defensible. His approach to language learning remained strictly philological, without any additional benefit accruing from familiarity with phonetics. As a result, while his English vocabulary was more than adequate and his syntax caused no difficulty, his intonational curve, in lectures more than in free-flowing conversation, never lost its obtrusively foreign contour, to the point of distracting auditors hypersensitive to pitch. In short, he remained all his life the "Altphilologe"—rather than the "Neusprachler," still less the "Sprachforscher"—which his early schooling predestined him to become; essentially, a reader and writer geared to visual rather than auditory perception of language.

The Posen regiment in which Kantorowicz served was sent to the Western front, where the young enlisted man was wounded in the Battle of Verdun. After his recovery he was assigned to the Asien-Korps which, though offering fewer excitements and less surrounded by legend than Erwin Rommel's Afrika-Korps was to become thirty years later, nevertheless afforded him the piquant opportunity of being stationed in the Ottoman Empire and observing at close range both the traditional fabric of mid-Eastern daily life and the tremendous potential impact of a small but superbly organized élite, such as were the Young Turks, amid an amorphous mass of indifferent drifters. Both experiences were to prove of incalculable value at later stages.

Kantorowicz, as an unabashedly patriotic German, undoubtedly suffered keen disappointment at the collapse of the Imperial army late in 1918, and the attempts at revolutionary social change attendant upon a humiliating military defeat caused him acute irritation. On two occasions he enlisted in volunteer corps to perform what he viewed as his duty. With his companions-in-arms he tried to bar bands of overzealous Poles from seizing too large a slice of territory in his native Posen; then, while briefly enrolled in the University of Munich, he took an active part in the suppression of the ephemeral, ill-fated Marxist "Räterepublik"—an episode which led many Bavarians to overreact by swinging to the extreme right, thus preparing the ground for the abortive Hitler-Ludendorff Putsch of 1923. In counter-revolutionary Munich the young Kantorowicz may have unwittingly rubbed shoulders for a moment with elements of the population from which the first Nazi shock and élite troops were eventually recruited.

As was customary among Germany's restless and adventurous students, Ernst soon moved to a third university, with somewhat less hazy ideas of just what kind of knowledge he intended to absorb. This third academic experience, which in 1919 took him to Heidelberg, turned out to be decisive. There may have been several reasons for his choice: the general beauty and renown of the picturesque "Neckarstadt," the advantage of temporary seclusion from nerve-racking urban life, the reputation of individual holders of university chairs in certain disciplines increasingly significant to him, and the tempting proximity of some celebrated disciples of Stefan George (not to mention the poet's periodic visits to that mecca of academicians). Finally, Ernst's sister, married to a local scholar, Arthur Salz, happened to reside in Heidelberg and, what is more, the couple was occasionally privileged to play host to the elusive poet.[6]

In view of Germany's general prostration during the postwar period the famous tradition of publishing doctoral dissertations (practically unaltered) was provisionally suspended. Thus Kantorowicz's thesis, submitted in 1921, remained in typescript form. This circumstance deprives his biographer of a chance to read the autobiographic sketch (*curriculum vitae*)— obligatory for printed dissertations—which, despite the usual conventionality, might shed some light at least on the externals of his study and possibly also on some of his preferences and anticipations. No such essay from Kantorowicz's pen has been preserved in the archives of

[6] As a result of the dispersal and displacements which occurred a quarter-century ago, members of the Salz family have become established in this country, with Columbus, Ohio, serving as the new headquarters (a niece, Beate, temporarily worked in the Museum of Anthropology at the University of Pennsylvania). Other kinsfolk of Kantorowicz are scattered from coast to coast, including a close cousin who resides and practices nursing in Stockton, California.

Heidelberg, but we do know the title of his thesis: "Das Wesen der muslimischen Handwerkerverbände." The topic implies the twenty-six-year-old author's attempt to blend his personal recollections of life in Turkey with his newly awakened active concern with economics (to be specific, "Nationalökonomie" and "Wirtschaftsgeschichte") dating from his brief association with the Munich campus.

Yet the subject of the dissertation does not begin to exhaust the feverish pitch of intellectual curiosity Kantorowicz experienced at the height of his student years. Among his more polished seminar reports, the one on "The Divine Honors of Alexander of Macedon" is, as his life-long friend and colleague Friedrich Baethgen correctly stresses in his masterly necrology, far more indicative of Kantorowicz's future predilections than the topically somewhat inconclusive dissertation. The Alexander theme, however, failed to mature into a full-length monograph. Interestingly, Kantorowicz was much later to cross, at Berkeley, the path of another scholar obsessed by the idea of devoting a major study to the same historical figure—a project which, to complete the parallel, also fell through, but indirectly bore rich fruit.[7]

---

[7] At the time when María Rosa Lida de Malkiel, a Hellenist and—at a later phase—Hispanist of Argentine background and training, and Kantorowicz were both Berkeleyans—they met several times in 1948-51, but their acquaintance remained casual—she was laying the groundwork for a monograph on Alexander. In the end, hers remained unfinished also, but from it she carved out a semitechnical book (*La idea de la fama en la Edad Media castellana* [1952], eventually translated into French [1968]) and a half-dozen exceptionally valuable articles and notes, which were, for the most part, channeled through *Festschriften*. Ironically, each of them was unaware of the other's parallel concern with the Alexander legend, though, as I can testify, M. R. Lida de Malkiel, with characteristic conscientiousness, made it a point in that context to read Gundolf's *Cäsar: Geschichte seines Ruhms* (1924).

The nominal director of Kantorowicz's dissertation was one of the senior professors of history on the local scene, Eberhard Gothein (1853-1923), who is likely to have stimulated and impressed the tyro not as an expert in Muslim economy (which he by no means was), but by virtue of a certain affinity of tastes and inclinations. Strictly speaking, Gothein was something of a "polyhistor," not infrequently stooping, in his memoirs and monographs, to forbiddingly narrow, almost parochial, problems in the history of Baden (the grandduchy that sponsored the University and the Academy of Heidelberg), to say nothing of a topic as unappealing in the context of lofty *Geisteswissenschaften* as the development of Rhenish navigation in the nineteenth century. By way of compensation, Gothein published profusely—and no doubt lectured entertainingly—on such magnetic personalities and such arresting themes as Ignatius Loyola; the Christian-social Jesuit state of Paraguay; the cultural development of South Italy; Raphael and the abbot Gregorio Cortese; or, for that matter, the impact of Plato's political science on the Renaissance. He also delved into politically and religiously tinged popularist movements before the Reformation. As early as 1889, at the peak of the German-style atomization of knowledge, Gothein even had the foresight and the courage to launch a truly programmatic pamphlet. An excellent guide to his generous scattering of tenuously connected writings was retroactively provided by the two-volume posthumous collection, *Schriften zur Kulturgeschichte der Renaissance, Reformation und Gegenreformation* (Munich and Leipzig, 1924), assembled and edited by his junior Heidelberg colleague Edgar Salin—now, after his transfer to Basel, the last surviving of Kantorowicz's personal friends recruited from the George camp.

The germaneness of some problems—if not necessarily approaches—cultivated by the older Gothein (his son Percy will yet cross our path) to many of Kantorowicz's most characteristic and cherished studies requires no laboring. One recognizes at a glance the same proclivity toward Italy, suggestive of an irrepressible *Drang nach Süden*; the same concern with the ideas of antiquity reawakened in the Renaissance; the same loving attention to the fine arts, especially painting; the same wonderment at the constant interplay of political thought and religious orientation. Yet one cannot help finding Kantorowicz far more restrained, rigorously selective, self-demanding in his commitments, and distinctly less prone to facile generalizations than was this favorite teacher of his.

At no stage of his career, least of all during his early Heidelberg years, did Kantorowicz strive to cut the umbilical cord linking medievalistic investigations to classical research. Thus, on balance, his most influential professor turned out to be the classicist Alfred von Domaszewski (1856-1927), a slightly controversial personality (Baethgen calls his manners "scurrilous"), but undoubtedly a solid and prolific researcher. I have scanned this expert's bibliography, in an effort to determine what streaks in Kantorowicz's multi-layered *œuvre* could possibly be traced to his impact. Domaszewski clearly favored Roman over Greek history. He was visibly engrossed by the imperial period (witness his "magnum opus" *Geschichte der römischen Kaiser*, published in two volumes in 1909, and such delayed echoes as *Die Consulate der römischen Kaiser*, 1918); by Roman religion (his *Abhandlungen zur römischen Religion* go back to 1909); by the organization of the Roman army (he did a relative beginner's edition of Hyginus Gromaticus' [?] *De munitionibus castrorum* in

1887; *Die Rangordnung des römischen Heeres* in 1908, at the midway point; plus two late monographs, *Bellum Marsicum* in 1924 and *Die Phalangen Alexanders und Cäsars Legionen* in 1926); by archeologically slanted art history (*Zwei römische Reliefs*, 1910); by the interplay of history and literature (*Zeitgeschichte bei römischen Elegikern*, 1919); and by the intersection of military and religious studies (*Die Religion des römischen Heeres*, 1895). This impressive thematic range must, of itself, have been exciting enough for Ernst; but more beneficial was the training in the technique of detailed textual analysis, conducted meticulously and with respect for minute bits of evidence (*Akribie* was the Greek label, in German disguise, for this virtue, one often extolled by Continental philologists), which the two-year association with a very mature Domaszewski afforded the young acolyte. Characteristically, the older man, approaching the concluding stage of his own development, was then examining in monograph after monograph every conceivable aspect of the *Scriptores Historiae Augustae*: the text's general geography, its topography of Rome, its anthroponymy, its chronology, its concept of the state, etc. This immersion was a perfect example of patient, unhurried, stereoscopic inquiry—worthy of emulation on the side, I repeat, of technique, if not of content and inspiration. As if all this were not enough, Domaszewski also happened to have written, in collaboration with R. E. Brünnow, a three-volume work on Roman antiquities in the Middle East (*Die Provincia Arabia*, 1904-09), based on extensive field work (1897-98) scrupulously distilled. This was a major side-line which must have had singular appeal for the erstwhile incipient Turcologist in Kantorowicz.

If Gothein's guidance was good for width of scope and

diversity of illustration, and if apprenticeship with
Domaszewski provided the much-needed corrective of
unvarnished workmanlike experience, that is, sharp
focus, there remains to be identified the academic factor
which channeled Kantorowicz's energy in the direction
of his great work on Emperor Frederick the Second
(1215-50). This last major influence was Karl Hampe
(1869-1936), a medievalist of exceptional merit and
productivity, whose specialty, ever since his doctoral dissertation (Berlin, 1893), had been, opportunely enough,
the closing stage of the Hohenstaufen period in all its
glory and subsequent horror. He was particularly interested in the dramatic intertwining of the threads of
German and Italian history at this crucial phase, and the
unique role of Dante against this incomparable backdrop. Much of Hampe's activity involved precise and
self-denying archival research, which allowed him to
unearth, especially in Capua, a treasure-trove of epistolary material.[8] But he certainly did not lack the power
of synthesis, as is evidenced by such bold temporal projections as his great triptych: *Deutsche Kaisergeschichte
in der Zeit der Salien und Staufer* (1909); *Herrscher-
gestalten des deutschen Mittelalters* (1927); and *Das
Hochmittelalter; Geschichte des Abendlandes von 900
bis 1250* (1932). In the early 'twenties Hampe reached
the pinnacle of his reputation, and a grateful Heidelberg clinched the wide recognition of his prestige by
making sure that he was elevated to the University Pres-

[8] Is it mere coincidence that the concluding (fifth) part of
Hampe's *Mitteilungen aus der Capuaner Briefsammlung* (Heidelberg, 1910-24) is entitled "Zur Gründungsgeschichte der Universi-
tät Neapel," an event whose seventh centennial was commem-
orated with special solemnity in George's Circle and one which,
in particular, deeply moved the young Kantorowicz? See the
Preamble, phrased in lapidary style, to his *Kaiser Friedrich der
Zweite*.

idency (1924). Characteristically, Hampe's "Rektorats-rede," published in expanded form the following year, dealt with posterity's view of Emperor Frederick the Second. Whether or not Kantorowicz agreed with Hampe's specific interpretation, the event itself, rich in implications, must have induced a euphoric mood in the younger man, who was already deeply engrossed in his own briskly advancing book on the very same historical figure.

What Hampe did for Kantorowicz—though he was far more than a mere trail-blazer—was to instill, in a wide community of intellectuals, fresh general interest in the splendid Hohenstaufen period of German history; to sharpen his readers' and students' awareness of the charismatic "Kaiser" concept in its medieval setting; to focus attention on the ruler-scholar-artist Frederick the Second as probably the most scintillating figure of the German Middle Ages; and to have reserved a niche for Dante as a crown witness to the legend, surrounding the monarch upon his death. All this was accomplished despite the fact that he himself was neither a literary scholar nor a chronicler of ideas, but an unpretentious general practitioner of history. Lastly, Hampe (and especially his faithful junior associate Baethgen) may plausibly have established, for Kantorowicz, the all-important link to the celebrated Berlin archives, the Monumenta Germaniae Historica. Much later, when Kantorowicz's book on Emperor Frederick ran into stiff resistance on the part of hard-line academicians, the chivalrous Hampe, in a signal display of generosity, used all the authority vested in him as the unexcelled senior expert to write a by no means hostile appraisal of that unorthodox venture by a younger and, all told, far more successful man.

Since Kantorowicz at no time showed any predisposi-

tion to become a *littérateur*, it was, one gathers, un-
adulterated historical curiosity which drove him to select certain scholarly problems for closer inspection and
to enroll in lecture courses and seminars conducted by
professors who had a knack for attacking and, if at all
possible, solving them. Also, the hospitable home of
Eberhard and Marie Luise Gothein (she was a scholarly
connoisseur of all manner of garden arrangements and
even had relevant book-length publications to her
credit) happened to serve as a meeting-ground for a
local chapter of George's followers, as is amply known
from independent attestations. This group behaved in
a deliberately clannish fashion, forming a kind of exclusive sect or colony within the otherwise fairly fluid
campus population. The members of this coterie were
noted for appearing frequently in groups; for patron-
izing certain boarding houses and eating places; for
dressing more nattily than anyone else, for tying their
four-in-hand with a special flourish; for seeming, in general, to strike a certain pose; and for maintaining a pronounced coolness and formality in their almost reluctant
relations with outsiders, especially those not considered
for tentative recruitment and ultimate initiation. Although the superficial impression produced by the self-
contained élite group as a whole bordered on arrogance,
it was, on the other hand, very well known that some
of Germany's, and specifically Heidelberg's, ablest aca-
demics formed part of the Circle and derived much of
their moral fiber, fierce independence, and—not least
—inspiration from this invigorating partnership. Half
a century ago, the tone-setting luminaries of the Heidelberg chapter, which forgathered in the salon of the
highly literate and sophisticated Frau Gothein, were
the spell-binding literary historian Friedrich Gundolf
and the almost equally magnetic, distinctly younger

sociologist Edgar Salin, around both of whom many serious and enthusiastically devoted students clustered in crowded lecture rooms.

How these "chosen ones" and "men of destiny" really felt in their splendid isolation and what they said in their unguarded moments can now be quite accurately pieced together from memoirs, diaries, and letters.[9] Those who prefer the outside view of the emergent situation can also fall back on appropriately independent and, it would seem, trustworthy eye-witness reports. For a sharply etched picture of the motley crowd of students and their professors who converged upon turbulent Heidelberg around 1920 one may turn to the chapter "Horen der Freundschaft" (pp. 259-310) in Carl Zuckmayer's masterly recollections, *Als wär's ein Stück von mir* (Vienna, 1966). A few of Zuckmayer's neatly chiseled paragraphs afford a glimpse of the venerated poet himself, observed during his strolls. On campus one sees Gundolf delivering his apparently dull lectures on romanticism (which were later collected into a book); and among his students or auditors one detects the strikingly beautiful, sultry Elisabeth ("Elli") Salomon, who, though earning her doctorate in a different field, even-

---

[9] This particular cycle of memoirs presumably started with the slim volume of recollections of George's publisher and lifelong friend Georg Bondi (1934); it is still in full swing. The most important epistolarium has been the corpus of letters exchanged between George and Hofmannsthal (1938; rev. edn., 1953). The latest innovative element in these attempts at reconstruction, added after the death of Gundolf's widow in Oxford (1958), has been the publication of three volumes of letters centering about Gundolf. Interesting also, on account of the side light it casts on these major protagonists, is Lothar Helbing's prefatory essay "Gundolf und Elli," ushering in two lectures of hers delivered in England at the height of the last war and only recently made accessible; see *Stefan George: Zwei Vorträge* (Amsterdam: Castrum Peregrini Presse, 1965), pp. 5-33.

tually (1926) became his wife. Salin is likewise in the
picture, as is an ugly, embittered, clubfooted dwarf
called Joseph Goebbels, crouched in a corner and feeling
universally despised. All this is described against the
colorful background of iconoclastic artistic shenanigans,
radical left-wing agitation, and the inchoate conglomer-
ation of right-wing rowdies and hooligans.[10] As for Kan-

[10] At the risk of skirting the domain of sensationalism, I am
duty bound to mention the fact that Hitler's future Minister of
Propaganda, Joseph Goebbels, also gave his version of Heidelberg student life in his half-novel, half-diary, *Michael*, completed
in 1921, when he was twenty-four, then published (probably after
a revision) eight years later. For an essayistic analysis of the budding demagogue's fling at fiction ("not literature, but a document"), see S. Spender, *European Witness* (New York, 1946), pp.
176-95; for a dispassionate study of Goebbels' sources (Goethe's
Die Leiden des jungen Werthers, Nietzsche and Dostoyevsky, and
expressionism which Goebbels, pathetically, was later to condemn
and try to extirpate as so much "degenerate art"), see M. Bonwit,
"*Michael*, ein Roman von Joseph Goebbels, im Lichte der
deutschen literarischen Tradition," *Monatshefte für deutschen
Unterricht* 49 (1957): 193-200. Samples (in authoritative translation) of Goebbels' actual diary entries traceable to 1925-26 are
displayed in L. P. Lochner's Preface to his selection and edition
of *The Goebbels Diaries, 1942-43* (New York, 1948), pp. 3-30.
Heidelberg was the eighth (and last) German university at which
Hitler's diabolically cunning aide—the only intellectual within
the original hierarchy—enrolled and which conferred on him the
doctorate. As a discharged soldier, Michael, the hero, is the
starkly idealized image of the author, who, being a cripple, was
barred from military service. Piecing together Michael's constant
ranting against "Überbildung" and "Fach-" or "Spezial-wissen-
schaft" and Goebbels' well-known attempts to ingratiate himself
with Kantorowicz's friend Gundolf, one realizes what some restless, aimless, migrant German students were expecting of poet-
professors associated with George and how the vicious anti-Semites
among them must have seethed with anger upon discovering that
the closest approximations to their ideal of academic leadership
—men like Gundolf and Kantorowicz—happened, of all backgrounds, to be Jews. When, ten years later, these drifters had the
power to translate their fury into action, they used a double-
barreled weapon by silencing, banishing, or wiping out the unwelcome witnesses to their own juvenile confusion and, worse, by

torowicz, he was still too young and inconspicuous to catch the beginning playwright's roving eye during the latter's all too brief stay at the banks of the Neckar River.

Never, I suspect, was a young and highly promising man absorbed more smoothly into the George Circle than Ernst Kantorowicz; and this association was to color, albeit in varying degrees, the remainder of his life. Everything seemed to predestine the blossoming of this friendship: his independent wealth provided a welcome margin of leisure and freedom of movement; the earlier connections of his poetically gifted cousin Gertrud (pseudonym "Gert Pauly") as well as those of his sister and brother-in-law (the Salz ménage) furnished the family links and the social setting; his own growing expertise in ancient and medieval history involved the kind of specialized knowledge that George and the men around him were the last to despise at that moment; Ernst's academic status as a brilliant disciple of Eberhard Gothein (and his distinctly close personal friendship with the latter's less than brilliant son Percy, a would-be Romance scholar who was to perish at the hands of the Nazis in 1944) rounded out the astonishingly bright picture. Add to this, as supplementary features, first, the coincidence that George's early glorification, in his poem "Gräber in Speier," of Emperor Frederick (or "Friedrich der Grössere," as the members of the Circle wittily called the Hohenstaufen Kaiser, to distinguish him from his namesake, the Prussian King Frederick the Second, who impressed them far less favorably) was now echoed by solid professional his-

---

injecting, with devilish shrewdness, some of the Circle's noble ideas and metaphors into the new, relentlessly enforced ideology. For further implications see below.

torians of the rank of Hampe; and, second, the circumstance that Ernst's closest personal friend at the height of his Heidelberg years, Woldemar Graf Uxkull-Gyllenband (to whom he almost effusively dedicated his "magnum opus" in 1928), had been in touch with the Berlin sector of George's Circle as early as 1918 or 1919.[11]

In view of this situation it seems proper to indulge in an excursus and to outline George's influence on the humanities, as they were cultivated at German centers of learning before, during, and shortly after World War I. We shall try to steer a middle course between the impressionistic, hence somewhat superficial (not to say flippant), treatment by Zuckmayer and the heavy-handed, dogmatic approach of a blindly obedient devotee like Friedrich Wolters.[12]

There is no exaggeration in stating, with retrospec-

---

[11] This young aristocrat-sportsman (who, in 1939, perished in an automobile accident) seems to have been reckless in real life; morose and impenetrable at social gatherings; but, as if by compensation, scrupulous and somewhat pedestrian as a researcher (he was a classicist, with a special commitment to archeology). He and his slightly older brother Bernhard (who died—apparently a soldier's death—at the age of nineteen) were junior habitués at some of the meetings of George's friends in war-time Berlin. See Boehringer, *Mein Bild*, pp. 160-68, 170f, 178-80, 234 (2nd edn., pp. 167, 178-80, 183, 191, 298, and Tables 149-51, 153f); Salin, *Um Stefan George*, pp. 34, 53, 55, 58, 133, 243, 257, 306, 308f, 311, 358; Thormaehlen, *Erinnerungen*, passim (see Index, p. 296*b*).

[12] The clashing reactions to Wolters' long-delayed and ill-advised book divided the Circle, as had few earlier publications bearing the Master's personal seal of approval. At that time, the dissensions were hushed up; but today, incontrovertible evidence has become available. See Salin, *Um Stefan George*, p. 209; G. P. Landmann, *Stefan George und sein Kreis*, Supplement, p. 274; K. Wolfskehl, *Briefe und Aufsätze, München 1925-1933*, ed. M. Ruben (Hamburg, 1966), pp. 297 (Wolfskehl) and 302 (Gundolf). For additional vignettes and candid snapshots of Wolters, see Boehringer, *Mein Bild*, 2nd edn., pp. 252-55 and 262f.

tive serenity, that during those fateful years one could hardly find an intellectual in German-speaking territory who was not somehow affected (indeed, aroused) by Stefan George's poetry—its artistic kernel, its ideological message, and its outward appearance down to idiosyncrasies of spelling and typography, which to many seemed provocative to the point of exhibitionism. Not a few reactions were boundlessly enthusiastic, many more were frankly antagonistic, but the vast majority of writers and readers thus stimulated seemed pathetically split in their responses. An eloquent witness to this fascination marked by inner cleavage is the poet-critic Albrecht Schaeffer (1885-1950) who, though professionally moored to Leipzig's Insel-Verlag, for a brief while strained to hover at the very periphery of the Circle. We owe to his versatile pen a shrewd and perceptive two-hundred-page essay on George's poetry—"Stefan George" in *Dichter und Dichtung; kritische Versuche* (Leipzig, 1923), pp. 297-501—an essay rich in overtones of uninhibited admiration. Simultaneously he did not mind stooping to write a sensational novel—*Elli; oder, sieben Treppen; Beschreibung eines weiblichen Lebens* (Leipzig, 1919)—a *Schlüsselroman* which, so trustworthy observers report, involved a threadbare and far less than friendly disguise of the Circle, maliciously grouped around that sensuous and sensitive girl who was to emerge seven years later as Friedrich Gundolf's wife.

The crest of Stefan George's life falls into three rather sharply delimited periods, though one discovers certain overlaps. The first, characterized by strictly artistic gropings and accomplishments, deserves to be called experimental. This period aligns the poet with the French symbolists (whom he revered as his masters), with their followers in other countries, with the Spanish and Latin American "modernists," and with similar groups of rebels, innovators, and iconoclasts who were concerned, above all (not unlike their painter friends), with reforming the TECHNIQUE of their chosen medium. During this phase, George's most prominent, if not closest, friend and his most valuable ally was the precocious Austrian poet Hugo von Hofmannsthal—a talented, fine-honed man of exceptional delicacy and receptivity, but of limited creative strength. The journal that served as the clearly recognizable mouthpiece for this, by and large, aesthetic movement was the *Blätter für die Kunst*, exclusive to the point of being editorially impenetrable—indeed, commercially almost unavailable—save for those properly introduced, screened, and initiated.

After the turn of the century and until the outbreak of the Great War there occurred a major reorientation in George's life and propensities. Without entirely abandoning his quest for novel art forms and his ceaseless search for delicately strung "schöne Seelen," especially among unspoiled, receptive adolescents, the poet—now metamorphosed into the Master—became more and more concerned with the breeding of an intellectual, explicitly academic, élite. This cadre, he dreamed, should be entrusted with checking and, if possible, reversing certain unhealthy trends; specifically, with curing, through ministration or surgery, certain moral ailments of our corrupted, materialistic mass civilization. After George thus joined the loose ranks of "Weltverbesserer," his prime attention was riveted on the universities, where he reckoned that his friends and adherents, by capturing standard-setting chairs in key disciplines (Germanics, classics, history, sociology), could exert a wholesome, steadying influence on select groups of malleable, warmly responsive students. The *Blätter*, though for a while continued, were gradually downgraded to playing a less prominent role than did a collateral series of jealously supervised scholarly books ("Bücher der Schau und Forschung") bearing the same emblem or signet on the front cover and issued preeminently by the same publishing house, Georg Bondi, which, discreetly enough, did not otherwise cater to contemporary literature. Also, there emerged a new, ephemeral venture, the *Jahrbuch für die geistige Bewegung* (3 volumes, 1910-12). Characteristically, that doctrinaire yearbook was piloted by two younger candidates for university professorships, Friedrich Gundolf and Friedrich Wolters, of whom the first before long became something of an archetypal George disciple ("Jünger"). Concurrently, the poet's concern with modern foreign literature, not to speak of other art forms, was steadily on the wane; the incidence of his travels abroad decreased sharply; and the constituency of the Circle, too, underwent a gradual change. After his unsuccessful romance with, or courtship of, Ida ("Isi") Coblenz, who in the end had the temerity to marry an "unacceptable" rival poet (Richard Dehmel), the Circle was gradually transmuted into a straight "Männerbund" and was not immune to the charge of militant misogyny.

The third stage, extending roughly from the outbreak of the war to George's death almost twenty years later, is marked by the poet's rapid aging, neatly traceable through the numerous photographs which have been preserved and are now readily accessible; by the decline of his artistic zest and power; by the weakening of his few remaining friendships with major independent literary figures; by his increased concern with a mystically conceived rebirth of a purified Germany (*Das neue Reich*, 1928); and by the ever heavier demands of such tasks as the conversion of promising young men to his ideals of stringency, aloofness, and near-asceticism (in matters intellectual) and the conquest of influential academic outposts and citadels. The poet's commitments had truly moved full circle: from a revolutionary, as regards artistic form, he had become a traditionalist, a believer in cultural organicism (i.e., change within a pattern of historical continuity), in brief, a conservative, at least on the increasingly important political level. The *Blätter* (1892-1919) now came to an end, even though their elegantly stylized signet continued to be imprinted on a swelling flood of scholarly books, dealing as a rule with "cultural heroes," e.g., Plato, Winckelmann, and Nietzsche. Of the older followers some of the most outstanding, including Gundolf, clearly resented the Master's firm, indeed stiffening, grip on their lives and patterns of thinking and slipped away, sometimes not without a painful struggle.[13] The new vintage of faithful followers contained, understandably, few individuals of conspicuous originality, because the atmosphere within the Circle, marked by a growing number of taboos ruthlessly enforced under threat of expulsion,[14] was by now widely known to be stifling. Of the

[13] There exists a whole literature, which cannot be digested here, on the increasingly strained relations between George and Gundolf. Relevant to our subject is the fact that, after the "classic" friendship between Master and Disciple had cooled off, George deliberately avoided going to Heidelberg when Gundolf was in residence. When he did spend a season or just a few days in the "Neckarstadt," he occupied a study, whose shelves were breaking under the weight of books, in a scenically located house owned by Ernst Kantorowicz and Woldemar Count Uxkull-Gyllenband. This situation doubtless required no little diplomacy and flexibility on the part of the two younger scholars.

[14] These taboos are well known and require no circumstantial discussion. Any compromise with modern theater was inadmissible; fiction was but marginally tolerated; experimental lyrical poetry was unmentionable; painting ended with Böcklin; philosophy meant Plato, Schopenhauer, and Nietzsche, but neither

younger men who, after the exertions and frustrations of the war and of the war's immediate aftermath, elected to gain inner strength by qualifying for admission to George's inner sanctum, some, like the dynamic and immensely gifted Max Kommerell, after ten years of loyal service or bondage, broke away, fleeing from the unwaveringly stern Master's *Bannkreis* ("magic circle"). What still others, the independents, enjoyed most was a kind of indirect or tangential relation— a loose, non-committal but nevertheless sincere and very profitable association with just one prominent member of the Circle. Thus, the poet-novelist-doctor Hans Carossa was an intimate friend of Ernst Bertram, i.e., of one of George's most dependable paladins, while the critic and literary historian Ernst Robert Curtius was,

---

Descartes, nor Spinoza, still less Leibniz; music was non-existent unless it revolved around George's poetry; modern foreign literature of any tone and persuasion was frowned upon.

How the inhibiting, not to say stifling, influence of a personality cult could narrow down a captive scholar's creative urge and spontaneous range of curiosity is best illustrated with the bibliography of Ernst Bertram (1884-1957). While, as a young man, Bertram could afford to explore not only such "orthodox" writers as Stifter (1907), Hofmannsthal (1907), George himself (1908, 1913), and Nietzsche (1910-11, 1918), but also a few of their "heterodox" counterparts, e.g. Thomas Mann (1907, 1917-18), the Austrian novelists (1909), and even Flaubert (1911), he scrupulously refrained from taking such eyebrow-raising liberties after World War I. See H. Buchner's bibliography of Bertram's writings appended to the posthumous selection: *Möglichkeiten, ein Vermächtnis* (Pfullingen, 1958), pp. 273-82. Only after his definitive break with George did Gundolf muster the courage to give public lectures on Rainer Maria Rilke and Frank Wedekind, and even these appeared in print with a certain delay; thus, it was through Elisabeth Gundolf's endeavors that her husband's lecture on Rilke, delivered in Essen on June 3, 1931, eventually saw the light of day in Vienna as late as 1937.

As a consequence of such repressions, those of George's scholarly friends relatively best shielded from conflicts of conscience were classical philologists and archeologists.

for decades, in close touch with Friedrich Gundolf; but neither Carossa nor—demonstrably to his own regret —Curtius ever became full-fledged members of the Circle.[15]

It is the contention of this paper—all told, its central thesis—that, in sober and critical retrospect, Kantorowicz proved to be the most significant product of that vintage. The irony of the situation lies in the fact that he achieved the distinction of such high stature not through his proximity to George, which might have entailed servility, but through his relative independence, rooted in originality, self-reliance, and, above all, intelligence. Unquestionably George, through his absolutist demands on his friends, especially those younger and weaker than himself, at first inspired them, filling their uncommitted lives with a purpose, then all too

[15] At this distance, in time and space, it is difficult to define just what kind of initiation led to membership in the Circle. Initially, there did exist a nominal, very loosely organized "Gesellschaft für die *Blätter für die Kunst*" and the hard core of the Circle simply included the contributors to that journal and to the books marked by the signet on their front cover as germane to its aims. Later, however, even this tangible frame disappeared. Members were, apparently, those addressing George as "Meister" and, where the difference in age so warranted, those addressed by him with the familiar "du." They were invited to attend certain readings of his poetry; encouraged to submit their writings to him for criticism and possible publication; and they were understood to be willing, in return, to accept and uphold a certain fairly rigid scale of values, canon of taste, and standard of behavior and, undoubtedly, to pledge—in the best Germanic tradition —personal loyalty vis-à-vis the poet and all fellow-members. From the scholars consistently junior to George who joined his Circle as admirers, one must sharply distinguish certain senior professors (mostly aestheticians or literary historians) whom a still very young George accepted as his academic well-wishers or "Gönner" (such as Max Dessoir, Reinhold Lepsius, Erich Schmidt, and Georg Simmel). These, realistically enough, he did not seek to restrain in their associations, bonds of personal friendship, or intellectual commitments.

often stunted their growth, eroded their substance, and ended by literally enslaving them. Those who, like Hofmannsthal, Gundolf, and Kommerell, attempted to shake themselves loose, achieved freedom at the cost of a painful estrangement, if not a downright quarrel, which left a long and bitter aftertaste. This fate Kantorowicz escaped—as before him only Karl Wolfskehl had done with comparable deftness—by combining steadfast personal loyalty and a knack for averting irritation with genuine intellectual strength of his own, a liberal dosage of common sense, and (not least) flawless taste. Therein lies the measure of his mettle. It may be stated parenthetically that, in Kantorowicz's case, "intelligence" involved a fine amalgam of four ingredients: German "Geist" (characterized by effervescent enthusiasm), Old French "mesure" (the choice of judicious limit), modern French, in fact Mediterranean, "esprit" (quick wit and readiness to let it sparkle in the right social context), and Latin "acumen" (cognitive incisiveness, analytical sharpness). A harmonious combination of these four qualities is found in pitifully few exemplars of the human species.

What was the secret of the hypnotic power George brought to bear on so many susceptible individuals at that particular juncture? There were, clearly, certain elements in his background and in his doctrine or program that literally mesmerized the German youth left aimlessly drifting and deeply frustrated by an exhausting and, on balance, pointless war. For those who had witnessed, and inwardly experienced, the collapse of every dimension of an established order and who could not reconcile themselves to such shallow substitutes as the cluster of new isms—materialism, relativism, skepticism, cynicism, opportunism—George's heroic message and sermon, with its contemptuous deprecation of mundane success and recognition, its stress on sterling character, unalloyed quality, and genuine merit, its dauntless championship of many endangered ideals and ridiculed virtues of yore, offered a much-needed mooring amid the raging storm. This steadying moral counsel, directed toward the reshaping of an individual's total life-pattern, now took precedence in George's blueprints over the vindication of strictly aesthetic causes. But the fact that the preacher was also a poet of signal distinction (even though, as insiders knew, past his peak of creative genius) and that in his youth and early manhood he had acted as a bold innovator of artistic forms undoubtedly enhanced the fascination he was now exerting on groups of young humanists. Similarly, the latter-day Tolstoy, however vehemently he inveighed against his own earlier advocacy of art for art's sake, indisputably derived much of his appeal as a reformer from the brilliance which his novels and stories, later in part disavowed by himself, continued to radiate in an appreciative nation and beyond. Unlike the Russian moralist, George was satisfied with having shifted his emphasis, and he never bothered to condemn his own early modernist experiments. For an artistically refined, nay spoiled, young man like Kantorowicz, capable of an aesthetic approach to life and culture but sensing the narcissistic sterility of such an approach without the correlate of a fixed and lofty set of moral values, the almost quixotically chivalric world of Stefan George and his legendary paladins and squires must have loomed as a new order of knights. The conversion to these ideals of an individual of young Kantorowicz's upbringing, connections, sensitivity, exposure to wartime hazards, and historical flights of fantasy may well have been instantaneous and compulsive.

If George's gradually congealing existentialist philosophy was to be projected onto the spectrum of political credos, then it could be assigned only to that spectrum's conservative wing. Democracy, with its inherent espousal of the majority opinion, and socialism, with (among other liabilities) its inherent menace of an all-leveling mass civilization, were both profoundly repugnant to this century's poet-aristocrat par excellence. But the subdued or veiled conservatism George urged upon his followers was unique and (not unlike T. S. Eliot's in this respect) radically at variance with most of the reactionary and vulgarian rightist movements. Granted that it extolled certain attitudes peculiar to the past; granted that it reflected, in beguilingly stylized form, the charm of folk belief and unspoiled rural life; granted that it tended to disregard contemporary foreign cultures, focusing its enthusiasm (aside from ancient Greece) on Greater Germany alone; granted that the poet's delicately archaizing vocabulary, purged of any admixture of irksome loan-words, implied a wistful longing for the roots of German *Wesensart*; and granted that the joint impact of all these parallel features suggests a conservative stance; one must, in fairness to George, counterbalance this image by placing equal stress on those ingredients which pointed in a different, not to say opposite, direction. He was not—at least not until 1920—narrowly patriotic, and he displayed restraint (indeed overt pessimism, if not defeatism) during World War I: he refused to endorse the Kaiser's militarism, expansionist imperialism, and industrial capitalism, and he identified himself with medieval and classical (i.e., pre-Prussian) German culture, projecting into it, as enriching and ennobling elements, Plato, Vergil, and Dante for good measure. He thus welcomed a Mediterranean strain to offset the Nordic heritage. In short, George's ideal, far removed

from the familiar goose-stepping and bureaucratic Germany of the Hohenzollern, was the romantically em-
broidered, mythically exalted land of the Hohenstaufen.

Speaking of George's private slant of conservatism
as part of the background that fostered Kantorowicz's
equally unique style of scholarship, it would be disingenuous to omit from discussion the role played in the
Circle by a strong contingent of Jews. The premise of
our analysis must be the self-evident fact that, ever since
the emancipation of Jews under Napoleon, anti-
Semitism in varying degrees of intensity was rampant
among European conservatives. Understandably, the
majority of educated Jews, under the circumstances,
were hesitant to join the conservative ranks. Intellectually active German Jews, like their cousins elsewhere,
tended to be cosmopolitan and articulately liberal, not
infrequently gravitating toward some form of left-wing
radicalism. The exceptions to this rule were few, unless
one includes here converted Jews, half- and quarter-
Jews, and other highly assimilated groups, almost in-
distinguishable from the bulk of Germans.

It is, then, a matter of no mean surprise—the paradox has often been tangentially mentioned, but seldom
if ever elucidated with the necessary candor—that no
less than one half of George's immediate followers were,
according to authoritative estimates, either Jews, by religious or ethnic standards, or at least of partially Jewish ancestry. What increases one's astonishment is the
further discovery that the ranks of the poet's Gentile
friends included several mild, and a few violent and
irate, anti-Semites. George himself, estranged from the
Catholicism of his family and his own childhood and
best classed as a neo-pagan, was at all times completely
indifferent to Judaism (starting with its classic distillate

in the Old Testament), but he undeniably felt attracted to Jewish men (like Wolfskehl, Gundolf, and Kantorowicz) and, even more consistently, to Jewish women. He was, in turn, destined to galvanize many of them. He himself was acutely aware of the tension between these two neatly polarized groups of his companions and admirers and, in a famous and fateful poem included in *Der Stern des Bundes,* evoked this haunting example of indissoluble love-hatred.[16]

My guess, based on observation and introspection, is that the young George—that richly sensuous poet whose visions gravitated toward the exuberant south, who was enamored of Romance languages (as an adolescent he even devised a new one for his private poetic exercises) and literatures, and who was excited by the temptation of verbal experiments—typified, within the matrix of German culture, that "Mediterranean strain" which, as a result of century-old ties and affinities, had become almost irresistibly appealing to the artistically responsive, intellectually alert Jews (and descendants of Jews). As this particular bond of allegiance weakened, in consequence of George's withdrawal from the Romance world (Dante excepted) and his reorientation toward an "endangered" Germany, another, unrelated fascination made itself felt. George's aloofness and a certain clannishness of his partisans may have subliminally

[16] I am aware of the margin of hazard in allowing subsequent events to color, through hindsight so to speak, one's reconstruction of earlier stages. Let us grant that before Hitler's actual advent to power the sporadic frictions within the Circle, between certain less than compatible members, were mild and confined to an intimate, almost impenetrable realm of each person's private life. After the explosive events of 1933, however, the character of the relations must have changed abruptly—a cleavage further dramatized and accentuated by the aged poet's death just a few months after the upheaval.

appealed to the scions of a proud, stubborn, fiercely independent stock trained in self-reliance and accustomed to living in small, hermetically closed communities over a period of two millennia.[17]

[17] This paradoxical convergence of Jews (including an occasional Zionist) and anti-Semites upon the same Circle explains certain bizarre contradictions and accounts for many agonies. The beginnings of this imbroglio are traceable to Munich's "Kosmische Tafelrunde," which, at the turn of the century, brought together in friendly conviviality two staunch Jew-haters who later repudiated George, Ludwig Klages and Alfred Schuler, and the ardent Zionist Karl Wolfskehl.

Of greater relevance to the period when Kantorowicz was an active member of the Circle is the fact that Friedrich Gundolf's widow, Elisabeth, when exiled to London, felt so harassed by her fellow-expatriates' accusations of George's and, by implication, her late husband's pathetic roles as unwitting harbingers and even abettors of the new dictatorships, that she made it a point, in 1944, to prepare, and conceivably to deliver, a lecture of formal rebuttal (see "Stefan George und der Nationalsozialismus," *Stefan George: Zwei Vorträge*, pp. 52-76). In that allocution she lodged a plea—carefully supported by citation of chapter and verse—to regard George as a resolute, inveterate opponent of Hitlerism, indeed, as the embodiment of a significant alternative (p. 76: "eine von mehreren Antithesen") to the new totalitarian barbarity. Her logic was unimpeachable, so far as the evidence of the passages adduced is concerned; also, given certain tragic circumstances surrounding the rift between Master and Disciple and her undeniable personal share in this estrangement, her low-key performance in 1944, which kept all passions and grudges under firm control, was nothing short of stoic.

The unhealable sore spot in this situation is the fact that it is equally possible—if not, indeed, distinctly easier—to assemble from the same poet's impassioned rhetoric such visionary passages as seem to stamp him as the precursor and trail-blazer of Nazism in all its unbridled violence. Understandably, this alluring possibility was seized upon and exploited, at least during the fateful Spring of 1933 (hailed as "Deutscher Frühling"). What must have exacerbated the bitterness of this experience for some witnesses, like Kantorowicz, was the aggravating circumstance that such counterfeiting was perpetrated not only by despicable small-time opportunists, but also by highly respected members of George's innermost circle, who thus clearly manifested their disloyalty toward former friends during a crisis of unspeakable

It is high time that we return to Kantorowicz, whom we left earning his doctorate at the age of twenty-six, despite the interruption of the war and its aftermath. The span from 1921 to 1927, when the first volume of his work on Emperor Frederick appeared, must have been a period of hard work, but also of zest bordering on euphoria. The outward circumstances favored such a mood: a talented, inspired, physically fit man of independent means,[18] Kantorowicz did not need to engage

---

poignancy. To cite but one example: Ernst Bertram, suddenly catapulted to a university presidency, contrived the device of tracing the "German Revolution" to George's poetry in an address attended by thousands in Cologne ("Deutscher Aufbruch: Rede an die akademische Jugend") which subsequently appeared not only in two educational journals (see entry 56 in Buchner's previously mentioned bibliography), but also, a fact the bibliography coyly hushes up, in such a mass-circulation medium as the *Kölnische Zeitung*. (I distinctly recall that hundreds of copies of the issue here incriminated were sold in Berlin's leading downtown book stores patronized by professors and university students.) For further details, see Hildebrandt, *Erinnerungen*, pp. 272ff.

[18] Even those who, like myself, met Kantorowicz when he was approaching the age of fifty recall the dashing figure he cut and can well imagine how striking his personal appearance must have been fifteen years earlier, at the time he was finishing his *magnum opus*. Of medium stature, slim, agile, virile in his gait and movements; gesturing with elegant restraint; showing a neatly profiled face characterized by instantaneous responses; blessed with a low, vibrant voice; speaking without undue haste (but quick in sharply pointed repartee); dark-haired and free from baldness; endowed with an intense, piercing gaze which could, on occasion, become warm and inviting; repressing complaints; refraining from the appeal to gross sarcasm and vituperation; and subtly hiding beneath his aplomb a deep-seated melancholia, due perhaps to dissatisfaction with himself—he was secure in his enjoyment of the friendship of appreciative men and visibly successful, at will, with discriminating women. He was the handsome embodiment of an Italian aristocrat or even an Oriental prince charming.

R. Boehringer's corroborative testimony invokes the similes of a cavalier and a fencer (*Mein Bild*, p. 186): "George sagte von ihm, er sei, was die Franzosen einen Chevalier genannt hätten,

in drudgery as an obscure college teacher or perform some menial service as university assistant or cataloguer in a library. Nor was he obliged to curry favor with whimsical, cantankerous senior professors to have his book accepted, first as a routine "Habilitationsschrift," perhaps a mere "travail de patience," opening the way to a coveted *venia legendi*; and later in a dust-gathering monograph series. He could afford to be a "Privatgelehrter," unhampered in the free exercise of his intellectual predilections, and his book could thus, in certain respects, be boldly experimental and mark a long-overdue departure from accepted practice. Privately, he was more than happy to submit its drafts to the judgment of experts and to consult fellow-scholars in all humility. Moreover, he read sections of it aloud, at the informal gatherings of his friends—in Berlin and in Heidelberg—presided over by the revered poet, who also made it a point to go over the text with a fine comb. (George was a superb editor, down to minutiae of proofreading.) The results of a project so auspiciously undertaken surpassed, however, the author's fondest expectations.

The personal reasons for Kantorowicz's triumphant mood in the early and mid-'twenties must have been even stronger. He had in hand the subject for a far-flung investigation which lay at a kind of magic intersection of several lines which to him were all crucially important. The setting and the historical moment he chose to investigate—the Crusades; a struggle for hegemony between Papal and Imperial forces; dynastic strife within a badly split Germany; and the polar-

---

und er sei so ganz Chevalier, wie man ihn nicht mehr sehe. Geschmeidig und doch männlich fest, weltmännisch, elegant in Kleidung, Geste und Sprache, hatte und hat Kantorowicz etwas von einem Florett-Fechter."

ization of ambitious, undaunted North Italian cities and the unique South Italian symbiosis of Arabic, Byzantine, French (Angevin), and Imperial German cultural streaks—were in themselves worthy of a saga, if not of a fairy tale. The *dramatis personae*—a German King and Roman Emperor who was born and died in Italy, the most powerful figure ever seated on the Papal throne (Innocent III), Sicilian and Aragonese princesses elevated to the rank of queen, a domineering and sophisticated chancellor viewed in his rise and downfall, to cite just a few conspicuous protagonists— could hardly have been more exciting, measured by the yardstick of expert and lay curiosity alike. More important, the political and cultural issues at stake were so gripping as to have captured the attention of Dante, a near-witness, in the past, and of Stefan George in the present. Moreover, European, in particular German, medievalistic scholarship had isolated this intricate complex of problems as a real key issue, clamoring for continued attention and improved inspection. Further, these same issues, by way of a separate dimension, concealed a relevant message for the intellectual leadership of our own time, a message inviting sagacious rephrasing. Finally, certain components of the situation— Frederick's yearning for the revival of an Italy-centered *imperium*, the presence and even prominence of Saracens and Jews in his Empire[19]—indisputably ap-

---

[19] The book on Frederick contains a scattering of noteworthy statements about the position of non-conformist Muslims and Jews, within the framework of the new concepts of "Staat" and "Empire" (see the Index, p. 642a). Most of them are innocuous enough and merely serve to convey the picture of motley crowds and the local *Mischkultur*. On the other hand, I refrain from speculating how the author may have felt about certain more controversial passages if he happened to reread them after 1933. See esp. pp. 244-46: "Denn nachdem er durch die Sarazenenverpflanzung die staatsfeindlichen und staatsverwirrenden Gifte

pealed to the classical scholar, to the widely traveled
student of Muslim culture, and to the strongly assimilated, but not entirely enucleated, German Jew in the
youthful historian.

The appearance, in 1927, of *Kaiser Friedrich II* had
the effect of a bombshell. Here was a fairly young man
—without so much, by way of preliminaries, as a single
learned article or book review to his credit, without a
doctoral thesis readily available for critique and circu-
lation—who, in a luxuriously printed 650-page book
devoid of footnotes, bibliography, and any other "ap-
paratus," offered an ornately styled, intensely personal
interpretation of a legend-ridden figure . . . and, all at
once, attracted thousands upon thousands of readers
bored by dry monographs, yet scornful of merely glittering, gaudy "biographies romancées." The book's
success was immediate; a second generous printing appeared the following year, opening the way for translations into Italian and English, and laying the ground
for a third printing in 1931, which before long likewise sold out.[20] But the academic Establishment, some-

---

der Muslims paralysiert hatte . . . ; Die Übertreter wurden mit
Güterkonfiskation oder, wenn sie arm waren, durch ein Brandmal
auf der Stirn bestraft—keineswegs aus religiöser Gehässigkeit,
sondern wegen der Ordnung im Staat." When the book was reissued in the German Federal Republic, Kantorowicz omitted the
Preamble, judging it "zeitbedingt," but left the remainder
untouched, alleging his inability to filter the flood of recent
investigations. One wonders whether the implied espousal of
enlightened absolutism which could be construed as a forerunner
and model of obscurantist totalitarianism did not constitute an
additional deterrent.

[20] The translation into Italian (two slim volumes) appeared in
1939, E. Lorimer's English version as early as 1931 (republished
in 1957, then again in 1967); these ventures involved only Vol. I
of the original (i.e., the interpretive part). The rumor of a
piracy in the German People's Republic turned out to be un-
founded, but a publisher residing in the German Federal Repub-

what as in the cases of Johan Huizinga's enormously
popular book on the waning of the Middle Ages, or,
for that matter, Arnold Toynbee's monumental undertaking, sensed a challenge and decided to mete out an
exemplary punishment to the defiant newcomer. In an
unsparingly abrasive review abounding in vitriolic re-
percussions, its influential spokesman Albert Brackmann, a scholar of formidable strength, denounced Kantorowicz as a mythographer rather than a historian.[21]
Other unenthusiastic specialists spoke of metahistory
or detected harmful definitional flaws amid the
plethora of pleasing metaphors.[22] Even critics recruited
from the ranks of personal friends (like Baethgen), who
could vouch for the challenger's intellectual honesty,
as tested by the "Kleinarbeit" which he had simply
elected to deëmphasize at the final stage, had a hard
time championing his cause and affixed a stamp of only
partial approval.[23] At a meeting of historians in Halle

lic launched an authorized edition after the war; see the preceding
footnote. The three pre-war editions of Vol. I (1927, 1928, 1931)
ran to a record-breaking total of 10,000 copies (see G. P. Landmann, *Stefan George und sein Kreis*, p. 140).

[21] For full details on the controversy between Brackmann (at
that juncture easily the most influential historian teaching at the
University of Berlin and a co-editor of the tone-setting *Historische
Zeitschrift*), R. Konetzke, and Kantorowicz, see my necrology
(1964) in *Romance Philology*, esp. pp. 6-8.

[22] Hampe (see note 25, below) quotes the Church historian W.
Köhler's negative reaction (1930) in the latter's book *Historie und
Metahistorie* and cites a still very young H. Baron (who was later
to join the staff of Newberry Library in Chicago) as wondering
whether Kantorowicz had any clear notion of the kind of "Antiquity" toward which his favorite medieval emperor gravitated in
his nostalgic visions.

[23] F. Baethgen's critique of the second printing (1928) of the
book appeared in *Deutsche Literaturzeitung* 51 (1930): cols.
75-85, and has been absorbed into the reviewer's omnibus volume
Mediaevalia: Aufsätze, Nachrufe, Besprechungen, Part II (Stuttgart, 1960), pp. 542-48. More compact than Hampe's meandering

the book became a butt of severe, no doubt caustic, attacks.

Kantorowicz, thus provoked, retaliated;[24] but far more effective than his rebuttal in silencing part of the

---

review article (see below) and chiefly concerned with underlying problems of methodology, it still makes excellent reading forty years after the original publication date. Transcending the limits of his assignment, the critic takes to task not only the author for occasional spasms of ecstasy and signs of insufficient self-criticism, but also the narrow specialists in the opposite camp for their pathetic inability to satisfy the reading public's legitimate demands and expectations. He then examines the inherent hazards of untrammeled subjectivism as opposed to those of a misguided quest for objectivity (through the untenable equation of the securely ascertainable with the truly significant) and, in the end, vigorously affirms the wisdom of engaging, under controlled conditions, in premature syntheses, with a view to counterbalancing the prevalent aridity of microscopic research and to experimenting with new and bold perspectives.

Baethgen's research is relevant to Kantorowicz's writings above all because, not unlike Walter Goetz and certain other German historians, he dealt on numerous occasions with Dante, at the risk of trespassing on the domain of literary scholarship. Particularly worthy of notice is the overlap with Kantorowicz's studies (1927, 1931, 1937)—which he adduces again and again—in his critical essay (1955) "Dante und Petrus de Vinea," reprinted in *Mediaevalia*, Part II, pp. 413-41. Important, too, is his extraordinarily substantial necrological article (1937) on Karl Hampe, an item opportunely absorbed into the same volume (pp. 480-93); as is his considerably later Kantorowicz necrology (1964), in which he reëxamined not a few of the same issues, seen this time from the vantage post of a man even more chastened through all manner of experiences and turns of fortune.

[24] Brackmann's aggressive review (originally a Berlin Academy lecture) provoked Kantorowicz's somewhat strident rebuttal "'Mythenschau': eine Erwiderung" in the *Historische Zeitschrift* 141 (1930): 457-71, which in turn led to Brackmann's appeasing surrebuttal, *ibid.*, 472-78. In the latter the critic deprecatingly referred to Baethgen's far more constructive reaction (see note 23, above). No doubt as a conciliatory gesture, Brackmann, in his capacity as co-editor of that key journal, shortly thereafter consented to publish Hampe's appraisal, a shade less cordially worded than Baethgen's and far more circumstantial; see below.

criticism was his production of what a luminary of Gundolf's prestige and such other George disciples as had preceded him in publishing unannotated monographs had never succeeded in accomplishing. Four years later, he issued a fairly thick supplement volume, containing only skeletal documentation plus a string of excursuses. Thus, the charge of impressionism and superficiality was removed, at the cost of four additional years of straight *Quellenforschung*—research performed at a feverish pace and this time unsweetened by the injection of elegant formulas and engaging metaphors.

After the publication of the Supplement, K. Hampe subjected the two-volume set to searching, dispassionate scrutiny in a masterly thirty-five-page review article which may well rank as the model of an impartial but by no means uncommitted balance sheet. Since that paper—aside from standing on its own feet as a superb clarification of an ensemble of specific historical problems—also represents the most trenchant critique of the young, but already seasoned, Kantorowicz's general approach to historiography and to new-style *Geisteswissenschaft*, it invites a liberal slice of attention in the context of this essay.[25]

[25] "Das neueste Lebensbild Kaiser Friedrichs II," *Historische Zeitschrift* 146 (1932): 441-75. It would, I venture to think, be most rewarding—mainly for those engrossed in the methodology of historical reconstruction—to see assembled for easy consultation and cross-indexed the stimulating, spirited reactions of Baethgen and Hampe (even, possibly, for good measure, Brackmann's angry attack flanked by Kantorowicz's counter-arguments). This material, properly sifted and critically weighed, might either appear as a separate pamphlet or as a supplement to a new edition of Kantorowicz's book. A compressed version of the book, ideally with an Epilogue from the pen of a younger scholar particularly attuned to such a delicate task, is another urgent desideratum. Cf., for one near-parallel, the useful condensation and revision—this time by the author himself—of H. Baron's *Crisis of the Early Italian Renaissance* (1966).

Placing both volumes in the mainstream of Frideri-
cian studies (those of the pioneers Huillard-Bréholles,
J. von Ficker, E. Winkelmann, and many younger
workers) and correctly gauging the relation of the high-
spirited 1927 venture to its 1931 Supplement, slightly
anticlimactic through sheer meticulosity, Hampe dis-
closes a startling paradox pervading the entire corpus
of these studies of the early thirteenth century. While
microscopic research has appreciably narrowed the margin of doubt concerning particular events and individual cross-connections, the pendulum has, for over a
century, been swinging with increasing wildness as regards the total interpretation ("Sinndeutung") of the
Emperor's personality, his entourage, and his reign.

Within this web of contradictions, Hampe thinks
Kantorowicz's book stands out by virtue of the author's
gift for synthesis, stylistic prowess, artistic intuition, and
exemplary exploitation of every conceivable source, however remote, to say nothing of the commendable avoidance of polemics and an admirable standard of over-all
tidiness. The book is not entirely aprioristic and con-
stitutes no obnoxious livre à thèse; however, Hampe
claims, it suffers from overinterpretation ("stark konstruktive Neigung," p. 445), insufficient restraint, and
an ineradicable—if gratifyingly witty—subjectivism. By
way of rebellion against the stifling orthodox study of
the ambiance, which was then fashionable, Kantorowicz
—in this a follower of Nietzsche [and, let me add,
of Carlyle]—may have overreacted by lifting a powerful personality, a man of genius, onto too high a pedes-
tal, and making the environment subservient to his
hero's "demon." Also, as Hampe points out, he has not
wholly eschewed the danger of confusing history and
myth—two domains, which, easily separable in the case
of a Caesar or a Charlemagne, tend to be blurred as

soon as saints, founders of religions and orders, and rulers or statesmen deeply immersed in religious struggles and disputations occupy the center of the stage. Any accurate historical reconstruction of Frederick's personality is almost unattainable, since his edicts and letters have been rhetorically stylized, hence adulterated, by the well-schooled staff of his chancery. Meritorious as one must deem Kantorowicz's eagerness to seize upon such shreds of oblique "mythic" information as legends, prophecies, fables, and anecdotes—which convey the exact local color and the authentic flavor of the period—he has too strongly identified himself with this make-believe world, operating, in the end, with number symbolism (p. 449) and cultivating other scholarly irrelevancies.

Adjoining exposed areas ("Gefahrenzonen") or weaknesses pointed out by Hampe include an excessive willingness to invoke the mysterious survival of pristine myths ("uralter Mythos," p. 450) where less glamorous alternatives are available; occasional indulgence in introspective ethnopsychology, which Kantorowicz himself must later have sorely regretted (pp. 450; 453, note 4; 463, note 1; 465); poetically suggestive, but analytically hazardous, projections of attitudes and relations onto a later or an earlier time-level, as if in tribute to a certain immanence or immutability ("so vermag ich auch mit der sonstigen, dichterisch vielleicht eindrucksvollen Konstruktion historisch nichts anzufangen," p. 451); a too suggestive, flamboyant formulation, redolent of the author's general aestheticism which seduces him into using an almost Baroque, even pompous, style (p. 466),[26] and his excessive vulnerability to

[26] It is not uninteresting to assemble the labels that a fault-finding Hampe tagged to his long inventory of objections to Kantorowicz's style (and styling): ". . . zu gehäufte . . . Verwen-

the lure of fine literature (as seen in the infelicitous chapter-heading "Wanderjahre," used in reference to the five years, 1215-20, Frederick spent in Germany, which clearly echoes the title of Goethe's masterpiece, p. 452); an inordinately minute depiction of lavish detail-studded scenes ("Kleinmalerei," p. 453) and an overelaborate dissection of abstruse doctrines, such as the Emperor's "Staatsmetaphysik" (p. 458); an inclination to favor Roman-Italian over French prototypes [as if, let me add on my own, to counterbalance J. Bédier] (pp. 453; 455, note 3; 457); a strained, overstressed confrontation of Frederick and Francesco d'Assisi, which would be more appropriate in legends or, for that matter, in the writings of a visionary like Dante, than in a sober scholarly monograph (p. 455); a too rashly posited "law," apropos of crusades, involving the inescapable roles of East and West in the rise of Western Empires, from Alexander of Macedon to Napoleon (p. 455); an unwarranted insistence on the difference between Fred-

---

dung solcher Rhetorik," "ein Missverhältnis zwischen Historie und Mythos" (p. 448); "die Gefahrenzonen" (p. 449; Baethgen detected "Schwierigkeiten und Gefahrenquellen . . . in drei Richtungen"); "die konstruktive Neigung des V[er]f[assers]" (p. 450); "übereilt," "recht unzutreffend bezeichnet" (p. 452); "gewaltsam übersteigert" (p. 453); "übersteigerte Bewertung seines Genies," "reichlich aufgebauscht" (p. 454); "geistvoll und anziehend, wenn auch nicht ohne einen gewissen konstruktiven Zwang," "zum mindesten in manchen Ausdrücken übersteigert," "zu sehr betont" (p. 455); "allzusehr zugespitzt" (p. 457); "gelegentlich zu weit gehen kann" (p. 458); etc. True, these demurrers and qualifications are, again and again, interspersed with the warmest commendations. Though both Baethgen and Hampe drew the line between poetry and scholarship at a considerable distance from the border favored by Kantorowicz, these sober historians were by no means insensitive antiquarians or arid specialists. They simply placed the search for unvarnished truth above the more glamorous search for relevance ("Sinn").

erick's absolutism and the enlightened, liberal rationalism of seventeenth- and eighteenth-century monarchies.

Nothing better characterizes the contrast between Kantorowicz and Hampe than the former's ("idealistic") willingness to view the Emperor's Sicilian experiment in political structure as emanating from a certain intrinsic metaphysics, whereas the latter, in a "realistic vein," sees local real-life conditions and older traditions as the prime controlling factors, later philosophically rationalized by that brilliant chancellor Petrus de Vinea (p. 457). Hampe also disagrees with the pervasive idealization of the Emperor's character (pp. 463f.) and, in his dissent, candidly endows the monarch with many adverse traits: outbursts of anger, sallies of arrogance, spells of vindictiveness, erroneous strategy stemming from poor judgment, and the like, denying him above all the power of unerring divination (p. 465). With Franz Kampers (1929) and against Kantorowicz, Hampe, in conclusion, does recognize Frederick as the trail-blazer of the Renaissance (p. 469)—even in its progressive rather than its merely restorative facets.

Despite all these reservations, consistently free of sarcasm, Hampe stresses time and again the brilliance of the whole book and the excellence of individual sections, especially Chapter VII, "Caesar and Rome." Averring that the skeleton bequeathed by Ficker and Winkelmann has now emerged generously filled out with flesh and blood (p. 467) and very graciously begging forgiveness for tearing certain controversial passages from their context in an effort to winnow out objective history and to discard the embroidery of legend (p. 472), he grants that what fundamentally separates author and critic may well be a difference of temperaments (p. 475). In conclusion he calls the younger scholar's disquisitions "stets geistvoll und glänzend formuliert" (p. 472), and cheerfully admits the book's charm (p. 474) and originality (p. 475).

The extraordinary reverberations of Kantorowicz's *magnum opus* soon began to mold his academic career.[27] The fall semester of 1930 witnessed him teaching medieval history at the relatively young and experimentally inclined University of Frankfurt, with the rank of Honorarprofessor, which still placed him at the periphery of the faculty. Two years later he was promoted to the coveted chair (i.e., a full professorship with certain executive powers attached to it) in the field of his advanced research, as a successor to Fedor Schneider —though technically, as a student, he had earned his spurs in other subjects. There was a scintilla of irony in this switch; but it was even more ironic that, no sooner than he had established himself in the academic teaching profession, the advent to power of the Hitlerites, at first in coalition with the conservative monarchists, almost immediately weakened this arch-conservative's precarious foothold in the university. True, his excellent war record made it possible for him to discharge his routine duties for a while, but only under humiliating conditions and in an indescribable atmosphere of chauvinistic bedlam (the full flavor of which the writer of these lines personally savored that summer, albeit in Berlin).

In November 1933 Oxford's New College issued Kantorowicz an invitation to spend one year in England, as a kind of senior research fellow. Amid all the chaos and a thousand disappointments he was still hesitant

[27] The biographic data in this section are based in part on Baethgen's necrology, which—appropriately—involved a bit of "Quellenforschung," in part on personal recollections of Kantorowicz's Berkeley friends.

to break off his commitment in Frankfurt, especially vis-à-vis a small circle of devoted and enthusiastic junior initiates. But even though he was willing to swallow his pride, the rampaging squads of goons and stormtroopers among the academic brownshirts, eager to push forward the frontier of the Cultural Revolution, now put an end to his teaching. So he went to England on a limited leave of absence, and the fruits of his stay there are embodied in a fine, lengthy article marking his gradual transition from a German- to an English-speaking public.[28] Upon returning to his homeland, he found that Hitler's formal elevation from the chancellorship of the Reich to the presidency or headship had created a new climate. All professors in good standing were now expected to swear an oath of personal allegiance to *Der Führer*. This Kantorowicz decided not to do; recoiling for the first time from an unwelcome, not to say obtrusive, loyalty oath, he tendered his formal resignation in October 1934, after just three years of active service. In the end, however, he decided to remain in Germany except for travels to France, Belgium, and Italy. This hesitation almost cost him his life.

The reluctance of so meritorious and so eminently successful a scholar as Kantorowicz, then in the prime of life, to leave his native Germany spontaneously, even in the face of ignominious treatment, and to seek elsewhere a position worthy of his talent and promise certainly calls for comment. Several plausible reasons for his wavering come to mind. While he would have been barred from teaching after the enactment of the "Nuremberg Laws" (1935), his property was not immediately confiscated and he could, for a while, travel freely—

---

[28] "Petrus de Vinea in England," *Mitteilungen des Österreichischen Instituts für Geschichtsforschung* 51 (1937): 43-88; reprinted in *Selected Studies*, pp. 213-46.

a privilege of which he did avail himself. He had a comfortable apartment in West Berlin's secluded Schaperstrasse and visibly enjoyed the use of his private library, patiently collected with the finesse of a connoisseur. A small estate near Plön in the lake-studded "Mecklenburgische Schweiz" remained his property, and some close relatives were also living out their lives in the inhospitable country, despite the degradation to be endured. Advanced research was still possible, although only because those archivists and paleographers who constituted the hard-core staff of the Monumenta were too gentlemanly and too aloof from politics to interfere with an ostracized scholar's daily visits. Finally, there may have been a glimmer of hope that the nightmare would soon come to a harmless end: Kantorowicz's deep-seated German patriotism had not yet completely evaporated, and some of his many friends recruited from the circles of higher Prussian aristocracy maintained unswerving loyalty toward him, all risks notwithstanding, as if to prove their independence amid all the servile conformism. A clinching argument may conceivably have been that his one-year visit to England, for all its friendliness, convinced him that he was not suited for living and working abroad, at least not on a permanent basis.

The years 1933-38 must have been the dreariest in Kantorowicz's life, punctuated as they were by the defection of many a trusted friend of long standing[29] and,

[29] There is hardly any need for ferreting out unsavory details which are off the record. On the record, however, is the fact, by no means isolated, that a book by K. Hildebrandt originally titled *Norm und Entartung des Menschen* (1923), flanked by that same year's parallel study *Norm und Entartung des Staates*, reappeared in 1939 under the new composite title, enriched by a bouquet of racism: *Norm, Entartung, Verfall; bezogen auf den Einzelnen, die Rasse, den Staat*. Significantly, the turning point

worse, by the gnawing realization that his own and his group's implied extolment—on the level of lofty discourse and through the enchanting prism of the Middle Ages—of autocracy and authoritarianism had paved the way for the acceptance by countless weak-kneed or uncritical intellectuals (above all, university students) of the new, unspeakably brutal variety of tyranny. In this depressing atmosphere of disillusionment and remorse, Kantorowicz's own technical research, not surprisingly, made headway far more haltingly than might otherwise have been anticipated in view of its brisk start.[30] Toward the end of the baneful year of the German Revolution George passed away, in voluntary Swiss exile. Kantorowicz, as has now been established in minute detail, took an active part in the unusual rites surrounding the poet's funeral—an event which to him,

---

goes back to 1928, when the author published three lectures under the title *Staat und Rasse*. In his *Erinnerungen*, pp. 120-24, 245f, 247, Hildebrandt tries to reduce his involvement to a mere infelicity of wording (*Rassenhygiene*, he argues, to him meant merely 'eugenics') and even claims credit for a subtly hidden polemic with A. Rosenberg (cf. my note 32, below). In this he is disingenuous, as I can assert from personal observation of his lectures (Berlin, 1933). Hildebrandt, Thormaehlen, and others of their ilk all flirted with the "völkische Bewegung," without mustering the courage to espouse it in all its hideousness or to reject it at heavy risk to life, limb, and career. Only the brothers Stauffenberg took that ultimate irreversible step.

[30] The Autobibliography (1965) lists, for the mid- and late 'thirties, only a slender pamphlet (*Die Wiederkehr gelehrter Anachorese im Mittelalter*) and the text of an erudite radio lecture bursting with timely innuendoes which a daredevil Kantorowicz delivered under dramatic circumstances, outwitting the Third Reich's monitoring officers ("Deutsches Papsttum"). To this must be added the item mentioned in note 28, above. For a lively and sympathetic sketch of Kantorowicz at Oxford, there are now available to us—as Arthur R. Evans, Jr., reminds me—C. M. Bowra's highly readable *Memories, 1898-1929* (Harvard University Press, 1967), pp. 286-91, 294-96, 303-305, 329; photograph, p. 244.

more than to the other participants, must have con-
noted the end of an era.[31] Far less transparent, to this
day, are the moral and the ideological implications of
George's withdrawal from the German scene after
the seizure of power by the National Socialists.

In their search for prestigious cultural patrons of
their movement, which still reeked of the gutter and
beer garden, the more pretentious Nazi leaders, flushed
with easy victory, were tempted to seduce into meek collaboration that proud and aged outsider George—who
appeared to them engagingly fanatic and, above all, un-
stained by any contact with the odious, venal culture of
the Weimar Republic. With a dramatic flourish, Goebbels hastened to offer him the honorary presidency of
Germany's Dichterakademie. Another faction of the
party (strongly entrenched in the old Munich headquarters), mindful of George's suspiciously close association with Jewish intellectuals over an unbroken
period of forty years, strongly demurred, but obviously
lost out in the ensuing struggle.[32] It is a fact that in the

---

[31] On George's death and burial see Thormaehlen's accurate
array of data (*Erinnerungen*, pp. 288-90). Kantorowicz, one of the
pall-bearers and participants in the solemn vigil, may have come
all the way from England. As background reading for this account
I recommend Hansjürgen Linke's *Das Kultische in der Dichtung
Stefan Georges und seiner Schule*, 2 vols. (Munich and Düsseldorf: Helmut Küpper, 1960), passim.

[32] A well-informed Thormaehlen (pp. 282f) describes the Nazi
ideologist A. Rosenberg, who had fallen under the sway of the
pioneer racist Dietrich Eckardt, as spearheading the opposition
to Goebbels' stratagem, which, on the other hand, received support from B. Rust, the new minister of culture and education.
Thormaehlen further muses that sometime before 1914 A. Schuler,
a disgruntled member of the Circle (see note 17, above), may have
met a very young and completely unknown Austrian yokel, Adolf
Hitler, as a stout drinking companion in a coachmen's pub attached to a Munich inn, and may at that time have sown in the
(frustrated and preconditioned) lad's head the seeds of "rationalized" vicious anti-Semitism. (The possibility that Hitler may

early 'thirties the increasingly self-centered members of
the George group remained unaware of, or insensitive
to, the dangers of the cataclysm looming on the horizon.
No George partisan at that turning point mustered the
strength to write a pamphlet, still less a book, remotely
comparable in exhortatory *élan* to Curtius' eloquent—
and sensationally successful—plea, *Deutscher Geist in
Gefahr* (1932).

In the first few months of the Revolution, George, as
has now become clear, took a distressingly ambiguous
stand toward the new regime. He found a pretext for
declining the major honor offered him, but patently derived pleasure from other, minor tokens of belated recognition; he was not unduly alarmed—judging from
remarks dropped in private conversation—by the pan-
demic ingredients of arbitrariness, violence, and cruelty;
he rejoiced at seeing part of his program and rhetoric
translated into reality, instead of disavowing the path
leading from *Das Neue Reich* (1928) to "Das Dritte
Reich" (1933); and he unequivocally regarded the vicious discrimination against Jews as, to be sure, regret-
table but, on balance, a matter of subordinate importance. What irritated him most was the fact—in retrospect, so trivial—that his sister had been requested to
prove the purity of the family's pedigree. At the poet's
last birthday party in fashionable West Berlin, the small
residue of the members of his group who gathered
around him viewed the emergent political situation as
basically salutary (since the pendulum had swung to the
right), shrugging off the all too visible excesses as so
many unavoidable temporary blemishes. It is difficult

---

have attended some of Schuler's lectures privately sponsored by
the publisher Hugo Bruckmann in the early 'twenties must now
be ruled out for cogent chronological reasons; see Boehringer,
Mein Bild, 2nd edn., pp. 249f.)

not to apply the tag of senility to George for his un-
heroic attitude and the stigma of indifference and
naïveté, if not of plain stupidity or opportunism, to
at least some of his youthful followers;[33] sensibility,
the hallmark of poets and aesthetes, had given way to
callousness, and the cult of moral fiber to bland acceptance of a *fait accompli*. Against this background of disappointment, vexing to a man as delicately strung as
Kantorowicz, one can readily see how his long-drawn-
out involvement with the Circle was bound to shrink
and shrivel to a nostalgic recollection of some deeply
moving encounters and experiences in happier years, a
treasure now irretrievably lost.[34]

The poetic formulation of this kind of disillusion-

[33] For George's, all told, less than impressive stance see Thormaehlen's report (pp. 281-87) of conversations overheard at the
poet's sixty-fifth birthday party, i.e., on July 12, 1933—a report,
be it said in fairness, depicting George as showing greater appre-
hension about the future than did his exuberant young followers,
who were carried away by the fresh winds of the "German
Spring." Distinctly more damaging is the last entry in E. Landmann's unretouched diary (Sept. 19, 1933): "Über das Politisch-
Aktuelle sagte er mir in Berlin, was er wohl allen Älteren sagte,
denen gegenüber er die Jungen in Schutz nahm, es sei doch
immerhin das erste Mal, das Auffassungen, die er vertreten habe,
ihm von aussen wiederklängen. Und als ich auf die Brutalität
der Formen hinwies: Im Politischen gingen halt die Dinge anders.
Bei der letzten Unterredung [i.e., Sept. 19] erklärte er, was die
Juden betrifft: . . . so ist mir die Judensach im Besonderen nicht
so wichtig" (p. 209). For additional stray shreds of information
on this painfully weak reaction see Hildebrandt, *Erinnerungen*,
pp. 232-34.

[34] Further fuel was added by such ostentatious and fulsome
joint dedications of learned books to the two leaders, Hitler and
George, as the one prefixled to E. Wechssler's *Jugendreihen des
deutschen Menschen, 1733-1933* (Leipzig, 1934). How George
reacted to such dual homages I do not know; Wechssler displayed
in the Romance Seminar Room of the Friedrich Wilhelm University a grateful Führer's citation. It is not difficult to imagine
Kantorowicz's anguish.

ment is found in Karl Wolfskehl's collection of poems *Die Stimme spricht,* perhaps the most powerful German-Jewish reaction in the 'thirties to the surge of anti-Semitism.[35] Kantorowicz, who lacked his inspired senior friend's religious convictions, Zionist excitement, and grounding in classical and medieval Hebrew,[36] could only mourn the total erosion of the pattern of his life. With this gloomy picture we must take leave of Stefan George's crumbling empire, except to recall that a junior member of the Circle, Count Claus von Stauffenberg—one of three gifted brothers conspicuously devoted to the aging poet—as if to redeem this shameful internal collapse of Germany's erstwhile élite, eleven years later volunteered to serve as one of the leaders of (and, subsequently, the prime scapegoat for) the German officer corps' unsuccessful conspiracy against Hitler. It was he, in fact, who planted the ill-fated bomb in the Führer's headquarters and thus, unwittingly, set in motion the final purge that engulfed himself and countless close friends.[37]

[35] Of particular relevance to Kantorowicz's experiences is Wolfskehl's poem *An die Deutschen* (Zürich, 1947), composed between 1933 (Rome) and 1944 (New Zealand). As the author's own explanatory post-script makes plain, the oldest stanza of this half-poetic, half-polemic "Auseinandersetzung" is: "Eure Kaiser sind auch meine." It ends with the evocation of, of all monarchs, Emperor Frederick the Second: "Und zum wahrsten Gibellinen / Friedrich, aller Kronen Kron, / Eilten, Guts und Bluts zu dienen, / Jude, Christ und Wüstensohn." Interestingly, it was Wolfskehl who revived the formula "Geheimes Deutschland" which dominates the Preamble to Kantorowicz's *magnum opus.* See Salin, *Um Stefan George,* p. 324.

[36] Though Kantorowicz's Judaism was far more subdued and residual than Wolfskehl's and even than Gundolf's, it breaks through in his intense intellectualism, in the cosmopolitan sweep of his curiosity, in a studied restraint from extremist positions and all manner of intoxication, and, generally, in a conciliatory attitude further tempered by steady concern for fairness.

[37] On the three brothers Stauffenberg—Alexander, Berthold,

The "Kristallnacht" of November 1938—to use the exquisite paraphrase for what, in coarser parlance, amounted to a pogrom—put an abrupt end to this uncertain, defeatist stretch of our historian's lifespan. Kantorowicz went into hiding; then escaped across the Dutch border with the help of some courageous Gentile friends; and, after a brief stop-over at Oxford, found himself transplanted to New York, an always overcrowded megalopolis which by then had become saturated to the point of surfeit with all manner of dislodged politicians, displaced scholars, and dispossessed representatives of the European middle class. Having never before been exposed to the needs and problems of a realistic wage-earner, an exhausted Kantorowicz had to learn fairly late in life—he was then forty-four—the indelicate and unceremonious art of job-hunting and soliciting assistance, in short, of "antichambrieren," in a context in which his charisma could no longer be relied upon to work. Fortunately, not all doors at which he was advised to knock proved unfriendly. The metropolitan Emergency Committee for Displaced Scholars granted him almost at once a modest one-year stipend which would have enabled him to spend a year of profitable research and adjustment at Johns Hopkins. But even before he made that move, Kantorowicz was lucky enough to be offered, and foresighted enough to accept, a lecturership at the University of California at Berkeley, where his strangely fragmented teaching career was to reach its all-time summit.[38]

---

and Claus (of whom two perished in the 1944 purge)—see the oft-quoted, indexed books by Boehringer (with photographs) and Thormaehlen; on Claus, see also Salin, pp. 324 and 339.

[38] While biding his time in the East, Kantorowicz attended an annual meeting of the Mediaeval Academy of America. The "lectureship" that California offered him implied no diminution of his academic status except administratively; all foreign schol-

In a way, Kantorowicz came to the West Coast unprepared. Advanced medieval and Byzantine studies, as understood on the Continent, were not exactly flourishing in between-the-wars America, so that Kantorowicz's connections with this country's native experts had been tenuous. Also, the general attitude toward the United States fostered in the George Circle was, for a variety of reasons, far from friendly or even so much as objective —judging from the available record of arrogant, sarcastic remarks; the one major exception was the humanistically-oriented social scientist E. Salin.[39] An enforced transfer to the western rim of the New World and the adjustment to an unfamiliar milieu amid the pressures of the busiest campus of America's most explosive state university must, consequently, have been extremely painful to an aristocratic scholar as spoiled and fastidious as was Kantorowicz. It is, therefore, all the more noteworthy that his gratitude and loyalty to the United States were unwaveringly sincere. Even in

ars newly engaged on that campus past a certain cut-off point were provisionally so categorized until the end of the war. (Several European necrologists missed this point.)

[39] See E. Landmann, Gespräche, esp. p. 172 (American universities); also pp. 201 (Negroes), 202 (evil effects of California's gold rush), 207 (collective type of human being produced by a mass-civilization), and the other passages recorded in the Index s.v. Amerika. Salin (b. 1892), on the other hand, submitted in 1914 and later published a Heidelberg dissertation titled Goldwäscherei und Goldbergbau am Klondike und in Alaska and that same year published, as Supplement XII to the Archiv für Sozialwissenschaft und Sozialpolitik, the obviously related monograph Die wirtschaftliche Entwicklung von Alaska (und Yukon Territory); ein Beitrag zur Geschichte und Theorie der Konzentrationsbewegung. In 1908 the young Gundolf devoted a review article to two publications involving Emerson. As early as 1920, Karl Wolfskehl, restless as ever, toyed with the idea of spending at least a few years in this country, despite serious misgivings; see the Letters Nos. 4 and 10 in Briefe und Aufsätze, München 1925-1933, ed. M. Ruben (Hamburg, 1966).

unguarded moments, when he could enjoy relaxed conversation with fellow-Europeans, he refrained from any wholesale condemnation of American culture, while occasionally voicing specific reservations.[40] Significantly, when offered a chance, after 1945, to return with high honors to his Frankfurt chair with further prospects of a truly meteoric career and an explosive range of influence, Kantorowicz declined, opting for continued service at Berkeley.

Kantorowicz spent a total of twelve years in California—not, to be sure, years of euphoria or ecstasy, but at least of intensive, deeply gratifying, and richly rewarding inquiries and human contacts. The need to express himself orally, as well as in writing, in a language of which he had a less than artistic command had a sobering effect: it filtered his verbal exuberance, so to speak, and helped him guard against any indulgence in such fireworks ("Überspitzungen") as his benevolent critics Hampe and Baethgen had warned him against in reviewing his earlier book. It is, indeed, the second central thesis of this paper that removal to an unfamiliar culture and the enforced adoption of a new vehicle of

[40] Privately, Kantorowicz found himself in disagreement with the positivistic strain in American historiography, i.e., with the widespread belief in the "dignity of facts" neatly established for their own sake and in isolation, or, as younger scholars would say, of "unstructured" facts. Perhaps he also lamented the atomization of knowledge. On one occasion, he deprecated the prevalent assumption, on this side of the Atlantic, that the "new and exciting" historical events were necessarily those occurring before our eyes, whereas European intellectuals derived their keenest satisfaction from reconstructing the mosaic of prehistory and earliest history, which they cherished as a reservoir of ceaseless surprises. Kantorowicz's view would have been better balanced had he taken into account the splendid work of American anthropologists; but unlike Olschki, who established a pleasant rapport with A. L. Kroeber, Kantorowicz had few if any contacts who might have enlightened him.

communication, imperfectly controlled at the start, can in the end have a purifying, cathartic effect on a certain type of strong-willed humanist. Kantorowicz emerged cleansed from his ordeal, and his style, including presentation and phrasing, became distinctly leaner and more chastened.[41]

He had a small following of carefully selected, enthusiastic students, who were thoroughly aware of the uniqueness of their teacher's qualifications and of their own unequaled opportunity. His reading of individual papers before faculty groups, his lecture courses, and, even more, his seminars were in a class by themselves; also, to put it colloquially, they "had real class." Some of his advanced disciples wrote publishable doctoral dissertations under his guidance and later became productive scholars in their own right; at least one, Ralph E. Giesey, engaged in gratifyingly close collaboration with his former teacher.[42]

[41] The switch to English involved not only a retreat from any excessive individualism, not to say mannerism, in stylistic matters, but also the renunciation of typographic pretentiousness. Henceforth the idea of separating text from footnotes became unacceptable to Kantorowicz; in fact, when the journal *Speculum*, for the sake of economy, started experimenting with this arrangement, he lodged a vigorous protest (at least in conversation), perhaps oblivious of the parallel in his own earlier practice.

[42] Two particularly faithful students, Michael Cherniavsky and Ralph E. Giesey, are responsible for organizing the posthumous volume of *Selected Studies*. Giesey's monograph, *The Royal Funeral Ceremony in Renaissance France* (and certain unpublished slivers of material collected in preparing it) nourished, through mutual agreement, Chapter VII of Kantorowicz's *The King's Two Bodies*. Other Berkeley students who, like Cherniavsky and Giesey, later succeeded one another as Kantorowicz's research assistants at the Institute for Advanced Study, were Robert L. Benson, Margaret Bentley Ševčenko, William M. Bowsky, William A. Chaney, George H. Williams, and Shafer Williams; their respective rôles are specified in the appreciative Preface to that book. Ihor Ševčenko was the expert, temporarily appointed

Kantorowicz, though no longer a young man, was sufficiently elastic—and enough of a conversational catalyst—to establish a new network of valuable friendships. Among the original Berkeley faculty he encountered upon his arrival, he greatly esteemed that versatile polygraph Max Radin (1880-1950), a jurisprudent by technical training, an essayist, cultural historian, and encyclopedically curious and competent humanist by avocation and self-improvement. Through the strangest of coincidences, the two friends discovered that not only their intellectual proclivities, but even characteristic segments of their biographic trajectories, bore a striking mutual resemblance.[43] In the conclud-

---

to a teaching position in Berkeley's History Department, under whose direction several dissertations stimulated by Kantorowicz but left unfinished at the time of his transfer were expeditiously completed. One of Kantorowicz's students at Princeton, Thomas N. Bisson, now teaches history at Berkeley.

[43] Like Kantorowicz, Radin was born in the Province of Posen, at Kepno (which he preferred to call Kempen), but his family immigrated to America when he was barely four years old. Radin went through the New York City school and college system, earning his Ph.D. at Columbia (1909) and reaching Berkeley (1919) via the City College. He shared Kantorowicz's intensive concern with Antiquity (*Marcus Brutus*, 1939) and with religion (*The Trial of Jesus of Nazareth*, 1931), but stressed more heavily the juridical aspect of past cultures (*Handbook of Roman Law*, 1927) and was far more actively interested in Judaism (*The Jews among the Greeks and the Romans*, 1915). He was not only fabulously prolific, but also slightly facile, stooping in moments of weakness to popularization (*The Law and You*, 1948) and even compiling reference works (witness the posthumous *Law Dictionary*, ed. Lawrence G. Greene, 1955)—weaknesses which Kantorowicz condoned in others, but strictly eschewed himself. While the project of a *Festschrift* for Max Radin came to naught, his brother Paul, a politically controversial anthropologist also connected with Berkeley for many years, was later honored with a magnificent volume *Culture in History* (ed. S. Diamond; New York, 1960). From personal experience I can readily see in Max Radin what—aside from human warmth and innate articulateness—fascinated

ing years of his stay in California, Kantorowicz's favorite project was an ambitious *Festschrift*, designed to honor the much-admired senior colleague on his retirement (and seventieth birthday). The plan failed to materialize, Max Radin died that same year, and Kantorowicz moved away to the East, somewhat reluctantly if not under duress. But when, in more than a lustrum of additional concentrated labor, he expanded the slender article originally earmarked for inclusion in that miscellany into a major hard-cover book—namely *The King's Two Bodies*, which was the fruition of his final large-scale venture—he made it a point to dedicate the book to the memory of Radin, evoking in his Preface with perceptible nostalgia the flavor of his Berkeley years, which marked the peak of his prime of life and another treasure irrevocably lost.

In addition to its members of early vintage, for the most part of old American stock, the Berkeley faculty at that time sheltered a rather motley crowd of foreign (overwhelmingly Central European) intellectuals, not a few of them refugees, with whom Kantorowicz maintained cordial social and academic relations. The "Arbeitsgemeinschaft" that effectively tied, indeed welded, them together throughout the 'forties was the newly founded *Colloquium Orientologicum*, which sponsored monthly one-hour evening lectures on campus followed by formal periods of lengthy discussion, with intellectually spiced social gatherings in divers pri-

---

Kantorowicz. No other student of jurisprudence in the American West would show the same unquenchable historico-philological curiosity and a comparable finesse and *Einfühlung*. If Radin occasionally discussed with me, a rank beginner at the time, subtle issues of Old French and Old Provençal exegesis, I can readily imagine how stimulating must have been his wide-ranging conversations with a historian in his prime.

vate homes frequently added for good measure.[44] In these contexts Kantorowicz, then still exuding strength and verve, was invariably the star performer, charming everyone by the latitude of his knowledge, the pointedness of his queries, and the elegance of his manners as a gastronomically refined host. His leadership, rooted in initiative, came naturally and was universally accepted as a matter of course. At these meetings one readily identified a kernel of regular participants, as distinct from an equally welcome fringe of occasional visitors; guests from other universities, including foreigners, particularly enjoyed watching the proceedings of this cosmopolitan group. At a typical session in the late 'forties one could expect to see the Austrian art historian, archeologist, and reconstructor of ancient caravan routes and oasis cultures Otto J. Maenchen (d. 1968); the German polyglot Orientalist and former museum director from Berlin Ferdinand D. Lessing, a close associate of Sven Hedin's and an expert in Tibetan and Mongolian, quite apart from his familiarity with exotic religions and traditions in visual arts; the worldly Russian Sinologist Peter A. Boodberg, a scion of Baltic nobility; the Dante and Marco Polo scholar, also a specialist in the records of Renaissance science, Leonardo Olschki (whom a very young Kantorowicz had run across in Heidelberg); the Sinitically oriented sociologist Wolfram Eberhard and his scholarly wife, both from Berlin; the self-centered Polish-Russian devotee of comparative literature Wacław Lednicki; the German authority on Romanesque art Walter W. Horn, a loyal disciple of Erwin Panofsky's; the much younger Göt-

[44] On the early history of the *Colloquium*, in general, and on Kantorowicz's generous share in the incipient phase of that venture, in particular, see my earlier statement in *Romance Philology* 18 (1964-65): 12-14.

tingen-born Hispanist (and, later, convert to Old Chinese studies), Hans H. Frankel and his father, the noted Ovid scholar, who would come over from nearby Stanford; the German-trained student of the Middle East Walter J. Fischel, imported via Israel; the Argentine Hellenist, medievalist, and Renaissance scholar María Rosa Lida de Malkiel; the explorers of ancient science and philosophy Ludwig and Emma Edelstein, both of Heidelberg background, who later went to Johns Hopkins; and many other celebrities. They all mixed very animatedly with a no less lively crowd of Americans, among whom Harold Cherniss, the specialist in ancient Greek philosophy (whose path was later to cross Kantorowicz's again in Princeton at the Institute for Advanced Study) deserves separate mention. Somewhat aloof from this close-knit philological coterie stood a younger man of exceptional brilliance and intensity, again from Germany, the musicologist Manfred Bukofzer. Neither a "Salonlöwe" nor a habitué of the Colloquium but a compulsive, many-sided researcher, Bukofzer teamed up with Kantorowicz in 1946 to produce a joint hymnological monograph—narrow-gauged but of major importance because it straddles Late Antiquity and the Middle Ages—on the *Laudes Regiae,* i.e., religious and royal acclamations.

Not surprisingly, this community's general state of happiness, security, and protection from both rote and coercion, visible throughout the 'forties and especially after the conclusion of the war, was reflected in a rapidly growing number of shorter publications by Kantorowicz (see items 11-27 of the Autobibliography). As late as 1948 all these studies were worded in English. Typical of the pioneering spirit informing this phase of his production is the fact that numerous articles, notes, and book reviews appeared in early volumes of newly launched periodicals, such as the *Journal of the Warburg and Courtauld Institutes, Medievalia et Humanistica, Comparative Literature, Medieval and Renaissance Studies*. A few years later Kantorowicz also lent his support to *Romance Philology*, a fledgling quarterly then struggling for recognition. Distinctly older publications, including *Harvard Theological Review, Art Bulletin*, and *Classical Philology*, also received their proper share of occasional or even sustained patronage, and one instance of joint authorship, with George L. Haskins, is likewise on record. Characteristic of Kantorowicz's *noblesse* and ability to cultivate academic friendships—both traits inherited from the years of his zestful participation in the George movement—was his readiness, here observable for the first time and later even more strongly accentuated, to reserve some of his finest writings for all manner of homage and testimonial ventures,[45] a practice which was a notoriously poor "investment," as he surely realized. Topically, the articles show an astonishing amplitude, ranging from the history of ideas (e.g., "Plato in the Middle Ages," "The Problem of Medieval World Unity") to salient chapters of Papal history, hymnology, and, above all, the iconographic projection of the medieval conceptual cosmos.

It is otiose to speculate where this idyllic existence in the "Athens of the West" would eventually have led, just as it is gratuitous, nay, morbid, to muse what direction Kantorowicz's life and research might have taken had he, through a caprice of circumstances, been acceptable to Germany's dogmatic rulers in 1933. Kan-

[45] The roster of friends and colleagues so honored, over the years, includes the following names: Alfred Weber (1948), Albrecht Bernstorff (1952), Karl Reinhardt (1952), Albert Mathias Friend, Jr. (1955), Ernst Langlotz (1957), Erwin Panofsky (1961), P. Thomas Michels, OSB (1963), Theodor Klauser (1964).

torowicz was so satisfied with having, at long last, achieved a certain equilibrium and was so distinctly, so radiantly at ease in Berkeley that no overtures from other universities, not even a feeler or tentative offer from the University of Chicago—undoubtedly lucrative —could deflect him from the straight path. It is against this background of contentment that one must judge his sudden alienation from, and his ultimate severance of all ties with, the Berkeley campus as a result of the infamous Loyalty Oath controversy.

The history of that crisis (1949-51), which for the first time made Berkeley known the world over as the scene of a *cause célèbre* in regard to academic freedom, has been chronicled elsewhere[46] and need not be reviewed here. In retrospect, it is not unfair to sum up the events by stating that the Regents, administration, and faculty literally blundered into an almost pointless head-on collision. Initially, a large section of the faculty was disposed to resist the Regents' stiff (and, quite obviously, both unwarranted and offensive) demand, triggered by the intolerance of the "McCarthy Era," for each professor's explicit declaration of political loyalty, a show

[46] The best-known and by far the most readable book-length treatment of the issue, *The Year of the Oath: The Fight for Academic Freedom at the University of California* (Garden City, N.Y.: Doubleday, 1950), by George R. Stewart in collaboration with other professors at the University of California, has the disadvantage of amounting to a mere mid-way report, confined as it is to the events of the opening year of the estrangement (1949-50). It was the bitter aftermath, as regards both formal litigation and the chilling of personal relations between erstwhile friends, that added poignancy to the crisis. Kantorowicz's own position and motivation were outlined in *The Fundamental Issue: Documents and Marginal Notes on the University of California Loyalty Oath* (San Francisco, 1958). Included in both books is a dossier of documents, among them Kantorowicz's Statement read before the Academic Senate on June 14, 1949, and his letter to President R. G. Sproul dated October 4, 1949.

of patriotism enforced under threat of dismissal regardless of tenure. As the pressure of the unbending Board of Regents increased, numerous recalcitrant faculty members, unable to withstand the tightening of the vice, humiliatingly enough, reversed themselves, and therein lies perhaps the essence of the tragedy, because deep rifts developed, especially among intimate friends, between the apostates and the perseverers. Kantorowicz and his alter ego Olschki, mindful of the scandalous complacency of German scholars in 1933, belonged to the necessarily small nucleus of those who, to the bitter end, refused to compromise with the Establishment. Kantorowicz, of course, vividly recalled his brush with an earlier loyalty oath issue (1934). With the noted psychologist Edward C. Tolman, he acted as the dynamic spokesman for the most articulate—or, as their opponents felt, most obdurate—faction of liberals and, in the end, successfully sued the Regents. The affair may have cost him five of the best years of his life, in terms of energy sapped. His vocal stewardship of an avowedly liberal cause, startling (as he himself admitted) against the backdrop of his own earlier staunch, indeed militant, conservatism, gave unusual poignancy to his stand. The widely quoted letter that he addressed on that occasion to an unhappy President Robert Gordon Sproul and the forty-page pamphlet that he wrote, privately issued, and distributed, presumably at his own expense (see note 46, above), made him overnight a hero in circles which would never have bothered to look into his esoteric scholarly writings.

One component of Kantorowicz's forthright position, almost overlooked twenty years ago but extraordinarily relevant under today's changed conditions, is the fact that his stand against outside constraint and interference was dictated by his deep, abiding respect for the dignity and relative autonomy of learning and teaching "for their own sake"—a reverential attitude toward the crystallization and transmission of knowledge (in which it is, incidentally, permissible to recognize a faint echo of ancestral Judaism,[47] reinforced by a legacy of German idealism). By the same token, Kantorowicz unequivocally declared himself against campus strikes, as being detrimental to the cause of learning, hence counterproductive. He failed to perceive any cogent analogy to the labor–management relationship. By staging a strike, he argued, teachers and students hit, first and foremost, themselves, irresponsibly depriving each other of a potentially unique chance for a great cognitive experience (and, in the process, unwittingly dignifying the role of administrative bureaucrats).

In 1951 Kantorowicz transferred permanently to the East, accepting—after the brief interlude of a Visiting Scholarship at the Dumbarton Oaks Foundation (a mecca of Byzantinists)—concurrent invitations from Princeton's Institute for Advanced Study to take a professorship in its School of Historical Studies, and from Princeton University to serve on its staff as a Visiting Lecturer with the rank of Professor. This joint membership in two distinguished communities of scholars was clearly the highest honor that the New World could bestow on any humanist of unusual merit, and the general feeling was that Kantorowicz indisputably—indeed, amply—deserved it.

From 1951 until his death, at the age of sixty-eight, on September 9, 1963, his life remained outwardly un-

---

[47] I was criticized (by O. J. Maenchen, among others) for having overstressed this submerged streak in my 1965 Necrology. Perhaps I should have emphasized its subliminal character; its reality seems to me undeniable. See also notes 36 and 43, above.

eventful.[48] Faithful to his resolve to steer clear of marital bonds, he nevertheless thoroughly enjoyed a rich social life, being surrounded by a growing number of buoyantly youthful followers, whose presence in a way compensated for the loss, through death, of such older, irreplaceable friends as Bukofzer and Olschki. He was now within easy reach of vital centers of learning in the Boston-Cambridge and the New York City areas, a fact which may have enlivened his contacts with colleagues, art collections, and research libraries. Also, he crossed the Atlantic more frequently, as when, in 1955, he attended a Congress of Historians held in Rome and enjoyed something of a private reunion with a few select friends from Germany whose conduct throughout the critical period he had reason to respect. He realized that he was deeply rooted in an older German culture which, though swept away by the tide of history, at no time ceased to haunt him; hence his increasing willingness to write articles—real gems or, as he would have put it, showcases ("Kabinettstücke") of scholarship—for *Festschriften* in tribute to those of Germany's truly outstanding senior scholars who were worthy of his continued esteem and affection. Yet this freedom from petty rancor, which Baethgen so appreciatively emphasizes in his necrology, neither detracted from his determination to channel the bulk of his research into the mainstream of American scholarship (it was Princeton University Press that, in 1957, published *The King's Two Bodies*), nor diminished an undercurrent of sadness at the thought that his life had failed to shape up the way he had hoped and that the world in which he now lived was so vastly different from the one into which he had been born. Kantorowicz never re-

---

[48] For a few random glimpses of Kantorowicz's life at Princeton, see the all too succinct necrology in *Speculum* 39 (1964): 596-97.

turned to Berkeley; I saw him once briefly, on business, in San Francisco, in the early 'fifties, and he was rumored to have spent an occasional summer with friends, at the shore of Lake Tahoe. The University of California did not, to my knowledge, honor or commemorate his twelve-year performance in any tangible way; but many learned societies showered him with attentions, and it is reported that, since his death, his bust adorns a contrite University of Frankfurt.

It remains to append to our thumbnail sketch a few comments on the American phase of Kantorowicz's research. This far-flung part of his not inordinately bulky *œuvre* includes, we recall, two monographs (*Laudes Regiae* and *The King's Two Bodies*) plus an estimated fifty articles, notes, and book reviews—some in English, some in German, and one item available only in Spanish translation—of which approximately one half are now readily accessible in a *de luxe* volume, which he himself helped to plan shortly before his demise.

First of all, does one detect any common denominators (or, at least, red threads)? I should think that several pervasive features can be identified. All these inquiries are unapologetically monographic, heavily annotated, uncompromisingly difficult. One finds among them no glib essays, no facile, premature syntheses, no textbooks, no condescending studies of "haute vulgarisation." The papers, whether long or short, testify to repeated, almost stubborn, rewriting. We recall that an "Urfassung" of *The King's Two Bodies* (1957) was available for publication before 1950; Kantorowicz would never have irresponsibly affixed his "imprimatur" to a rough draft. I can cite an even more striking example of doggedly tenacious elaboration. The kernel of one major paper, "Oriens Augusti—Lever du Roi," which appeared as late as 1963 (perhaps posthumously), is traceable to a magnificent "intimate" lecture or "causerie" that Kantorowicz delivered before Berkeley's *Colloquium*, in my presence, fully thirteen years earlier. Given this peculiarly slow rhythm—which, in part, accounts for the thoroughness, even luxuriance, of his documentation—Kantorowicz, at the time of his death, must have been feverishly at work on numerous concurrent, possibly overlapping, projects; in fact, not a few of the informal pledges he incidentally made in his last book (1957) have remained unredeemed. Can his executors and intellectual heirs be persuaded to salvage and open this locked treasure-trove of almost-finished studies?

Another recurrent trademark is the interdisciplinary character of Kantorowicz's research, with artful interweaving of the individual strands and with ever heavier emphasis placed on the tapping of exotic, auxiliary, and ancillary sources. As the three signers of the *Speculum* necrology astutely observe:

> Already he had begun to understand the importance of theology, ritual, and symbolism for the study of mediaeval kingship. . . . He turned to the study of ancient ruler-cults, religion, Roman public law, Christian theology, and early mediaeval ecclesiastic history . . . a monumental work of history, constituting a great synthesis of art, literature, religion, theology, ecclesiology, numismatics, and political and legal thought. . . . The erudition ranged widely in subject matter and in time and space, from Antiquity to the age of the Tudors, from the Near East and Byzantium to Britain.

Still another idiosyncrasy—fundamentally a weakness in the opinion of some observers, who measure by the author's own earlier standard—was Kantorowicz's consistently inductive approach, which bade him favor prohibitively narrow topics. These, it is true, he knew how to render fascinating by the discovery of hidden implications and by his consummate skill in using mutually corroborative techniques and bits of evidence or illustrations. Kantorowicz cannot, however, be entirely absolved of the charge of excessive miniaturization; he may have carried too far the avoidance of broad themes comparable in range to the reign of Emperor Frederick. Even his most ambitious and triumphantly successful work of this period, *The King's Two Bodies*, represents a sophisticated embroidery on a theme which originally, by his own admission, could have fit into a middle-sized article. Despite one's admiration for each richly adorned specimen of Kantorowicz's scholarship, one is left wondering why, in forty years of intensive labor, he shied away from boldly starting out with a broad canvas, at least on some particularly auspicious occasions. His best friends can each offer only unsubstantiated conjectures regarding this stubborn retreat from monumentality.

A final and positive hallmark of Kantorowicz's studies, one in which the foreground of George's insistence on "Geist" and of German expertise in "Geisteswissenschaft" conceivably blended with the very remote Judaic background of intellectualized religion, was his steady concern with spiritual traditions, culminating in his inquiries into theocracy. In this concept and in its congeners he recognized the hard kernel of medieval culture at its most haunting and compelling. Hence his insatiable curiosity about Dante, and relative indifference to Shakespeare and even to Goethe; hence his eagerness to see the record of contemporary literature and fine arts as a kind of manifestation or emanation of the irreducible conceptual nucleus.

The two book ventures invite separate characterizations. The *Laudes Regiae*, a cross-temporal, cross-topical study of liturgical acclamations (especially "Christus vincit, Christus regnat, Christus imperat") and medieval ruler-worship, focuses attention on Carolingian France, but displays a tremendous sweep in the ferreting-out of prototypes, genetic connections, and typological variations, down to the ludicrous degeneracy of the sacred formulas in Fascist Italy. The monograph, virtually completed in 1941, mainly reflects Kantorowicz's readiness to strike out in two new directions: toward Byzantium in the Southeast and toward England in the Northwest. The latter, viewed through a medievalist's prism as a peripheral or marginal cultural area in relation to more progressive Continental Europe, once again turns out to be a priceless repository of Occidental patterns rapidly overlaid in the more centrally located countries along the more frequently traveled thoroughfares. Several threads tie this exuberantly documented work, enriched by Bukofzer's musicological excursus, to the author's earlier *magnum opus*. In post-war Germany, the parallel studies of B. Opfermann and R. Elze, although confined to "Herrscherakklamationen," generated such intense curiosity about the subject that Kantorowicz's learned treatise, in steady demand, was reissued in 1958.[49]

---

[49] For summaries and critical reactions, turn to F. E. Cranz, *Speculum* 22 (1947): 648-51; R. Folz, *Revue d'histoire et de philosophie religieuses* 30 (1950): 229-35; and H. Grundmann, *Historische Zeitschrift* 188 (1959): 116-19; also, to Baethgen's aforecited necrology, pp. 9-12, which felicitously supplements his own earlier review, originally published in *Deutsche Literaturzeitung* 71 (1950): 368-74, and later absorbed into the miscellany *Mediaevalia*, II, 557-81.

All critics of *The King's Two Bodies*—for which Kantorowicz was awarded the Hawkins Medal—agree that this is a book of immensely complex structure, whose message it is practically impossible to reduce to a simple formula.[50] The less puzzling subtitle: "A Study in Mediaeval Political Theology" presumably yields a more reliable and more immediately satisfying clue to

[50] *The King's Two Bodies* elicited a spate of critical reactions. On this side of the Atlantic it was reviewed in *Speculum* 33 (1958): 550-53, by W. H. Dunham, Jr.; and in *Romance Philology* 15 (1961): 179-84, by Cecil Grayson, an Oxonian Italianist who, understandably, was chiefly interested in the Dante material (*De Monarchia; Purgatory*, xxvii, 142). The various German reactions—typically, more circumstantial—were, in turn, summarized and assessed by Baethgen in his necrology in conjunction with his own authoritative appraisal, in bird's-eye view, of the book (pp. 10-12). Of these reactions only E. Reibstein's, in *Zeitschrift für Rechtsgeschichte* (Germ. Abt.) 76 (1959): 378ff., contains serious objections. W. Fesefeldt in *Göttingische Gelehrte Anzeigen* 212 (1958): 57-67, carefully digests the book, then, toward the end, attempts to isolate and define the chosen issue's dynamics and the deeply concerned author's subdued passion ("doch spürt der Leser auch die Leidenschaft, die mit dem Begriffe 'politische Theologie' das Feuer zweier dynamischer Denkformen in eine Einheit zwingt"). Fesefeldt concludes by praising Kantorowicz's filigree precision and ever-present command over the vast congeries of data painstakingly assembled. R. M. Kloos, in *Historische Zeitschrift* 188 (1959): 358-64, emphasizes the book's general orientation toward Elizabethan England, where the fiction of the monarch's two bodies—the perishable piece of physical reality and the immortal enshrinement of *dignitas*—has its real roots, then places on record his admiration for the author's accomplished artistry ("glänzende Essays bei souveräner Beherrschung des Stoffes, kühne Interpretationen bei strenger geistiger Disziplin"). Technically the most searching critique was contributed by the Jesuit F. Kempf, "Untersuchungen über das Einwirken der Theologie auf die Staatslehre des Mittelalters," *Römische Quartalschrift* 54 (1959): 203ff.

I have here examined Kantorowicz's latter-day writings somewhat cursorily, because I expect to supplement these sketchy remarks with a full-sized review of his *Selected Studies* in the quarterly *Romance Philology*.

Kantorowicz's thinking. The *Speculum* reviewer praised it as a great book and a major classic; six years later that same journal's team of obituarists spoke of a masterpiece of art, of reason in the writing of History, and of a many-splendored work of literary art. For a foreign-born, foreign-trained, foreign-inspired scholar to have produced a book so described presupposes a most unusual reservoir of talent and exercise of will-power, jointly conducive to a virtuoso performance.

From this tightly woven tapestry of a spiritual history of European monarchy I wish to pluck just two threads. By shedding significant light on the traditional concept of the Crown in England, Kantorowicz, as a historian, acquitted himself of his debt toward the two English-speaking countries to which he owed so much as a man —his bare survival and his professional rehabilitation. And by devoting an important section of his book to Dante, he reverted to a favorite subject broached in his portrait of Frederick (a theme of which he almost became a captive) and thus vindicated the unbroken continuity of this intellectual commitment, endearing himself to Romance philologists in the process.

Ever averse to superficially glittering formulations, Ernst H. Kantorowicz hardly deserves a treatment that would tend to reduce his multi-faceted personality, the many vicissitudes and tragedies of his life, and his fine-spun, if slightly esoteric and elusive, writings to any sort of simplistic formula. His problem was, from the start, to reconcile certain conflicting strains in himself, and the difficulty grew more acute as new and unforeseen experiences increased the number of elements that had to be balanced against one another. It can perhaps be argued that, to the humanist-at-large, as opposed to the specialized historian, Kantorowicz's two most conspicuous accomplishments were first, to have assimilated just the right dosage of poetic inspiration for the lasting benefit of his own serious scholarship; and second, to have turned the painful, enforced weaning from his native culture, his familiar environment, and his cherished linguistic vehicle into a self-imposed filtering and chastening of topic-selection, analysis, and style of presentation.

Index

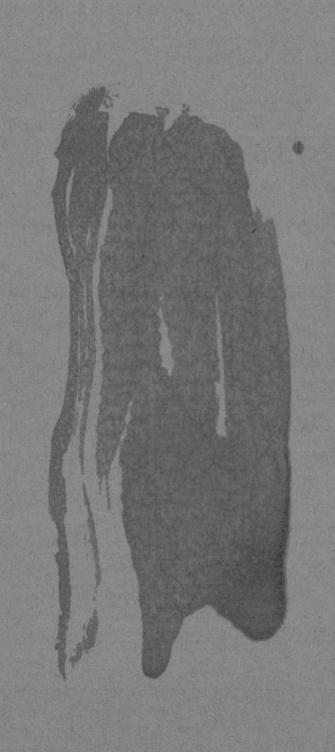